The Defence of
British Trade
1689–1815

The Defence of
British Trade
1689–1815

PATRICK CROWHURST

DAWSON

First published in 1977

© P Crowhurst 1977

Wm Dawson & Sons Ltd, Cannon House
Folkestone, Kent, England

British Library Cataloguing in Publication Data

Crowhurst, P
  The defence of British trade, 1689–1815.
  1. Great Britain – Commerce – History
  I. Title
  382'.0941   HF183
  ISBN 0–7129–0699–1

Printed in Great Britain
by W & J Mackay Limited, Chatham

To
Helen, Lesley and
Janet

Contents

List of Maps		9
List of Abbreviations		11
Acknowledgements		13
1	French privateering and British trade 1689–1815	15
2	The organization of convoys and their departure	43
3	Marine insurance	81
4	The Northern States and Canada	104
5	The Southern States	138
6	West Indies	170
7	East Indies	206
Notes		249
Bibliography		265
Index		275

List of Maps

1 French privateering ports   16
2 The Baltic   51
3 The Mediterranean   53
4 North American Trade   105
5 North American ports   106
6 Massachusetts Bay   107
7 Newfoundland trade   109
8 Chesapeake Bay   142
9 British Ports   149
10 West India trade   171
11 West India ports   173
12 East India trade   207
13 East India ports   209
14 Far East India ports   210

Abbreviations

Cal.S.P.Dom.	*Calendar of State Papers, Domestic*
Cherbourg Archives	*Archives de la Marine, Cherbourg*
Exeter R.O.	*Exeter City Library, Record Office*
IOR	*India Office Records*
Rennes Archives	*Archives départementales d'Ille-et-Vilaine, Rennes*
SRO	*Scottish Record Office*

Acknowledgements

This study has been assisted by grants from the Social Science Research Council, the British Academy and the Sir Ernest Cassel Educational Trust. The grants have helped me to visit record offices in England and France that I should not otherwise have been able to visit. I also wish to express my appreciation for help from Professor G. Williams of Queen Mary College, University of London, who has read successive drafts of the manuscript and whose extensive knowledge of eighteenth century naval and maritime history has helped me to understand many problems. Any errors in this work are of course my own.

In addition I wish to acknowledge the help I have received from the staffs of archives listed in the Bibliography, especially those of the Public Record Office, the Reading and Manuscript Rooms of the British Museum, the Scottish Record Office, the Archives Nationales, the Archives départementales d'Ille-et-Vilaine, Rennes and the Archives départementales des Basses Pyrénées, Pau. I am also grateful to the Secretary and Archivist of the Society of Merchant Venturers, Bristol, for allowing me to consult the Society's records.

Many others have given generous help at different stages of my work. I wish to mention especially Professor G. S. Graham, Professor R. Davis, Mr H. Slechte of the Gemeente Archief, Rotterdam and Mrs Alice Carter of the London School of Economics.

I am also most grateful to the publishers for their help in preparing the manuscript for publication.

Finally I acknowledge my considerable debt to my wife for her constant support and encouragement, which has sustained me through this study, and to my two daughters whose youthful incomprehension of the significance of this work has helped me to keep it in its true perspective.

Acknowledgements

1

French Privateering and British Trade 1689–1815

THE PRINCIPAL THREAT to British trade in the wars between 1689 and 1815 came from a large number of French privateers that put to sea from St Malo, Dunkirk and other ports along the French coast. At times other nations joined the attack against Britain: the American colonies at times after 1775, Holland, the Scandinavian states and Spain. The naval forces of these states never threatened British trade directly, although between 1694 and 1713 the French formed small commerce raiding squadrons of frigates and some line-of-battle ships which did considerable damage to English commerce. This commerce war varied in intensity, reaching a peak between 1694 and 1713, declining in the mid-eighteenth century and then assuming a major role in the Revolutionary and Napoleonic wars between 1793 and 1815. The subject of privateering, especially French privateering, is surrounded by myth and legend, for the major privateering captains performed what their compatriots regarded as acts of daring and courage and became national heroes. Privateering for most of the period replaced naval activity as the subject of popular interest in France, unlike in Britain where the reverse was true. Gradually the myth is being stripped away, and the reputations of the popular figures – Jean Bart, the Chevalier de Forbin and others – is being examined more closely so that an assessment can be made of the size and intensity of the French privateering threat to British trade in this period.

St Malo has long been regarded as one of the most famous of all French privateering ports. It had the geographical advantage of lying at the western end of the English Channel, through which most of English trade passed in war and peace. There was ample opportunity for attacking English merchant shipping. Equally important, it had a large reserve of hardy, experienced seamen, most of whom were experienced deep water sailors. At one time it was thought that during the wars with England sailors and merchants were drawn to privateering in the hope of booty – contemporary literature emphasized the number of rich prizes that were brought into the port. Recent evidence casts doubt on the theory that the major cause of privateering was its attractiveness.[1] Apart from a few spectacular successes which made the fortunes of those who fitted out and sailed the ships, the majority do not seem to have made any profit, and a number suffered losses. What seems to have motivated those who

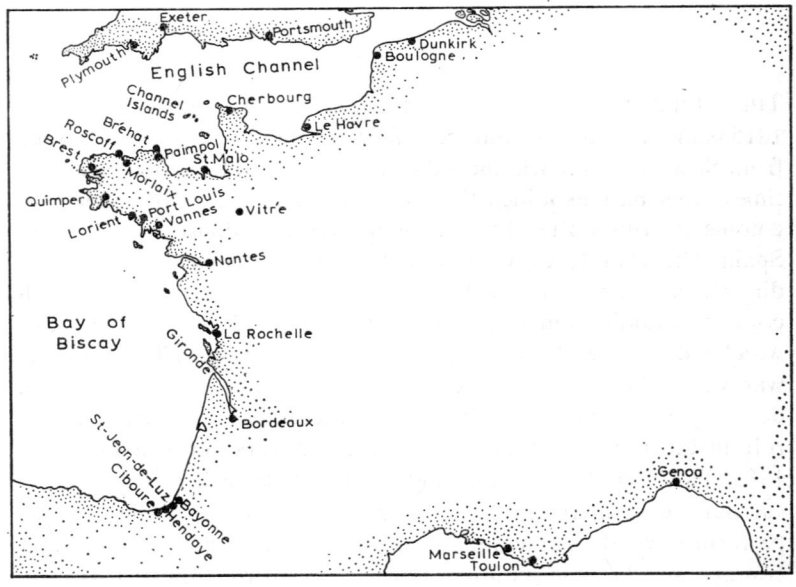

1   French privateering ports

financed these ventures – the *armateurs*, not all of whom were merchants – was the difficulty of continuing any other form of economic activity. In peacetime St Malo sent ships to the Newfoundland coastal fishery and to the Grand Banks as well as to the Caribbean and Mediterranean, but in wartime this became dangerous and very expensive to insure. This sharply reduced the opportunities for profit, and in the wars between 1689 and 1713 the alternative appeared to be privateering.

The extent to which St Malo was dependent on commerce or privateering becomes clear when her trade is examined in detail. A large country such as France, with poor internal communications, relied heavily on sea and river transport; St Malo acted as the entrepôt for most Breton commerce. As early as the second half of the sixteenth century Rennes, the principal inland town in Brittany, contained an important mint for which bullion was brought from Spain via St Malo. Breton linens, especially from Vitré, were sent in exchange. This developed into a trade with the Mediterranean and the French Biscay ports, and St Malo supplied most of northern France with Mediterranean products and wine. More important in the long run was the Newfoundland cod fishery, to which large numbers of boats were leaving by as early as the end of the sixteenth century.[2] This also fitted the established pattern of Mediterranean trade of selling the dried catch in exchange for Mediterranean goods. It was this development of long distance trade that gave St Malo its distinctive character, and to which the coastal trade acted as a feeder by supplying items such as linen, cider and salt for export overseas. This commerce flourished during the seventeenth century, with the result that by 1687 St Malo possessed 117 large sea-going vessels, which was more than any other French port.[3] Her merchants were reputed to be so wealthy that when the Compagnie française des Indes orientales was in financial difficulties in 1708, it turned to St Malo merchants for support. Underlying this prosperity was the commercial drive of the mercantile community, some of whose members initiated trading ventures in the South Seas and in the Indian Ocean, though in the long run none proved successful. The Compagnie pour la Mer du Sud, founded by Noel Danycan de l'Epine and Jean Jourdan in 1698, flourished until 1716 when its activities were forbidden because they interfered with Spanish trade.[4] Unfortunately for St Malo this prosperity was seriously threatened by war with England. The annual fishing expeditions to Newfoundland were halted when the fishing stations were destroyed by English fishermen and the coastal and Mediterranean trade was interrupted by English privateers based on the Channel Islands. The result was a severe decline in trade during the War of the League of Augsburg: it fell 35 per cent and the price of salt dropped by 77 per cent.[5]

Under these circumstances, privateering offered the best chance of making money. Interest was stimulated by a number of Jacobites who fitted out vessels at the port, and the record of *armements* and captures indicates a dynamism about this war which represents a peak in St Malo privateering[6] *(see table p. 18)*.

It also emphasizes the weakness of the British navy, which on the outbreak of the War of the League of Augsburg was unprepared for the defence of commerce. The progress of the navy in trying to limit

Table 1.1 ST MALO PRIVATEERING 1688–97

	No. of ships fitted out	No. of prizes	No. of ransoms	Total prizes and ransoms
1688*	9	16	3	19
1689	28	65	5	70
1690	29	118	5	123
1691	34	98	0	98
1692	59	179	21	200
1693	41	110	27	137
1694	48	122	35	157
1695	65	124	48	172
1696	62	119	48	167
1697*	49	93	39	132

* Years of partly war and peace.
Source: J. Delumeau, 'La guerre de course française sous l'ancien régime' (Paper presented at the XIV International Congress of Historical Sciences, San Francisco, 1975), p 292.

the losses of English ships is indicated by the rise in the number of captured vessels that were ransomed after 1691; after 1692 it was apparently in the interests of privateer captains to ransom vessels for a sum approaching the value of the ship and cargo rather than send it to St Malo under a prize crew and risk losing it to an English privateer or warship. It is also striking that although French historians generally claim that the period after 1694 represents *l'apogée de la course*, in the case of St Malo this is only true of the number of privateers fitted out, not of the number of captures made by each. The peak in that respect is 1692, before La Hogue and the subsequent support of the French crown.

When war began again in 1702, privateers were again fitted out. Some trade survived, and though the numbers were small, merchant ships continued to sail to Newfoundland, to the Caribbean, to the whale fishery and to other French ports. After 1706 some of the more adventurous fitted out vessels for the South Seas, for the Spanish colonies in America and even for China. As a result the number of privateers declined sharply as did the number of prizes *(see table p. 19)*.

The years from 1706 are above all about the attempt by St Malo merchants to develop trade with the Pacific, and although the figures for fitting out merchant ships and privateers may not be wholly comparable – there is some divergence between those of Delumeau and Vignols for the number of privateers fitted out – the

Table 1.2 ST MALO PRIVATEERING AND TRADE, 1702–12

	No. of ships fitted out	No. of prizes	No. of ransoms	Total ransoms and prizes	No. of merchant ships fitted out
1702*	15	54	4	58	NA
1703	59	125	21	146	NA
1704	64	173	21	194	NA
1705	61	117	49	166	NA
1706	38	75	50	125	39
1707	35	20	19	39	56
1708	30	23	17	40	40
1709	39	30	6	36	22
1710	37	32	4	36	43
1711	15	29	9	38	33
1712	12	5	3	8	51
1713	NA	NA	NA	NA	88

* Years of partly war and peace.
Source: *ibid*; Rennes Archives, 1F 1930, Fonds Vignols, armements et désarmements à Saint-Malo, 1706–1739.

main trend is clear. The commercial interest in Pacific trade from 1706 is also reflected by, and may even be a product of, the rise in the number of privateers lost to British vessels because of the British navy's success at protecting commerce.

Table 1.3 LOSSES OF ST MALO PRIVATEERS AND MERCHANT VESSELS

	Merchant ships	Privateers	Total
1706	9	10	19
1707	9	14	23
1708	16	13	29
1709	2	23	25
1710	16	24	40
1711	5	19	24
1712*	7	10	17

* Year of war and peace.
Source: *ibid*.

The table emphasizes the risks taken by privateers after 1706: of 196 privateers (Vignols' total) that put to sea between 1706 and 1712, no fewer than 113 were taken, and the highest losses came after 1708.

In later wars privateering never reached the level of the years 1689–97:

Table 1.4 ST MALO PRIVATEERING 1744–8

	Privateers
1744	25
1745	42
1746	48
1747	23
1748	11

Commissions *en guerre et marchandises*, 113
Source: Rennes Archives 9B 435d. Vessels issued with a commission *en guerre et marchandises* were heavily armed merchant ships which only made prizes during their commercial voyages.

Table 1.5 ST MALO PRIVATEERING 1756–62

	Privateers
1756*	14
1757	29
1758	5
1759	2
1760	25
1761	9
1762	8

* Year of war and peace.
Commissions *en guerre et marchandises* 54
Source: *ibid*, 9B 435e.

Table 1.6 ST MALO PRIVATEERING 1778–82

	Privateers	No. making captures	Prizes
1778*	5	3	9
1779	4	4	16
1780	17	12	54
1781	20	11	89
1782	14	12	33

* Year of war and peace
Source: J-N le Coz, 'La Guerre de Course à Saint-Malo sous Louis XVI' (Diplôme d'Études Supérieures, Rennes 1957), p 121 and Table A.

Table 1.7 ST MALO PRIVATEERING 1793–1814

	Privateers		Prizes
	Registered	Captured	
1793	22	11	23
Year 4	5	5	0
Year 5	31	15	29
Year 6	28	9	38
Year 7	19	8	30
Year 8	24	7	29
Year 9	20	12	24
Year 11	10	7	4
Year 12	5	1	15
Year 13	4	1	12
Year 14	5	1	11
1806	18	5	21
1807	25	13	22
1808	21	6	12
1809	20	13	8
1810	23	12	15
1811	17	5	18
1812	16	10	16
1813	13	3	9
1814	1	0	0

Source: F. Robidou, *Les derniers corsaires malouins; la course sous la République et l'Empire, 1793–1814* (Rennes 1919), pp 41, 78, 88.

These figures indicate the level of St Malo's attack on British commerce and help to explain why British merchants were prepared to believe tales that 'swarms' of French privateers were 'hovering off the British coast'. These figures should however be used with caution. They indicate the number of privateers that were granted letters of marque each year; they do not show how many privateers put to sea in the course of each year, because they do not show how many cruises each vessel made. In the case of the War of American Independence, there is a record of sixty sailings by privateers, but an analysis of the register of commissions indicates that only about forty-eight ships put to sea, allowing for a few that were sold and renamed. This is an important consideration. It is from the record of privateers that put to sea that one may estimate, roughly, the level of profitability, and thus the measure of success against British commerce. If the figures of Janine Lemay are accepted for privateering at St Malo during the War of Austrian Succession and the Seven Years War – fifty-two and eighty-seven respectively – her figures for the average number of prizes taken – six and '2–5' – show that privateering was only moderately successful.[7] The evidence of the War of

American Independence supports this general view, because out of a total of forty-eight privateers only 201 prizes were taken, an average of about four per vessel.[8] The wars of the Revolution and Empire produced even fewer prizes, probably about one per privateer.

This is only one side of the picture however, and one needs to look also at the average size of these St Malo privateers. Using the tonnage figures given in the register of commissions as a guide, it is possible to divide the totals of ships into a number of categories. Using those adopted by Vignols, that is below 15 tons, 16–50, 51–100, 101–200 and over 200, it is clear that throughout the War of Spanish Succession, over half the privateers commissioned were over 200 tons – a significant proportion for the period, when the average merchant vessel was probably under 100 tons.[9] This was the great age of privateering at St Malo. In successive wars, *armateurs* were more cautious and on the whole the vessels registered for commissions during the wars of Austrian Succession and of American Independence were much smaller – in the latter war, thirty-two of the forty-eight privateers which put to sea were between 16 and 100 tons.[10] At the end of the period the numbers of privateers again increased, and the average size rose. During the Napoleonic War 41 of the 126 registrations were for ships between 100 and 200 tons.[11] However, as Professor Delumeau has shown, the average size of the privateers that put to sea from St Malo in the period from 1688 to 1813 declined from 188 to only 76 tons.[12]

Another important aspect of the St Malo threat to British trade was the type of crew that these vessels carried. In relation to their size privateers needed large crews for boarding vessels and crewing them once they were captured. This was a great strain on the available resources of trained seamen. Some experienced sailors may have been deterred from joining privateers by the risk of capture, but this is unlikely during the early wars when the British navy was weak. In the mid-eighteenth century the position had changed. The risk of capture was greater, and one writer has come to the conclusion that during the War of Austrian Succession and the Seven Years War the crews were of mediocre quality.[13] The captains were young, inexperienced and unable to command their ships effectively, and the crews mutinied, deserted and pillaged. This was probably too harsh a view. The expulsion of the Acadians from Nova Scotia in 1755 had provided St Malo merchants with many trained seamen and besides those who were usually employed in the Caribbean and coastal trades there were many cod fishermen who could not go to Newfoundland. These men were probably no more likely to mutiny than the crews of earlier privateers. It is more likely that the decline of the population at St Malo, from over 20,000 at the beginning of the period to about 10,000 by the mid-eighteenth century, and the demands of the navy and military service in the later wars, took men away from privateers. Furthermore, when the British navy was strong at the beginning of a war, as in 1756, it seized French shipping as soon as, or even before, war broke out. Admiral Hawke took around 300 vessels, manned by 6,000 officers and men and worth 30 million livres in 1756.[14] Not all of these were from St Malo, but they represent a significant loss of men and ships.

It is difficult to assess the profit of St Malo privateering. Few accounts have survived and it is hard to tell if these are representative. The most complete records cover the years after 1800 when Napoleon took an interest and asked for reports on its progress. In general terms it appears that, at least between 1 October 1806 and 1 May 1814, St Malo privateers gained more from the value of prizes than they lost in captured privateers:

Table 1.8 ST MALO PRIVATEERING 1 OCTOBER 1806 TO 1 MAY 1814

| | (Livres) | | |
	Value of privateers	Value of captured privateers	Benefit
1 Oct. to 1 May 1806/07	2,639,000	295,000	2,234,000
1 Oct. to 1 May 1807/08	2,334,000	285,000	2,049,000
1809–10 records missing			
1 May to 1 May 1810/11	5,735,000	1,690,000	4,045,000
1 May to 1 May 1811/12	2,446,946	480,000	1,986,946
1 May to 1 May 1812/13	3,689,666	210,000	3,479,666
1 May to 1 May 1813/14	1,099,750	963,000	136,750

Source: Robidou, *Derniers corsaires malouins*, p 125.

This appears to show a relatively healthy picture of St Malo privateering in the closing years of this period, though one may be certain that whether or not St Malo gained from the prize captures, many individual merchants made a loss. The value of the captured privateers represents the proceeds from selling them in a prize court, not the true value to their owners. A more representative picture may be gained from the example of Robert Surcouf, one of the most famous privateer captains in the Revolutionary War. After 1800 he became an *armateur*. Of fifteen cruises made by his eleven privateers, two cruises were made without any captures, one ship was laid up without making any prize, a further five made losses and only three made a profit. Fortunately for Surcouf one of his ships, the *Marsouin*, had a particularly successful second cruise and made a profit of 280,384 livres which more than compensated for his loss on other ventures. The final result was that his gross profits totalled 386,931 livres and his losses 184,715 livres, which gave him a net profit for 1803–14 of 202,216 livres.[15] Not all these vessels cruised in European waters; some went to the Indian Ocean. It is impossible to tell which voyages were profitable and it is difficult to translate the sums into contemporary figures. All that can be said is that Surcouf's final profit was less than the cost of fitting out one privateer, the *Napoléon*. This was a well-built ship, designed to cruise in the Indian Ocean with a crew of fifty, and cost 346,858 livres – a price raised by wartime inflation.[16] Few prize vessels were sold for as much as that, and it was more than a successful privateer captain might expect to get. The *Bougainville*, which had a crew of seventy-one, earned 23,643 livres for the captain out of a total profit of 309,909 livres for the first cruise in 1798. Its second cruise was also successful and the *armateurs* received 71,268 livres profit.[17]

Another important factor in planning a privateering voyage was the relative profitability of different types of vessel. The large, well armed and heavily manned ships cleared the seas of all but naval vessels. However they were expensive to build, fit out and man, and did not necessarily make richer prizes than smaller ships. One ship which made a loss was the *Speculateur*; its loss was 18,000 livres of 46,000 livres prize money. A second, the *Minerve*, made a profit of 39,840 livres of 178,440 livres prize money.[18] The more astute *armateurs* invested in smaller vessels and it is significant that the most successful period for privateering at St Malo was also a time when the crown supplied warships for commerce raiding. The warships attacked the convoy escorts and the privateers rounded up the merchant vessels; it was a powerful combination that the British Admiralty could only match by strengthening convoy escorts. This would weaken the naval squadrons and was not welcomed by the Admiralty, which preferred to destroy the French commerce raiders at sea.

It is easy to see why St Malo posed a serious threat to British commerce between 1688 and 1815. Privateers could cross the English Channel in a matter of hours and on a dull winter day cruise off a headland and wait for incoming trade or small coasters. The first sign of danger for the British was often the sight of the privateer in the lee of a headland. The men who sailed in these vessels spent much of their lives at sea, they knew the tides and currents, the winds and the coastline, and could send their prizes back to St Malo or a neighbouring port such as Bréhat-Paimpol or Morlaix-Roscoff. Whether or not the privateers were specially built – a matter about which there is some dispute – they could sail quickly with their large crew and were more than a match for any but the fastest British warships. Some of these privateers cruised off the south coast of England and in the Soundings at the entrance of the Channel to wait for trade returning from distant ports. Others, manned by cod fishermen and other deep-water sailors, cruised as far afield as off the coast of Ireland, venturing occasionally into the Irish Sea and Bristol Channel and even to round Scotland into the North Sea. Some went even further afield. *La Reine*, a St Malo privateer of 150 tons and a crew of sixty, sailed first to Dunkirk, then through the North Sea, round Scotland and on to Lisbon, where a further forty men were recruited into the crew. Then she cruised off the coast of Portugal and took three prizes, though one was subsequently wrecked in the Gironde while sailing for a French port.[19] In her cruise off the Iberian coast, the *Reine* was following a pattern of St Malo privateering established during the period 1689–1713 or even earlier.[20]

The other major privateering port was Dunkirk, the city of Jean Bart and the Chevalier de Forbin. For many years it was widely believed that Dunkirk was the major French privateering port, because of the attention which the Dunkirk corsairs received. Professor Bromley, in a perceptive study, has shown recently that St Malo privateers probably took more prizes. The records of the *Conseil des prises* show that for the War of the League of Augsburg, Brittany had 1,282 prizes and Dunkirk (with Nieuport and till 1706, Ostend) 993. Of the Breton prizes, the greatest number was taken by St Malo vessels. Even the other small Breton ports had close connections with St Malo. Dunkirk privateers cruised mainly in the North Sea, preying on fishing boats, coasters and the stragglers from returning convoys. In the War of the League of Augsburg, Dunkirkers seem to have taken more Dutch than British boats, but seldom took any of great value. About thirty put to sea each year. Each made several cruises and had their greatest hauls in the lengthening nights of autumn and the spring mists. Few cruised far from home before 1706; the favourite practice was to zigzag across the North Sea between the British and Norwegian coasts, many taking their prizes into the Norwegian ports. Britain tried to check the movement of these privateers by stationing a small squadron off Dunkirk, but navigation in the tidal channels was hazardous and ships were frequently blown off station by winds that brought the privateers out.

This was as true in 1759 as it was at the beginning of the period. From August to October 1759 Commodore Boys cruised off Dunkirk because the Admiralty had been told by the British consul at Flushing that François Thurot was about to put to sea with five frigates. Boys took every precaution: he made soundings of the channels leading to the port and tried to maintain a close blockade, but when he was blown off station in October, Thurot slipped out. He was later caught in the Irish Sea in February 1760 and killed in the battle that followed.

Dunkirk privateers had a reputation for valour that was second to none, and seem to have been more prepared to fight to take prizes than the crews at other ports. Although Jean Bart's heroic period is the 1670s, he remained a noted figure during the War of the League of Augsburg. He died of pleurisy in 1702. Other important privateer captains from this period to 1713 were Sausse and Baeteman. In the mid-eighteenth century Thurot maintained the reputation of the port. He first went to sea in 1745, aged eighteen, as a surgeon in a privateer and though captured and imprisoned in England managed to escape. In the course of the Seven Years War he captured sixty ships. In the Revolutionary and Napoleonic wars the tradition was carried on by Jean Blanckmann, Louis Leveille and others. After the success of the wars of the League of Augsburg and the Spanish Succession, Dunkirk privateering declined, as it did at other French ports bordering the English Channel. Although figures for Dunkirk privateering between 1744 and 1748 are incomplete, the record for the Seven Years War shows that a total of no more than twenty-four *armements* took eighty-five vessels.[21] For the 1744–8 war the record is of 137 vessels taken into the port, although not all of these were taken by Dunkirk privateers.[22] There is unfortunately no evidence of the number of privateers at Dunkirk in the Revolutionary and Napoleonic wars, but it is unlikely that *armements* were on the scale of the War of the League of Augsburg. This was fortunate for Britain, for the wars of the eighteenth century placed heavy demands on foreign supplies of timber for shipbuilding and fitting out naval vessels. The Baltic trade grew enormously during the course of the century, and convoys which had amounted to no more than twenty or thirty ships early in the century numbered approximately 1,000 by 1814. Attempts to control and ultimately prevent this trade through the Continental System failed because of the corruption of customs officials in the Baltic ports and the widespread use of 'neutral' (often disguised British) ships and forged papers. Apart from the small number of experienced and daring privateer captains already mentioned,

Dunkirk privateers played little part in commerce raiding on this strategically important trade route.

Other French ports participated in the *guerre de course* as well, though not on the same scale. Le Havre, a port that traded with the Caribbean, raised money for privateering by issuing bills which carried 5 per cent interest.[23] Huge sums were raised in this way and bills were sometimes issued for as much as 1,000 livres. Privateering attracted most of the young men, and even in 1745, when privateering had seriously declined, fishing boats had to put to sea with crews of elderly men. For example, the *Saint Philippe du Merliment*, a Cherbourg vessel, had a crew of eight that consisted of two aged 70, four aged between 51 and 57, a master of 39 and one of 22.[24] Of the other Breton ports, Brest played an important part in the early wars before 1713 when the naval vessels were fitted out for commerce raiding but took little part thereafter. Other smaller ports played a minor role. Vannes, on the south coast of Brittany, sent two privateers to sea during the War of Austrian Succession, and one during the Seven Years War.[25] In the first war, the *Hermine* of 35 tons was commanded by an 80 year-old captain. His only capture was a French vessel, the *St Vincent* of Port Louis, and when the *Hermione* was subsequently chased by a British privateer the crew took to their boat. A second privateer, the *Aigle Volant* of 135 tons, was no more successful. It was chased and taken by a British privateer before making any captures. In the Seven Years War the *Ville Hélie* put to sea in 1758 but took only one ship, the *Elizabeth* of Rotterdam, which was sent to the port of Vigo. The general lack of success in these ventures is a reflection not only of the efficiency of the convoy system but also, in the Seven Years War, of the close blockade of the Breton coast.

A more general view of privateering at the western end of the English Channel is reflected in the figures for prizes and ransoms sent to Port Louis during the wars of the Austrian Succession, the Seven Years War and the War of American Independence (Table 1.9).

Table 1.9

	British ships taken or ransomed	French or ally retaken	Tonnage	Value of boats (livres)	Value of cargo (livres)
1744–8	36	5	5,680	311,000	1,652,000
1756–63	27	7	2,200	128,170	263,190
1778–83	99	23	16,800	1,883,540	4,704,580

Source: R. Thomas Lacroix, 'La guerre de course dans les ports des amirautés de Vannes et de Lorient (1744–1783)', *Mémoires de la Societé d'Histoire et d'Archéologie de Bretagne*, xxvi, (1946), p 186.

Most, if not all of these prizes were made by privateers from a variety of ports, but the figures help to emphasize the scale of French privateering during these wars.

An indication of the privateering activity in the Breton ports can also be gained from the record of prize ships and ransoms taken to the ports:

Table 1.10 BRETON PRIVATEERING

	St Malo	Morlaix	Brest	Quimper	Vannes/ Port Louis	Nantes	Others
1695–1713	858	365	918	64	229	213	10
1744–8	72	36	54	6	19	14	5
1756–63	41	24	37	5	5	1	—

Source: Delumeau, 'Guerre de course francaise', p 283.

Although the two tables are not directly comparable, they suggest the comparatively small scale of Breton commerce raiding. Even during the period 1695–1713 the figures for all except Brest are insignificant when compared with the total recorded for Dunkirk – 2,793.[26] The true value of these ports was not revealed until the War of American Independence and the war with America in 1812, when the ports served as a base for a number of successful American privateers. The hallmark of these ships was their speed, the admirable way in which they could be handled and the distances they could travel. From the small Breton ports they cruised in waters where few Frenchmen had sailed: the Irish Sea and the Bristol Channel, as well as the more traditional hunting grounds for French privateers, the English Channel and the North Sea. John Paul Jones in the War of American Independence and Thomas Boyle in the later war both became legendary figures. The news that the former had been seen off Edinburgh in 1779 while on his famous cruise in the *Bonhomme Richard*, was enough to throw the city into a panic, especially as it had been deprived of a militia since the 1745 rising. Boyle's exploits in the *Chasseur* in the North and South Atlantic, the English Channel and the Irish Sea made him equally well-known. Other Americans, notably Conyngham and Wickes, cruised from Lorient, Nantes, Bordeaux and Dunkirk and the measure of their success is indicated by the American privateers *Crawford*, *Reprisal* and *Lexington* in capturing eleven British ships in five days in June 1777 between the Mull of Kintyre and Bardsey Island.[27]

This activity by American privateers helped to compensate for a lull in French privateering at Nantes during the War of American Independence. But this was not typical of the whole period. Although there are no figures for the War of the League of Augsburg – apart from a record of twenty commissions for privateering and *guerre et marchandises* – Nantes *armateurs* sent thirty-nine privateers to sea in the War of Spanish Succession.[28] The wars of the mid-eighteenth century told a different story. There were only nine privateers at sea in the Seven Years War and no more than three in the War of American Independence, although some Nantes merchants invested in St Malo privateers.[29] The lack of privateering activity does not indicate that the port was in decline; at the end of the wars in 1763 and 1783 trade quickly recovered and the number of ships at the port almost doubled between 1750 and 1792, from 120 to 230.[30] In fact, privateering was badly supported at the port because many merchants were able to continue trading, as the following table shows:

Table 1.11 NANTES PRIVATEERING

	Merchant ships fitted out	Privateers	Tonnage	Crew
1754	128	—	—	—
1755	77	—	—	—
1756	55	5	475	531
1757	36	2	400	317
			130	43
1758	13	—	—	—
1759	44	—	—	—
1760	11	1	24	25
1761	6	1	80	73
1762	14	1	100	23
1763	127	—	—	—
1776	178	—	—	—
1777	108	—	—	—
1778	127	—	—	—
1779	76	2	350	268
1780	66	—	—	—
1781	73	1	150	25
1782	59	—	—	—
1783	151	—	—	—
1784	191	—	—	—
1792	230	—	—	—
1793	98	16	3,310	1,675

Source: J. Meyer, *L'armement nantais dans le XVIIIe siècle* (Paris 1969), pp 79, 80, 83–6.

This shows that not only were few privateers fitted out at Nantes, but even those that put to sea were undermanned by comparison with privateers from other ports. Even Kerguelin-Trémarec, the famous explorer of the Indian Ocean in the late 1770s, put to sea in 1781 with a small crew, though he made a profitable voyage in the North Sea. He was a difficult man and often at odds with his superiors, but on this voyage he cruised at least as far as the northern Faroe Islands in the privateer *Comtesse Brionne* and took at least one prize, the *Lively* of Whitby, a whaler which he ransomed for 550 guineas.[31]

The results of this privateering activity were minimal. During the War of the League of Augsburg, six English, four Spanish and two Dutch ships were taken. In the War of Spanish Succession this increased to forty-three, of which thirty-nine were British, three were Dutch and one Portuguese. Thereafter the numbers declined sharply: the War of the Austrian Succession produced thirteen prizes, the Seven Years War seven and the War of American Independence none.[32] One reason for this poor showing is that in most, if not all cases, the privateers were fitted out to defend French trade rather than attack British commerce. There were enormous profits to be made in shipping slaves to the West Indian colonies, where wartime shortages pushed prices up, but the risks were high. Many made profitable voyages and as Chaurand said in 1783: 'We have won more in war than we could lose in peace'.[33] The French Biscay coast, as far south as the Gironde, was within the range of privateers from the Channel Islands and even Zeeland, who interrupted coastal trade and even entered rivers. Nantes lost approximately a quarter of all ships that sailed to the West Indies between 1705 and 1713, and half of these were taken by Zeelanders. It led to the suspicion, which was vigorously denied, that one of the prominent Nantes merchants, Jan Stalpaërt, who had been born at Bruges, was in league with the Zeelanders. This attack on French Biscay trade was so serious during the War of the League of Augsburg that a decree was enacted condemning privateer crews to the galleys when they were caught in French rivers.[34]

Nantes, like other Biscay ports, suffered a crushing blow with the outbreak of war in 1702, but after 1703 there followed a steady recovery until 1709. The period 1709–12 saw another decline, but trade recovered steadily after 1712.[35] The following table shows how the recovery of trade was matched by a decrease in the number of privateers fitted out (see table p. 31).

La Rochelle and Bordeaux suffered in the same way, and it is likely that the pattern of their privateering activity in this early and mid-eighteenth century period was the same. The rich trade of the Biscay ports with the Caribbean and West Africa continued to attract privateers and losses in the mid-eighteenth century were high. One of the principal merchants at Bordeaux, Abraham Gradis, tried to overcome this by hiring his ships to the king to carry stores to overseas garrisons. In this way he was paid for the hire of his ships and paid compensation if they were captured, as a number were in both the War of Austrian Succession and the Seven Years War.

Table 1.12 NANTES PRIVATEERING 1702–12

	Privateers		Privateers
1702	3	1708	0
1703	3	1709	0
1704	2	1710	2
1705	3	1711	7
1706	4	1712	3
1707	1		

Source: Péju, *La course à Nantes*, pp 94–5.

To the south lay Bayonne and her outport, St Jean-de-Luz, both Basque ports with a long history of deep-water sailing in whale fishing and freebooting in the Caribbean. The important point about privateering at these ports is that it does not conform to the established pattern of ports in the English Channel. While St Malo privateering enjoyed a peak between 1688 and 1713, a lull in the mid-eighteenth century and a gradual recovery thereafter, Bayonne and St Jean-de-Luz had indulged in very little privateering before 1713 and a great deal in the mid-eighteenth century. The generally accepted pattern of French privateering in this period does not apply to all French ports. Bayonne had none of the advantages of St Malo and Dunkirk. It lay far from the English Channel and privateers that cruised there would have to send their prizes to Breton ports or risk losing them on the longer passage to Bayonne. *Armateurs* did not welcome this; they liked to control the sale of prizes and distribution of profits and the managing owner made a small commission on this. The records of *armements* for the War of Spanish Succession – those of the War of the League of Augsburg have been lost – show how few privateers were sent to sea from these Basque ports *(see table p. 32)*.

In the two wars of the mid-eighteenth century many more were sent to sea *(see table p. 32)*.

Table 1.13 BASQUE PRIVATEERING 1702–13

| | Privateers | | | | Prizes | | | |
	Bayonne	St Jean-de-Luz	Other ports	TOTAL	Bayonne	St Jean-de-Luz	Other ports	TOTAL
1702	1	1	3	5	—	—	—	—
1703	—	1	—	1	—	—	—	—
1704	3	4	1	8	—	—	—	—
1705	3	2	4	9	2	—	2	4
1706	1	1	5	7	—	—	8	8
1707	—	2	3	5	—	4	—	4
1708	5	3	2	10	1	—	—	1
1709	8	1	1	10	4	—	—	4
1710	6	2	2	10	6	—	9	15
1711	9	5	1	15	4	1	—	5
1712	9	2	1	12	7	5	15	27
1713	—	—	2	2	—	—	3	3
TOTAL	45	24	25	94	24	10	37	71

Table 1.14 BASQUE PRIVATEERING, MID-EIGHTEENTH CENTURY

| | Privateers | | | | Prizes | | | |
	Bayonne	St Jean-de-Luz	Other ports	TOTAL	Bayonne	St Jean-de-Luz	Other ports	TOTAL
1744	11	3	1	15	9	1	2	12
1745	20	7	2	29	22	3	1	26
1746	27	3	5	35	36	11	6	53
1747	27	2	6	35	40	3	12	55
1748	20	1	4	25	27	3	16	46
TOTAL	103	16	20	139	134	21	37	192
1756	17	8	2	27	11	1	1	13
1757	52	13	8	74	44	13	12	69
1758	17	4	3	24	26	2	10	38
1759	13	6	2	21	14	11	19	44
1760	28	6	8	42	31	19	15	65
1761	48	12	7	67	62	25	32	119
1762	45	6	4	56	55	20	32	107
TOTAL	220	56	34	311	243	99	113	455

Source: Archives départementales des Basses Pyrénées, Amirauté de Bayonne, B Supplément, Nos 2–44, 1702–1762.

The wars of 1744–8 and the Seven Years War witnessed a remarkable increase in the number of privateers fitted out and this capital was certainly available earlier in the century as well. Nor can it be said that Bayonne, St-Jean-de-Luz, Ciboure and Hendaye lacked experienced deep-water seamen. Basque sailors had an excellent reputation as early as the sixteenth century when each year significant numbers went to the Gulf of St Lawrence to fish for cod and whales.[36] These men were held in such high esteem before the end of the century that many were employed in English and Dutch whalers as well. In the seventeenth century Bayonne continued to develop as a centre for the whale fishery – when the whales moved from the Gulf of St Lawrence into the Davis Strait off the coast of Greenland and off Spitsbergen, the whalers followed them. With the growth of the Caribbean trade Bayonne became prosperous, mainly because it was a centre for commercial development. Basque seamen were also involved in piracy against the Caribbean trade in the seventeenth century. It was these qualities – piracy and the skill, courage and determination shown by the fishermen in the northern fisheries as well as legitimate trade – which gave the Basques, and especially Bayonne men, their special reputation. It is not surprising that a large proportion of Basques lived by the sea since the coastal strip from the Landes to the Spanish frontier was generally infertile and barely supported the population.

Bayonne and the other French Basque ports also enjoyed significant economic advantages over other French ports. Their import duties were generally lower – a privilege dating from the time when the ports formed part of the British province of Gascony. These privileges were jealously guarded and Bayonne resisted the centralizing influence of Colbert in the second half of the seventeenth century. Bayonne used the advantage of lower duties to establish itself as an entrepôt between Spain and the countries of northern Europe, especially Holland. The port also gained from Colbert's efforts to foster French commerce and free it from Dutch control – a form of mercantilism not unlike the British Navigation Acts. The result was that Bayonne flourished as a commercial port; her merchants became more wealthy as Bayonne ships replaced Dutch ships in trade with Spain and Portugal. Also experienced sailors were attracted to serve in her ships. While this demonstrates that Bayonne possessed all the resources needed for successful privateering, it fails to explain why privateering only developed at this port in the mid-eighteenth century. The answer seems to lie in the counter attraction which legitimate trade exercized over merchants in the period 1689–1713, when Bayonne's commerce was not seriously disrupted by the Anglo-French wars. That the temporary collapse of trade could at times lead merchants to invest in privateering is borne out by the experience of St Malo where the wartime collapse of the cod fisheries drove many *armateurs* to support privateering.[37] Hopes of rich profits were seldom realized however, either at St Malo or Bayonne. During the period 1702–13 only seventy-one prizes were brought in to Bayonne and the other Basque ports against a total of ninety-four privateering cruises, and a further fifty made with *lettres de guerre et marchandises* which allowed them to take prizes during the commercial voyages.

In the long period of peace that followed the signing of the Treaty of Utrecht, the French government tried, with some success, to whittle away Bayonne's special privileges and the port lost ground to Bordeaux. Bayonne's trade with Portugal, a valuable though not vital prop to her economy, was slowly taken over by British merchants following the Methuen Treaty of 1703 – a process which accelerated after the coming of peace in 1714. Bayonne slowly declined. So too did her annual fairs, which had attracted merchants from France, Holland, Spain and Portugal and had made Bayonne the centre of much of the trade in Spanish merino wool, olive oil and Asturias iron as well as providing an outlet for Languedoc woollens and the famous Armagnac. Bordeaux steadily grew at Bayonne's expense.

The outbreak of war between Britain and France in 1744 gave Bayonne and her neighbouring ports a new lease of life. After the years of slow decline, here at last was an opportunity to make money. Figures for privateering at Bayonne, and to a lesser extent at St Jean-de-Luz, reflect this new interest. Some *armateurs* were able to send ships to sea within months of war being declared though in general the peak was not reached until the second year of war when new vessels were completed and commissioned. The number of Bayonne privateering campaigns increased significantly over those for the War of Spanish Succession though at St Jean-de-Luz, a smaller port, there was no marked increase. The capacity for privateering at that port had already been reached and the low figures for St Jean-de-Luz in both these wars indicate the limited economic resources of a small port. In the war of 1744–8, one may note a steady rise in the number of prizes brought to Bayonne between 1745 and 1747, a reflection of the growing competence of privateer captains, since the number of vessels remained fairly constant. The decline in privateering voyages in the final years of war reflects the unwillingness of *armateurs* to invest when peace was expected. Prize totals also fell.

The outbreak of the Seven Years War was greeted with enthusiasm by the Bayonne Chamber of Commerce, which claimed, in tones of patriotic fervour that the port would be the first to send privateers to sea.[38] By August 1756 there were six small vessels of between six and twelve guns and a frigate of twenty-four guns ready to put to sea. By the beginning of January 1757 the number of privateers at

Bayonne had risen to thirty manned by 4,710 men, while at St Jean-de-Luz there were fourteen privateers, manned by 1,383, men.[39] The early success of many of these ships acted as a magnet to draw men from ports throughout the western Mediterranean and as a result there was for a time no shortage of men to crew the privateers as soon as they were equipped. Indeed, the only factor which limited the numbers of privateers from these ports was the embargo on privateering in 1758 when the government tried to recruit more men for the navy.[40] The same was probably true of 1759, when only thirteen vessels sailed from Bayonne and six from St Jean-de-Luz, and the erratic course of privateering in this war is marked by the fluctuation of prize totals. The fall in privateering in 1758 and 1759 was followed by a recovery between 1760 and 1762 and the trend was the same in both ports. But the record of profitability revealed the speculative nature of such ventures. Of the total of seventy-nine privateers which are known to have sailed from the two ports during the course of the war only twenty made a profit on each of their cruises and a further sixteen made at least one loss.[41] The most striking figure is that of ships which made no profit at all – forty-three – or over half the total. At the same time, the difference in financial resources between the two ports is shown by the average tonnage figures for these privateers where the tonnage is recorded:

Table 1.15 AVERAGE TONNAGE OF PRIVATEERS

	Bayonne	St Jean-de-Luz
1702–13	124	91
1744–8	144	118
1756–63	135	80

Source: Archives départementales des Basses Pyrénées, Amirauté de Bayonne, B Supplément, No 2–44, 1702–62.

Although Bayonne possessed greater resources of capital than St Jean-de-Luz and her *armateurs* could afford larger privateers, both could draw on large numbers of seamen from the Basque and Mediterranean coasts. Jaupart states that the region has adequate supplies of suitable shipbuilding timber for the needs of these ports although it is likely that these consisted of pine rather than oak.[42] Ships built with the former would last perhaps five years, a quarter of the life of an oak-built vessel but this was usually long enough for wartime privateers. Pitch and tar were certainly available, though of unknown quality, as a by-product of the pine trees and cannon were made from the nearby Asturias iron. It was difficult to obtain flax and hemp for the sails and cordage, but supplies were obtained – probably from the Baltic on neutral Dutch ships.

One question that cannot be answered conclusively is whether, in this period of intense privateering activity, the merchants used trading vessels as privateers or built new ones specially for the purpose. It is impossible to be dogmatic on this issue. The main purpose of a privateer was to outsail the merchant ships it wished to capture and the warships that tried to take it. Merchant ships that were lightened during a chase by throwing their cargo and guns overboard seldom escaped a privateer, though the latter carried a heavier armament and more men – though not, of course, a cargo. It is possible that a privateer, specially built, could be faster than a merchant ship of approximately the same tonnage but it is equally clear that even if many were constructed solely for privateering, there were others that were pressed into service from trading which may have served equally well. It has been argued that the type of construction was less important than the size of crew because a large crew would handle the sails and rigging more quickly than the small crew usually found on a merchantman and could make the ship sail faster by making her more responsive to the changes in strength and direction of the wind. However this argument does not seem to apply to the privateers or slave ships that were caught and which carried large crews. At the same time privateering was largely sustained by the use of prize ships as privateers and it is the view of the present writer that the delay in putting privateers to sea after the outbreak of war – a common feature of the period 1689–1815 – indicates that merchants used this time to build new vessels. Some might have taken a considerable time to decide whether to participate in privateering.

Hesitation by the merchant would have been understandable. Privateering was a dangerous occupation, even by the standards of violence of the eighteenth century. Rich prizes were notoriously hard to find and catch. For a majority of privateering captains and crews the sea was an empty void in which they sailed for weeks and sometimes months without seeing another ship. The successful captain was a man who combined luck with considerable courage, because although the isolated merchant ship was easily caught, often without a shot being fired, there were some who put up a good fight. Most merchant ships were outsailed, outmanned and outgunned by almost any privateer and the crew meekly surrendered when escape was impossible – sometimes taking to the ship's boat and making for the shore if it was close enough. One example among many was the capture of an unnamed British vessel by the *St Joseph*, captained by Pierre Bonet, as reported in the Amirauté records in December 1760.[43] Her crew apparently made some attempt at defence and then escaped. A very different case was the fight between the *Flambeaux*, captained by Etienne Darnaud of Bayonne, and the *Sally* of Bristol.[44] The *Sally* was a much larger vessel – 150 tons against the 50 of the *Flambeaux*, and carried a crew of twenty-six (the size of the *Flambeaux*'s crew is not known). Most important of all, the *Sally* was a slaver on a voyage to West Africa and her crew were all able and determined seamen – slaving was not an occupation for the faint-hearted as there was always the risk of a slave rebellion on the Middle Passage. The *Sally* only surrendered after a three-hour fight.

Another notable struggle was that between the *Aigle* of Bayonne, 400 tons, captained by Martine Lafargue, and the *Falcon* of Bristol.[45] The *Falcon* was also a privateer, of 200 tons, carrying 160 men and armed with 20 six-pounder guns and 20 swivel guns. In spite of the difference in tonnage, the ships were evenly matched since the battle lasted an hour and a half. Losses were heavy on both sides: Captain Lafargue had his wrist severed and was wounded in the leg, and the second captain, Forestier, took command. Battles such as these, though uncommon, give a good idea of the risks in privateering and the qualities of leadership and determination exhibited by the most successful captains. To command a crew in sustained action demanded exceptional qualities of leadership.

An unusual battle was that between the British bomb vessel *Basilisk* and the *Audacieux* of Bayonne, captained by Jean Minbielle.[46] Unfortunately no record exists of the tonnage, armament, or size of crew of this privateer but according to the records of the Amirauté de Bayonne the *Basilisk* was a vessel of 260 tons and 14 cannon with a crew of 50. There was a violent struggle between the two ships and the *Basilisk* finally surrendered after her captain and eight men had been killed. These battles were however untypical of privateering. The prize was usually taken by fierce hand-to-hand fighting when the merchant ship tried to resist and handgrenades were widely used as a form of anti-personnel weapon to terrorize merchant seamen. But as has been noted already, few merchant ships tried to resist. The odds were usually heavily against them and if any of the crew were wounded they would not receive any compensation – there was no provision for merchant seamen at Greenwich Hospital and the small number of almshouses, and after 1747 a few provincial hospitals, were totally inadequate.

At the same time it must be stressed that *armateurs* who financed privateering did not want their ships to fight these fierce battles unless the prizes were particularly valuable. It was expensive to repair ships, especially in war when costs rose, and this cut profits. Captains who sought dramatic action of this kind could be a liability to their *armateurs*, though often this could not be avoided. Although most prizes surrendered without a fight, the successful privateer captain who patrolled the focal points of British trade ran the risk of meeting naval vessels appointed to protect British commerce. Thus the potentially fruitful areas for privateering were also the most dangerous and captains had to exercise judgement in selecting the areas and seasons for their cruises. The apparent ease with which some captains seized a succession of prizes shows that those who failed to take any ships were either exceptionally unlucky or cautious, or incompetent. It is also possible that there were some captains who were totally unsuitable, as at Vannes, where an 80 year-old captain was appointed to command the 35-ton *Hermine* in the 1744–8 war.[47]

As so few Bayonne privateers were captured this does not seem to have been a serious risk. In general Basque privateers cruised with impunity off Lisbon, Oporto, Viana and near the Straits of Gibraltar. Most prizes were stragglers from convoys or 'runners' – faster and better-armed ships which sailed independently. Until the earthquake of 1755 Lisbon was the centre of British trade with Portugal, although many ships also sailed to Oporto and Viana to the north for wine, olive oil and a variety of less important items. British commerce with the Mediterranean increased steadily during the eighteenth century – in contrast to the Portuguese which declined – and this gave Bayonne privateers the chance of further captures. The best opportunities were off the ports of Viana – the landing port of the Newfoundland cod fleet – Lisbon and Oporto, but there was a sandbar at Lisbon which forced shipping to wait outside the harbour for high tide. The Bayonne privateers preyed on a variety of trades as can be seen from the records of prizes captured. Many were from the outports, whose trade was only protected in British waters. The *Comte de Noailles* of Ciboure (Captain Michel Moliet) took five ships in 1747: two from London, one from Liverpool, one from Poole and another from an unnamed port.[48] There were also many examples of prizes from Bristol, Stockton, Lancaster as well as from Irish and Scottish ports.

Basque privateers also took vessels from New England, particularly Boston and Marblehead, which brought dried cod from the Newfoundland Grand Banks for the Portuguese and Mediterranean markets. These boats did not join the annual convoys of by-boats and fishing boats from St John's, Newfoundland, but arrived off the

Portuguese coast at approximately the same time, in October. These small vessels, sailing unprotected, were an easy prey for Basque privateers and the trade is reflected by the capture of the *Duke* of Boston by the *Cantabre* (Captain Joseph Duplat) in 1747, the *Seaflower* of Marblehead by the *Bellone* (Captain Dominique Lebat) in 1746 and the *Delight* of Boston by the *Jupiter* of Bayonne (Captain Jean Minbielle) in 1758.[49] Many of these and other vessels sailing to and from the North American coast were often blown off course and as the captains usually could not measure longitude sailed too far east and found themselves off the Portuguese, Spanish or even French coasts before they realized the mistake. Many of the latter were taken by privateers and ships with *lettres en guerre et marchandises* while they were setting sail from Bayonne or returning at the end of a voyage.

These records of captures should make it possible to estimate the degree of profitability of privateering at these Basque ports. In practice it is much more difficult because it is as hard to obtain details of the costs of fitting out privateers and of their voyages as it is to discover the profit from the sale of prizes or the ransoms. All that can be said at this stage is that of the seventy-nine privateers (not to be confused with successive privateering voyages) that put to sea from Bayonne and St Jean-de-Luz in the Seven Years War, only twenty made a profit on each of their cruises, a further sixteen made at least one loss and forty-three made no profit at all.[50] Yet profitability was a crucial issue for *armateurs*. Apart from the difficulty for contemporary *armateurs* to assess this from available methods of accounting, the lack of success indicated above resulted in a frequent change of captains, as *armateurs* tried to find suitable men. The appointment of Pierre Naguille for four successive years as captain of the *Labourt*, a 300 ton ship of St Jean-de-Luz, is in itself remarkable.[51] His record of success – twenty-seven ships taken – shows why this was done; he obviously combined success with cordial relations with his *armateurs*, though it is possible he kept his place because he was a major shareholder. Other men had more mixed luck. Jean Minbielle commanded four ships between mid-1757 and the end of the war.[52] One of these, the *Grunvel* (?), took no prizes but he had more luck with the others and his total by the end of the war was twenty-six, one of which, the *Frise* of Philadelphia, he ransomed for £4,000. Occasionally ransoms were higher and the record for this period seems to be the £10,000 paid for the *Success* of Jersey to Captain Samson Dufourcq of the *Samson* of Bayonne.[53] This is what made privateering so popular at Bayonne and other French ports:

the gambler's dream of sharing in a rich prize attracted seamen from the Mediterranean and other French ports. The harsh reality is that privateering made few men rich. Yet it proved a temporary relief for Bayonne, which otherwise would have declined further. The peace that followed until 1778 made little difference to Bayonne's sinking economy, but the war of 1778–83 once more opened the door to successful trade with Spain and Portugal. As trade increased to 24 million livres (1778–80) from the 13 million of 1770–6, there was little interest in privateering and few prizes were taken.[54] In other words, there was a return to the conditions at the beginning of the century. The trade between Bayonne and Spain thus dominates and controls the level of privateering and helps to explain why this should run counter to the pattern shown at other ports.

To the south of Bayonne and the other Basque ports, small Spanish rowboat privateers were occasionally to be found. However these were only a threat to British ships as they lay becalmed off the Spanish and Portuguese coast. Spanish ports were also used by French privateers to refit and dispose of their prizes, whether Spain was at war with the British or neutral. This led many British merchants to send their bullion to Britain on neutral shipping, and during the War of Austrian Succession and the Seven Years War much was sent on Dutch as well as British warships. British trade was also threatened at Madeira and the Azores as well as in the Mediterranean. Spanish ports within and outside the Straits of Gibraltar provided bases for French and Spanish privateers and at times these cruised in the Straits waiting for British trading vessels. Because the Straits are only eight miles wide at the narrowest point, between Tarife and Ceuta, navigation was particularly dangerous without proper convoy. At times British shipping was ordered to sail in the middle of the Straits so as to stay out of sight of French and Spanish privateers cruising off the coast. Once inside the Mediterranean convoys were protected by the Mediterranean squadron. The principal privateering base was Marseilles, from where considerable numbers of privateers sailed during the War of Spanish Succession. During the mid-eighteenth century it maintained its interests better than many other ports further north *(see table p. 41)*.

From Marseilles, privateers sailed to intercept British trade with Genoa and Leghorn, the two entrepôts for northern Italy. British trade with the Austrian Empire, conducted through Trieste and Ancona, was also threatened by French privateers from Marseilles and to a lesser extent, from Toulon where there were fewer privateers. These sailed off the coast of Sicily, in the Strait of Messina and

Table 1.16

	Privateers
War of Spanish Succession	146
Seven Years War	92
War of American Independence	76

Source: Delumeau, 'Guerre de course française', p 294.

watched for shipping from an observation post on the island of Zemba. To avoid them, British ships sailed close to the Algerian coast from Gibraltar to Tunis and thence via the island of Pantellaria to the coast of Italy. During the Napoleonic War, British trade with Austria and northern Italy was seriously disrupted by the French conquest of Italy and the closing of ports to British ships. Privateers, fitted out in Adriatic ports, formed an additional hazard.

There was also much British trade with the Levant through the ports of Alexandretta and Smyrna, with Corinth through the port of Zante and with Janina and Arta. As a result, although naval vessels escorted the large Levant Company ships to ports in Asia Minor and convoyed them back, those destined for the Greek ports and islands had to complete their voyages independently. The islands of the Cyclades through which these British ships sailed, provided a base for French privateers which were supported by French trading communities. For the early period however, British losses to French privateers were not too severe, but during the Napoleonic War they rose steeply. In August 1803 Nelson ordered two warships to cruise between Cape Matapan and the western end of Crete to protect commerce with the Greek islands, while vessels were also ordered to cruise off the south coast of Italy and the mouth of the Adriatic.[55] Later in the same year he supplemented this with convoys based on Malta and Gibraltar. Trade for Britain was first assembled at Malta, and these collected the remaining trade at Gibraltar. This worked well on the whole, but in February 1805 two French frigates, *Hortense* and *Incorruptible* met a British convoy defended by the sloop *Arrow* and the bomb *Acheron* off Cape Caxine.[56] In the fierce action which followed the British vessels were sunk after attacking the French frigates and the convoy was dispersed. Of the thirty-five ships in the convoy, three were sunk, three were captured and the remainder dispersed reaching Gibraltar, Malta and Algiers. This was the only serious setback however, and the threat from French privateers was checked by Nelson's system of trade protection and his decision to refuse to recognize as neutral any port that sheltered French privateers. The result was that trade was better protected, many ports were closed to French privateers and Nelson received the thanks of the merchant corporations of London.[57]

This makes a fitting close to a discussion of the French privateering attack on British commerce. During the period 1689–1815 this threat varied greatly in intensity from the wars of the League of Augsburg and Spanish Succession – the *apogée de la course*, as French historians like to describe it – to the less active Seven Years War. To a large extent the severity of this attack varied according to the strength of the British navy, the degree to which an effective convoy system operated and the opportunities for trade that were open to French *armateurs*. In some cases, the proximity to the focal points of British trade in the English Channel enabled privateers from St Malo and Dunkirk to wreak considerable damage to British commerce, but only when the privateers enjoyed the support of royal warships. To a large extent they were driven to privateering by the destruction of commercial ventures: the British attack on the French cod fishery at Newfoundland hit St Malo hard, and the proximity of British naval bases in the Medway prevented Dunkirk and Calais merchants from continuing trade in wartime. When this naval support was withdrawn during the mid-eighteenth century wars, *armateurs* were less willing to support privateering ventures in the ports and harbours along the English Channel, and Admiral Hawke's naval blockade of Brittany in the Seven Years War effectively checked French trade and privateering. Only at Bayonne was the pattern of activity different, but that reflects a pattern of trade that was successful early in the period and in decline by the mid-eighteenth century. Privateering offered a chance to reverse the decline, but in the long run it was unsuccessful, the harbour silted up and Bordeaux on a better river site, with excellent communications to the interior, replaced Bayonne as the entrepôt of south-west France. In the wars of American Independence and of Revolution and Empire there was some general recovery of interest, but it was on a smaller scale.

2

The Organization of Convoys and their Departure

THE GROWTH OF TRADE in the period 1689–1815 was crucial to the development of Britain. Commerce provided the capital for war finance in the period as well as the resources for launching and sustaining the Industrial Revolution. It was also respectable and commercial wealth carried considerable social prestige. At the end of the seventeenth century most rich men were merchants; the exceptions were a small number of lawyers and civil servants.[1] During the eighteenth century the number of important merchants increased; contemporary accounts suggest a rise from 2,000 in 1700 to 2,900 in 1750 and 3,500 in 1812. During the eighteenth century other professions produced wealth: doctors, estate agents, lawyers and a growing number of industrialists. This change in the social composition of the wealthy did not seriously weaken the power and prestige of the commercial class. Many merchants were members of parliament and some, after fulfilling important government contracts, were given baronetcies, though they had to give up commerce to gain them. It would be an exaggeration to claim that merchants as a group controlled government finances. Nevertheless throughout the period they formed a wealthy, influential and vocal group which was well organized and to which the government and the Admiralty had to pay careful attention.

During this period the composition of the group changed to include new men in London and the outports, but continued to be dominated by wealthy London merchants. When the period opened in 1689, the bulk of English commerce was in the hands of chartered companies: East India, Levant, Royal African, Hudson's Bay and a number of others. By the end of the period, in 1815, all but a few had disappeared. Only the Hudson's Bay Company remained in control of its trade, although it was challenged by the North Western

Company in Canada. The East India Company had lost all but its China trade and that monopoly was ended within twenty years. The chartered companies had been replaced by groups of merchants in London and by the outports who were free to participate in trade without the restrictions of company regulations. They formed associations in the ports and acted as pressure groups influencing government policy. They were led by energetic shipping magnates who were linked by bonds of interest and marriage. New men of this type were instrumental in making Liverpool and Glasgow the centres of successful trades with North and South America, West Africa and the Far East within the fifty years that followed.

The early chartered companies had played a major role in developing English trade in the sixteenth and seventeenth centuries. Overseas trade demanded considerable capital to build and fit out ships, purchase trade goods and carry the initial expenses of opening new trade routes. To safeguard the long term security and prosperity of these trades it was essential to grant merchants a monopoly of future profits as an encouragement. In this way English trade was opened with India, Russia, Turkey and elsewhere by companies chartered respectively in 1660, 1555 and 1583. In this respect, England was no different from other European countries, which developed eastern commerce through the French Compagnie française des Indes, the Dutch Vereenigde Oost Indische Compagnie and the Danish Asiatisk Kompagni. All were given commercial monopolies and all tried to exclude interlopers. When the companies prospered, other merchants tried to share in their trade. In England after 1688 the East India Company was challenged by rivals and this weakened its influence on the government. Although this did not change the way in which the Admiralty defended the company's ships, the challenge was of considerable significance. Before 1688 the company had enjoyed the support of the Stuart monarchy and its fortunes had been closely linked with James II. When he fled, the East India Company was discredited. Its rivals tried to force Parliament to rescind its charter and were able to gain the support of the new king. The dispute dragged on until 1698 when Parliament offered to grant a charter to whichever company offered a loan of £2 million. The old company gave £315,000 and kept its forts and Indian privileges, but its rivals were given the right to trade there. In 1702 the old and new companies merged and formed the United Company of Merchants trading to the East Indies. It was chartered by Godolphin's government in 1708. The older group of merchants had been forced to share their power and rights with newer rivals, but kept their privileges.

Other companies were less fortunate. The Royal African Company had been created in 1672 from the remains of the unsuccessful Royal Adventurers into Africa. This company was also in serious difficulties after the flight of James II. It maintained forts on the West African coast but could not meet these expenses. Nor could it service the company's debt of providing the credit needed to sell slaves in the West Indies. The company could not keep rivals from the West African coast; it lacked the resources to patrol the extensive area over which it claimed a monopoly, and there were merchants at Bristol who regularly sailed there, bought slaves and sold them at considerable profit in the Caribbean. These voyages were more profitable than the Royal African Company's for the Bristol merchants paid nothing towards the company's administrative costs. In war these interlopers received little protection from naval convoys – the Admiralty was only obliged to defend legitimate trade – but in practice this made little difference. The Admiralty was too weak to defend commerce in the face of heavy naval and privateering attack.

Other companies were also in decline or already defunct: the Levant Company and the Russia Company are examples. The result of this gradual collapse of the chartered companies is that there was a measure of uncertainty as to who were the most important figures in English commerce. Trade was also under attack, and English commerce was particularly vulnerable because her most important trade, with north-western and southern Europe, lay open to French commerce raiders. The earliest available figures for England's trade between the wars of the League of Augsburg and Spanish Succession show the main lines of English commerce:

Table 2.1 ENGLISH TRADE 1699–1701

	(£000)	
	Imports	Exports and re-exports
N.W. Europe	1,418	3,022
N. Europe	583	335
S. Europe	1,555	1,708
British Islands	430	367
America	1,107	851
E. Indies	756	136

Source: R. Davis, 'English foreign trade, 1700–74' in *The growth of English overseas trade in the seventeenth and eighteenth centuries*, W. E. Minchinton (ed), (1969), table p 118.

The greater part of English trade had to sail close to French ports. However their destinations were relatively close to England and the convoys could be escorted relatively quickly and easily to their destinations, provided there were adequate numbers of the smaller warships which were used for commerce defence. Unfortunately this was one of the weaknesses of the navy in 1689. The Admiralty also lacked experience in providing convoys for the growing number of ships sailing to European ports and distant waters. The idea of convoys was not new; merchant ships had been convoyed in the thirteenth century and there is evidence of organized convoys in the reign of Edward III, but in the late seventeenth century the system was still not working efficiently.[2] During the Anglo-Dutch wars the important coal trade from north-east England had suffered heavy losses because there were too few convoys. Some ships sailed without an escort in an attempt to reach London where the market price of coal was often higher than elsewhere. However they were often taken by privateers. Those that waited for escorts often had to wait many months which meant that no coal left the ports, forcing collieries to close.[3] In the War of the League of Augsburg the trade was little better defended and the price of coal rose alarmingly, to £6 a chaldron in London. In 1694 the government appointed nine ships to protect the trade, six on the northern and three on the western coast.

This improvement was not made until five years after the outbreak of war. It was not due to neglect or a lack of interest on the part of the Admiralty and the administration. When war broke out, naval resources were concentrated on the defence of England; William II ordered fifty line-of-battle ships to be concentrated in the English Channel and in the Mediterranean, to be supported by fifteen smaller vessels and fire ships.[4] They were to be given a full complement of men, and stocks of provisions and naval stores were to be held in the Mediterranean. Commerce was not neglected; William also ordered that the West India ships were to be given a convoy. Until the Battle of La Hogue in 1692 naval resources continued to be used in this way. The Revolution of 1688 was in danger and every effort had to be made to protect William from French attack. After that battle the English were able to turn from defence to offence, but for two years little more was done for commerce. In these early years of the war there was little reference to trade in parliamentary debates, even though the Spanish and American trades had suffered badly: 29 out of 59 ships were lost from the American and 21 out of 29 from Spanish trade in 1690.[5] Trade with the eastern Mediterranean had also suffered from attacks by privateers, losing ships and being delayed on their voyages. Many members of parliament were suspicious that the merchants were making excessive profits and that some were trading with the enemy and did not wish to debate merchants' grievances. The merchants' case was also hampered by rivalry between ports and even between the country gentry and merchants. Gradually however the status of merchants improved and the loss of the Smyrna convoy in 1693 was a national disaster which united rival factions in a bitter attack on government inadequacy. The Admiralty was attacked for failing to appoint convoys which it had ordered; in its defence on 10 April the Board supplied lists of convoys and cruisers that had been ordered since 25 January. The House discovered that although the list was impressive, it was also misleading; of the 59 ships shown as cruisers, 13 had not been used for this purpose and of the 32 named as escorts to convoys, 12 had not, as the Admiralty claimed, escorted coastal convoys but instead had escorted overseas shipping. Furthermore, some ships had been mentioned several times when they were transferred to new duties. The actual number of convoys appointed was closer to forty-three and not the number claimed by the Admiralty. Parliamentary anger at this deception could achieve little by itself. The root cause of the country's commercial misfortunes was a chronic lack of small craft suitable for escort duties and the absence was also felt by Berkeley when he bombarded French coastal towns in 1694 and 1695. As a result a Council of Trade was appointed in 1696 to ensure that English commerce was given adequate protection. Its purpose was to advise the king and the Admiralty on the number of convoys to be appointed for foreign trade and for the rest of the war help to organize a more effective defence of commercial vessels. During the War of Spanish Succession it continued to pass to the Admiralty information in the form of letters from colonial governors and merchants. This was useful, but what the Admiralty really needed was to be able to discuss with merchants when the convoys should sail and how large the escort should be. The Council of Trade could not do this, although it passed information, in the form of letters from merchants and colonial governors, to the Admiralty in an impartial manner.

There were also discussions between the Admiralty and merchants, though it was not always easy for the Board to know who to consult about some of the trades. In the case of the East India trade, the Board summoned the secretary or directors to the Admiralty and discussed with them how many ships would be sent and at what times. The secretary and directors of the company – or companies – were able to give precise information on shipping in their own trade and were able to make every effort to see that the Indiamen were ready at the appointed time. In the case of other trades, where there was no chartered company, it was not possible to hold consultations of this kind. The Admiralty tried to find out the names of the principal merchants and consult them. Unfortunately there was often rivalry between merchants and groups of merchants and it was by no means certain that the information supplied in this manner applied to the whole trade. For West India commerce, for example, there had been a number of different sailing dates for outward and return sections of the trade, depending on whether merchants wished to buy sugar at the beginning of the harvest or the end. Those who sent their ships to Barbados, where most of the sugar was partly processed, habitually returned later. In consequence, the Admiralty received a number of conflicting requests for convoys, depending on which merchants were consulted. The Admiralty did not have sufficient resources, in this or any other war during the period, to provide separate convoys for each section of the Caribbean trade. Another problem was that merchants tended to exaggerate the value of the cargo and the number of ships needed as a convoy. In the case of the Newfoundland trade, most of the merchants lived in western ports – Poole, Bristol and smaller ports in Devon – and therefore it was not possible for the Admiralty to consult the merchants. This trade was important. At the time it was regarded as a 'nursery of seamen', and the dried fish that was taken to Portugal, Spain and the Mediterranean was a valuable part of English commerce. In this case the Admiralty had to consult with the few Newfoundland merchants who lived in London, with members of parliament who represented the fishing ports, and through correspondence with the merchants in the western ports.

Following these discussions it was decided that the Admiralty should choose the dates on which to send convoys and the ships which were to form the escort. The details of the sailing dates had to be given to the merchants concerned. In the case of the chartered companies, this was comparatively straight forward. The Secretary of the Admiralty informed the company by letter and could rely on the arrangements being made to get merchant ships to the rendezvous at the correct dates. In the case of other trades, the Admiralty had to publish the details of sailing dates in a place frequented by the merchants. In the case of the outports, the Secretary wrote to a person of authority in the port and asked him to pass the information to the merchants concerned. In November 1689, the Admiralty decided at four days notice to send a convoy to the Canary Islands. The Secretary sent a notice to the Royal Exchange to inform merchants that the convoy would rendezvous in the Downs and sail on 5 December.[6] The Royal Exchange was an excellent place to display notices of this kind, for merchants from most branches of commerce regularly went there to discuss business and hear the latest news. However not every trade could be informed in this way. The colliers were not engaged in commerce in the usual sense and their masters were seldom seen on the floor of the Royal Exchange. When the Admiralty wished to inform them that a convoy would sail from the buoy of the Gunfleet for Newcastle, the Secretary sent the notice to Mr Arthur Shallott to be displayed at Billingsgate. In the case of shipping at the outports, there was sometimes a merchant society such as the one at Bristol – the Society of Merchant Venturers – or the Secretary wrote to a person of authority in the community. When the Admiralty wished to send orders for a naval vessel to escort ships from Leith to Newcastle, the Secretary wrote to the chief magistrate and asked him to give the Admiralty's orders to the captain of the first naval vessel that arrived at the port, and also to inform merchants of these arrangements.[7]

To some degree the Admiralty was not in complete control of convoy arrangements. Occasionally the king, William II, sent instructions under the royal sign manual or by Order in Council. The Admiralty was also subject to orders from two committees of the royal council: the Committee for the Affairs of Ireland and the Committee for Trade and Plantations, replaced by the Board of Trade in 1696. The Committee for the Affairs of Ireland was particularly important during the troubled years of the Catholic Rebellion from 1689 to 1692. It was logical that this committee should be in charge of arranging convoys for troops and supplies in the Irish Sea and it was given the right to order convoy escorts and arrange the disposition of naval vessels there.[8] Relations between the Admiralty and the Committee appear to have been harmonious and much information passed between them.[9] After the defeat of the Catholic army and the flight of Patrick Sarsfield there remained only one threat to English trade with Ireland, the Irish Jacobites. These men sailed on French privateers and provided first hand knowledge of the Irish coast. They also enjoyed the support and sympathy of many Irish Catholics in the coastal areas, especially in south-west Ireland, and they gained information and provisions from many Irish fishing boats. In 1692 this threat was considered so serious that a proclamation forbade fishing boats to put to sea for a month except from three named ports and with at least three protestants on board.[10] Detachments of troops were also posted in Valentia and Baltimore in order to prevent privateer crews landing and to keep the Tories in check. These small-scale measures could do little to control the privateers and in the War of Spanish Succession, raids on commerce and the coast continued virtually unchecked. At first they were of little importance – a few cattle were stolen for food. However, in 1708 and 1711 privateer crews raided Dingle and there were incursions in Baltimore and Bantry in 1704 and 1708. The damage was usually light but the government feared that it might encourage a Fifth Column.

This formed part of the severe threat to English shipping in the War of the League of Augsburg. The losses to these Irish-manned privateers may not have been very heavy compared with the more numerous vessels manned by French crews. But the area where the Irish boats operated, off the south and south-west coasts of Ireland, was important as many ships made a landfall there on their return voyages. English merchant losses were heavy. No accurate estimate of the total exists, though the Admiralty claimed that 4,000 were captured, and Pepys believed that all but about 500 of these were taken during the last four years of the war.[11] In the War of Spanish Succession privateers were again active and the Admiralty organized a convoy system as in the previous war. It was extremely costly in its demands on resources of men and shipping – half the sailors and two thirds of the naval vessels were occupied in protecting English trade.[12] The Admiralty continued to discuss convoy arrangements with companies and associations of merchant shipowners, and many strategic decisions regarding the strength of escorts and the disposition of cruising squadrons were discussed in the Cabinet Council. The coast was protected by small frigates and lesser craft, each of which patrolled a section of the coast. Other ships patrolled the North Sea and the English Channel to safeguard the important fisheries. The coastal trade was escorted by a number of standing convoys. The strength of the escort in the English Channel was increased to ships of fifty or sixty guns in an attempt to overawe privateers and to match the small French raiding squadrons which put to sea from Dunkirk. The most important coastal trade was between Newcastle and London. In previous wars this had not always been adequately protected. In the War of Spanish Succession it was given two and sometimes three groups of ships as standing convoys, each group consisting of two frigates, one of which was often a ship of fifty guns. One of the outstanding examples of commerce defence took place in 1707, when the *Nightingale*, 24 guns, from Stockton-on-Tees held off six Dunkirk privateers which attacked her

convoy off the Long Sand. This careful defence of the coal trade
roused the jealousy of other merchants: the Russia Company asked
for additional escorts for its convoys but was told that the Newcastle
convoys could not be touched.

Colonial trade was defended in these wars in much the same way.
Ships were stationed at the centres of colonial commerce and
additional protection was given by convoy escorts while they were on
the coast. Newfoundland was given up to six warships because the
coastal and Grand Banks fisheries demanded adequate protection
from the well-armed French fishing boats, and because the Grand
Banks was a focal area for all convoys returning to Britain from the
Caribbean and American coast. Boston and New York each had one
or two ships for local defence against privateers and pirates, and the
Chesapeake and Carolinas were defended by an additional cruiser.
The Caribbean trade was especially threatened by pirates – until
about 1715 – and British commerce was defended by a squadron at
Jamaica and by single ships in the Leeward Islands and at Barbados.

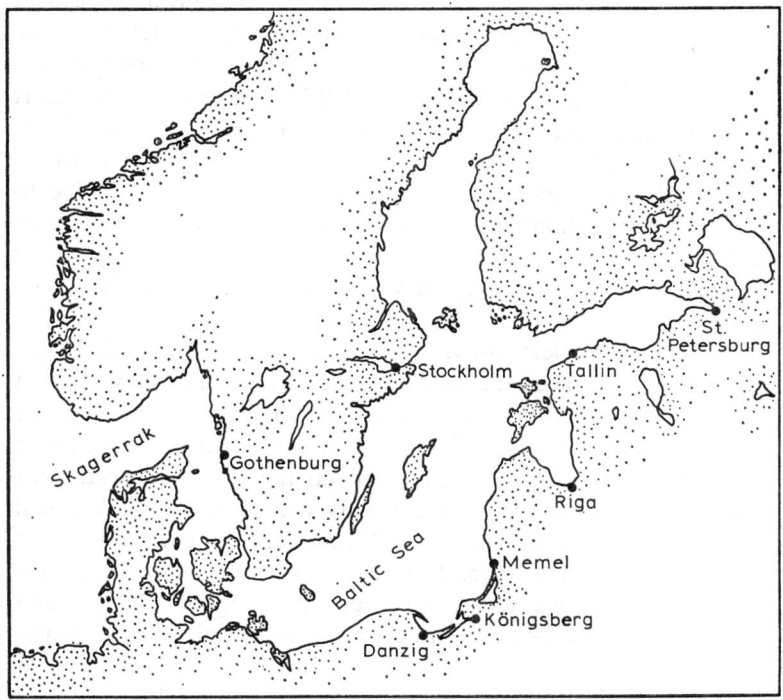

2 The Baltic

Slave ships were protected by a couple of frigates stationed on the Guinea coast. Efforts were made to safeguard the ships sailing across the North Sea and through the English Channel by providing large escorts at least for the major convoys. The Russia Company's fleet assembled at the buoy of the Nore and sailed north with naval escort, calling off the Humber and Tyne for any additional trade. The convoys sailed across the North Sea, followed the coast of Norway to the North Cape and were escorted into the harbour of Archangel. The Baltic trade, which was the most important strategically on account of imports of naval stores, had similar protection, usually to the Sound. At times, when it was feared that a French squadron was at sea, convoys were delayed until the French ships had returned to port – a caution that was necessary but which took up much of the trading season. If merchant ships had to put to sea, for example to reach a Baltic market before the port was frozen, the trade was escorted by the bulk of the North Sea squadron. In October 1806 Sir Edward Whitaker protected the autumn trade for Hamburg and the Baltic, escorting the Hamburg ships to within 50 miles of the island of Heligoland and the Eastland fleet 'clear of the Dogger Bank'. This apparently satisfied the merchants. The remaining ships from his squadron, two heavy frigates, strengthened a convoy to the Maas and then joined Whitaker at Goree to escort Marlborough from Holland to the North Foreland. Subsequently the convoy was again split up, part of it sailing to meet the returning Baltic trade at Elsinore, and another part sailing to the Elbe to escort returning Hamburg trade. The remaining two large frigates were sent in to port to refit. The Hamburg merchants had the choice of returning with this convoy or waiting until the frigates had been refitted.

The North American convoys were not so well defended, for the only hazard they faced on their outward voyage once they had left the English Channel and the Channel Soundings was a small number of privateers and occasional pirates on the American coast. The passage through the English Channel was the most dangerous part of the voyage and convoys were usually strengthened by additional ships from the western squadron which escorted them for the first 100 leagues of their voyage. The most valuable ships were the East Indiamen which were escorted through the English Channel and often as far as the south Atlantic by warships which subsequently sailed to St Helena to bring the returning Indiamen back to England. Commerce to the Mediterranean, Spain and Portugal was always strongly defended. Not only did these ships have to run the gauntlet

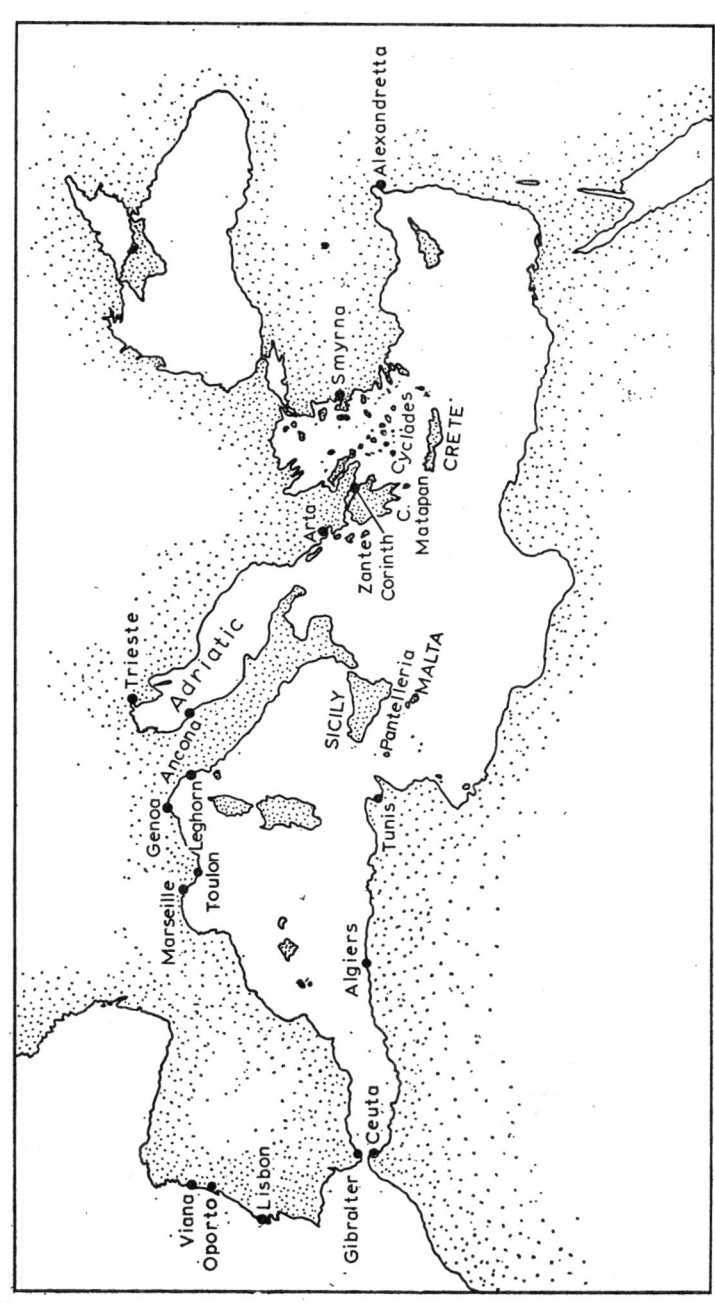

3   The Mediterannean

of the privateering ports in the English Channel, but they also had to pass the French naval bases of Brest in the Bay of Biscay and Toulon in the Mediterranean. The disastrous loss of the Smyrna convoy in the earlier war emphasized the dangers facing this commerce, and convoys were usually escorted in the War of Spanish Succession by ships of seventy or eighty guns as far as the Straits of Gibraltar. Once within the Mediterranean, convoys were protected by weaker escorts to Smyrna or Scanderoon. The Mediterranean was also the scene of important naval and military operations against the French, notably the attack on Toulon in 1707. Thus the passage of the larger line-of-battle ships from England to the Mediterranean in the spring and their return in the autumn was to some extent planned to coincide with the sailing of the main convoys. There were dangers in delaying the return of these large warships, for commerce protection or for any other reason, as the winter gales in the Bay of Biscay could cause severe damage. One extreme case was in October 1707 when Sir Clowdisley Shovell's flagship, the *Association*, and three other vessels were lost on the Gillstone Ledges off the Scillies as they were returning from the Mediterranean.

Although this elaborate system of commerce defence did much to cut shipping losses in this war, they still remained high. In the first few months of the war, many merchant ships were lost mainly through lack of adequate convoys for which the Prince's Council must take responsibility.[13] The Soundings squadron and the Newcastle and Irish trades were protected at the expense of the system of coastal defence and there was in any case a general shortage of cruisers. At first there was little criticism of the Admiralty in the Commons, for although there was widespread merchant dissatisfaction there were also deep divisions within the mercantile community. In 1704 and 1705 losses rose. In 1704 Du-Guay Trouin from Brest and Saint-Pol from Dunkirk cruised together in the Soundings. Their combined force numbered half a dozen warships, but they attracted many privateers. Together they captured over thirty prizes including a number of warships, for the loss of one small corvette.[14] Their principal success was in taking the *Coventry* and part of her convoy bound for Newfoundland about 200 miles west of Scilly. French victories were mainly due to the weakness of the Soundings squadron, from which ships had been taken to strengthen the Mediterranean force, and to the French interception of returning American convoys that were inadequately protected. The appearance of these French raiding forces in the summer demonstrated the weakness of a convoy system that relied too heavily on a strong western squadron, which in any case could not hope to intercept returning convoys and French squadrons at the same time. There were higher losses in 1705, which were ignored by the Commons but when in both 1705 and 1706 convoys were late reaching England there was serious concern. In late summer 1707 the French gained control of the English Channel when they captured many British merchant ships which were returning to port. Worst hit were the Spanish and Portuguese trades, and sixteen merchant ships were taken from a Russia convoy after the escorts had turned back for England. In 1708 public concern was such that a Convoys and Cruisers Act was passed.[15] This reserved forty-three naval ships for use as convoy escorts and cruisers, save in national emergency: 6 third rates, 20 fourth, 13 fifth and 4 sixth. A senior official was appointed as superintendent of cruisers and minor officials in outports were ordered to record the sailing and arrival of cruisers which were to be careened three times a year. Furthermore, Parliament was to be given an annual report on the working of the Act. It is tempting to see this as a turning point in the *guerre de course* – there were no more complaints from merchants for the rest of the war. But in reality the value of the Act was that it convinced the merchants that every effort was being made to protect their trade. It made little difference to the level of British losses which did not fall and reached their highest level in 1711. However the emphasis did shift from the English Channel to the Mediterranean. Total losses in this war probably reached 2,000 and may have been higher.

This was a heavy burden for British commerce to bear but losses of merchant ships were lower in the War of Spanish Succession than in the previous war in spite of the success of Du-Guay Trouin and Saint-Pol. To some extent this must be attributed to the more efficient use of naval resources for commerce defence and greater experience of the Admiralty and the naval captains. There was no lack of consultation between the Admiralty and the merchants about the number and timing of convoys. The problems were rather the shortage of suitable escort vessels and cruisers and occasional carelessness by the Admiralty in assigning vessels for convoy duty when they were due for repair. The Admiralty regularly received information about the movements of French privateers and warships from spies in French ports and from the captains of cartel ships. It was therefore able to regulate the sailing of convoys to try and avoid them. However this often delayed convoys for weeks and even months and in some cases trade suffered badly. In 1696 the Portuguese wine vintage was poor – the summer had been wet and the wine was sour when shipped. It was further delayed in Portuguese ports and much wine fretted and went off. Many English shippers suffered heavy losses.[16] In June 1707 a report reached the Admiralty that thirty-eight merchant ships at Ostend were waiting for convoy, and some had been waiting for up to eight months.[17] Under these circumstances convoys were frequently amalgamated. In October 1706 the Admiralty was informed that the Virginia fleet, consisting of 200 ships under the protection of four warships, had been sighted 300 leagues east of the Capes. No doubt some of these reports were exaggerated, but there can be little doubt about the dangers faced by ships hired by the Royal African Company. On their outward voyage, they sailed with convoys bound for the West Indies and were escorted safely through the danger zone of the English Channel and the Soundings. Some however sailed back to England with cargoes of gold, hides, ivory, wax and gum from Gambia, Sierra Leone and Sherbro. Of the nine ships that made this return voyage between 1702 and 1704 only three completed it, five were captured by the French and one disappeared.[18] Ships which carried slaves to the West Indies were more fortunate. After the slaves had been sold the proceeds were invested either in commodities or bills of exchange and shipped back to England under the protection of a convoy. Many of these were lost as well, but the company usually insured gold, silver and sugar and in any case hired rather than owned the ships, so that the burden of the loss of 114 ships was only borne partly by the company.

So far this chapter has been concerned with the convoys which escorted the London trade, but there were other convoys as well. Although London dominated the country's commerce and over half of all trade passed through the Thames, many outports enjoyed a greater prosperity than they do today. Several of the western ports which sent ships with the fishing fleet to Newfoundland each year were regarded as important towns. Weymouth had a 'great many good substantial merchants' who 'drive a considerable trade and have a good number of ships'.[19] The Admiralty could not afford to ignore the interests of these ports, although they did not receive as much attention as the principal London chartered companies. Nonetheless the Newfoundland fishery drew ships from Weymouth, Poole, Dartmouth and other western ports and was as carefully protected as the limited naval resources would allow. Convoys were arranged between the merchants and the Admiralty by correspondence, and where necessary merchants were supported by their members of parliament. The most important port in the English

Channel in the period 1689–1713 was Exeter, at that time almost at the peak of its prosperity as a serge manufacturing and marketing centre.[20] It had extensive trade with Holland, Flanders and north Germany, with which its merchants had close personal links, and managed to break the monopoly of London interests such as the Hamburg Company. When war broke out in 1689 merchants at Exeter and adjacent ports asked for separate convoys under the escort of two or more warships, but there is no evidence that these were given.[21] The naval resources were too meagre and merchants had to send their ships by coastal convoy to the Thames to join the London convoys for northern Europe. Similarly, the Exeter ships bound for Spain, Portugal and the Canaries, as well as more distant markets, joined convoys at Plymouth. The Admiralty tried to keep the merchants fully informed of convoy arrangements, but at times there were complaints that not enough warning had been given. Exeter's trade was hit hard by the war. In 1702, serge exports to Spain fell from the peacetime total of more than 1 million to only 217,238 lbs and in the next two years there were no exports to Spain. From 1705 there was a slow recovery, but even at the end of the war, serge exports were still under 1 million lbs. Furthermore, although the Bruges and Ostend commerce was well established before 1700, it did not develop as it should have done. This was due to a combination of poor wartime markets and inadequate convoys and it is particularly significant that Exeter's trade with Spain should have suffered so badly, for this was a trade especially vulnerable to French privateering attack.

Bristol was more fortunate. The port lay outside the main area of privateering attack, though Bristol ships were vulnerable when they were sailing to markets in the West Indies or North America and passing to the south of Ireland. Until about the mid-eighteenth century, Bristol was the second most important port in Britain, and her merchants were represented by the Society of Merchant Venturers. Bristol also had two members of parliament, one of which represented the Society, and so the Admiralty made every effort to satisfy Bristol demands for protection. Much of the city's trade was with the West Indies and North America and in 1692 the Society asked for a convoy to escort thirty or forty ships bound for Virginia, Barbados, the Leeward Islands and Jamaica. The merchants argued that the convoy should meet the trade at Bristol rather than at Milford Haven, Plymouth or Kinsale, implicitly rejecting any suggestion that Bristol ships should join the main convoys.[22] In 1702, even before war had broken out, the Society wrote to the

Bristol members of parliament urging them to ask for two convoys if war was declared and in June 1705 the Society resolved to lend the Admiralty £200 towards the cost of raising a crew for a ship which was being built to protect Bristol's commerce. Two years later, the Society's treasurer, Abraham Elton, and his co-owners of a merchant vessel, lent it free to the Society to accommodate sailors recruited to form the crew of an escort vessel. The same year the Society thanked its member of parliament, Sir John Duddlestone, for obtaining a convoy and also sent a present of wine to Captain Steward of the *Garland* when he arrived to escort the Virginia fleet. It is significant that these gestures of appreciation were made when much of British commerce was under strong attack by the French, and although they are earlier than the cruise of Saint-Pol and Du-Guay Trouin in the late summer, they reveal a close co-operation between the Admiralty and the Society. No other port on the west coast of Britain received comparable treatment. Liverpool was still a small port and did not get its own custom house until 1700, although the foundations of its later commercial prosperity had already been laid by its leading citizens. Nor was Glasgow's trade of any greater importance, although illegal tobacco imports were made before the Act of Union. More significantly, one merchant in Edinburgh, which was commercially more important, was still trading with France in 1711, four years after the Act of Union, and many others no doubt continued illegal activities of this sort during the war.[23]

The heavy losses suffered by British shipping during these two wars did not result in commercial stagnation. River navigation was improved and money was spent on harbour works at ports as diverse as Grimsby and Liverpool.[24] When peace returned in 1713, merchants were able to take advantage of these improvements and develop their commerce. The interval before the outbreak of war with Spain in 1739 was one of unparalleled prosperity, as the following table shows *(see table p. 59)*.

The increase in British trade is mirrored by a comparable rise in the number of ships owned by British merchants. Yet losses were lower in the wars of 1739–48 and 1756–63 than in the two wars at the beginning of the century. To some extent this is because there were fewer French privateers at sea and there was no French raiding squadron of the type used by Saint-Pol and Du-Guay Trouin with devastating effect. British naval supremacy was not seriously threatened in these wars of the mid-eighteenth century, and the Admiralty was able to devote large numbers of frigates and smaller vessels to use as convoy escorts and cruisers instead of using them

Table 2.2 OFFICIAL VALUES OF IMPORTS AND OF EXPORTS AND
RE-EXPORTS COMBINED FOR ENGLAND AND WALES

| | (£000) | | | |
| | 1713 | | 1739 | |
	Imports	Exports	Imports	Exports
N. Europe	1,756	3,340	2,256	3,634
S. Europe	1,536	2,126	1,341	2,851
Asia	932	94	1,297	271
Africa	12	112	43	220
British N. America	19	8	60	36
American Colonies	303	285	754	696
British W. Indies	792	358	1,567	246
Foreign W. Indies and S. America	2	110	65	209

Source: B. R. Mitchell and Phyllis Deane, *Abstract of British historical statistics*
(Cambridge 1971), p. 309.

for squadron duties. Yet the Admiralty must be given credit for
efficient convoy organization. Although there were few chartered
companies still trading by the mid-eighteenth century – the East India
and Hudson's Bay Companies are exceptions – the Admiralty was
able to consult other groups of merchants who represented the
major trades. Because the Admiralty was not short of suitable
escorts, it could afford to appoint many more convoys than earlier
boards had been able to do. This made the system more flexible and
for most of the time relations between the Admiralty and the
merchants in London and the outports were extremely cordial.
Parliament continued to supervise the defence of commerce. However
in January 1742, before war began with France, a petition was made
to Parliament by the London merchants. This demanded information
about the numbers of convoys appointed since the beginning of war
with Spain, the numbers of ships that had sailed with them, the ships
appointed as escorts, the notice given to traders and the times the
convoys had sailed.[25] After the House had resolved into a committee
of the whole House, it continued to hear evidence from the merchants and the Admiralty until the second half of February. During
this time the merchants continued to press for information about the
numbers of ships whose masters had disobeyed instructions, the
numbers which had missed convoys and much more. In fact the
questioning took on an increasingly waspish and unreasonable tone
and the Admiralty's moderate reply is worth quoting:

The trade to Africa and Newfoundland have had their annual ships, and we have heard no complaint from them. The trade of the West Indies has been so well protected by Vice Admiral Vernon, and the ships stationed at the islands, that we hear of no losses in those parts; and even in North America, where it is alleged that ships have been lately taken, the same is not imputed in the petition to a want of cruisers but of proper care in some of your Majesty's commanders stationed in those parts . . . since the declaration of war, there have been . . . six convoys to the West Indies, and eleven home; four convoys to North America, and three home . . .[26]

This attack seems to have been inspired by partisan motives and is the only one recorded during these wars.

The Admiralty seems to have been able to appoint convoys for London and outports shipping whenever these were requested. In May 1746 the Mayor of Lynn asked for a convoy for ships from his own and neighbouring harbours to Newcastle. The Admiralty agreed to send the *Swift* sloop.[27] Another convoy was appointed for only nine ships which sailed from Oporto in November the same year, and in December 1745 the Admiralty was prepared to leave the *Fly* sloop cruising off Plymouth for three weeks when the ships transporting tin were delayed. There were many similar examples in the Seven Years War. This profusion of convoys, after the relatively small numbers in the earlier wars, had many advantages. The chief was that it avoided the single annual convoy for some trades, which produced a serious glut and lowered prices for merchants and planters. It provided the opportunity for merchants to space out their purchases, especially of perishable commodities, and it was particularly valuable to outports merchants whose markets were smaller than those of the London men. Another result was that convoys sailed to a timetable and merchants were spared heavy demurrage charges for ships waiting in port. It also helped the Admiralty to use its ships more efficiently, for the Board could be more certain when ships would reach their destinations and arrive back in British ports. This did not result in a large increase in convoys to distant markets such as the Caribbean and North America, although one or two more were generally appointed than in the earlier wars. The increase was almost entirely in convoys to the Baltic, European and Mediterranean markets, for the voyages were generally brief and ships could be recalled quickly in an emergency.

This increase in the numbers of convoys appointed made it imperative that merchants should be fully informed of the escorts available. In the cases of convoys quoted above, the merchants who had requested protection were informed by the Secretary to the

Admiralty that a convoy would be appointed. However, to use these escorts efficiently other merchants had to be informed as well so that requests would not be duplicated. This presented certain difficulties. In the earlier wars the Admiralty had been able to arrange convoys by consultation with the representatives of chartered companies and the chief London merchants in other trades. By the mid-eighteenth century most of the chartered companies had been eclipsed by independent commercial interests. The Admiralty arranged convoys by consulting the chief London merchants in each trade and relied on notices in the Royal Exchange and other commercial centres to inform the other merchants. This only served the London merchants. At the outports the merchants were informed by the commercial press. This was a relatively new development, and its growth had reflected the increase in commercial activity in the country. Much of the information published by newspapers was inaccurate gossip, but one newspaper editor tried to ensure that his news was accurate – the editor of *Lloyds List*. In the course of time this became the organ of Lloyds Coffee House and was one of the reasons for the rise in prosperity of that institution and of its reputation as a centre of the growing insurance activity among London merchants. By the end of the Seven Years War *Lloyds List* carried a considerable amount of information about London shipping, including news of convoys, and this was pirated and reproduced in the provincial press. Although it seldom gave much warning of the departure of convoys, merchants knew when they usually sailed and could use this information as confirmation. The accuracy of this newspaper was the product of close co-operation between Lloyds Coffee House and the Admiralty, which was of considerable importance later in the century. Lloyds received much of its information on convoys from the Secretary to the Admiralty, who used *Lloyds List* as a means of informing merchants outside London of Admiralty decisions.

Although commerce was relatively well protected in these wars, the merchants were seldom satisfied that their ships were adequately defended and usually asked for large numbers of escorts. This anxiety also showed itself in two features of wartime commerce: a shift of trade to Bristol and Liverpool and a tendency to use neutral shipping. In the case of Exeter, the other western port that had been important at the beginning of the century, this was now declining because of the cheaper Norwich cloth exports. From 1745 Exeter's Dutch trade began to decline.[28] It is a symptom of this fall that Exeter's merchants apparently no longer asked for convoys for their ships and at least one merchant – Samuel Milford whose accounts for 1760 have survived – was using neutral vessels, to ship goods to Hamburg and Leghorn.[29] The other important western ports, Bristol and Liverpool, were relatively safe from privateers. Bristol ships needed protection during the early part of their voyage when sailing to the south of Ireland. In each of these wars the Admiralty stationed a warship to escort shipping through the danger zone. The Board also put the captain under the orders of the Master of the Society of Merchant Venturers. This was a practical measure designed to ensure that convoys sailed whenever they were required, but it also demonstrated the understanding between the Board and the Society, for such a situation was fraught with difficulties if there was not complete mutual understanding. For the first three years of the War of Austrian Succession, Bristol ships sailed without escorts, but in March 1742 the frigate *Sapphire* arrived at Bristol. This provided a defence in the seas off the Irish coast for outgoing ships until France entered the war in 1744. In that year the Bristol merchants petitioned the Admiralty for a ship to be stationed off the African coast to protect slavers and from time to time, sometimes independently and sometimes in conjunction with other ports, asked for convoys for the Jamaica and African trades.[30] Protection was usually given, but the Admiralty expected that Bristol should contribute seamen to the navy. In 1746 the Board complained that whereas the City of London allowed impressment, Bristol did not; in any case, many Bristol seamen had sailed on privateers, and in the course of the war, over a thousand were employed in this way.[31]

In 1755, when it seemed that Boscawen's action would lead to French reprisal, the Society of Merchant Venturers asked for two escorts for their ships. The Admiralty reply was apparently encouraging and by April 1756 the frigate *Prince Edward* had arrived in Bristol. In the Society's view this was not enough, for whenever the escort was away Bristol's trade was defenceless. In 1759 the Admiralty finally conceded and sent two vessels, the *Alarm*, 32 guns, and the *Aldborough*, 20 guns, on condition that the Society provided the crews. It proved difficult to recruit the 380 men required, for the Admiralty insisted that its agent should continue to impress men for the navy. Within a month the Society asked that the marines who had helped to sail the ships to Bristol should be left on board, but the Admiralty firmly refused. Thereafter, apart from the replacement of the *Aldborough* by the larger *Looe*, 32 guns, there were no more requests for convoys. As a final concession to the Society, the Admiralty stopped impressment in December 1759 and ordered its agent to impress men only from incoming ships. At times this too was disputed by the Society. In 1758 men had been taken from a ship returning with a convoy from the West Indies and the ship was later lost at sea. The Society was indignant, but Nugent persuaded the members not to press their complaint; the practice of pressing seamen from returning merchant ships was well-established. The loss of the merchant ship was unfortunate, but the Society was lucky in the choice of escort commanders sent to protect Bristol trade. Captain Saumarez of the *Antelope*, 54 guns, captured a French 64 in the Bristol Channel in 1759 and Captain Lockhard of the *Tartar* 28, helped to take some French privateers. Both men were rewarded by the Society with plate to a value of one hundred guineas.

Other ports on the west coast of Britain escaped relatively un-scathed. Liverpool and Glasgow did not receive any convoy protection and the only time that their trade was in danger was when privateers were sighted off Tory Island on the north west coast of Ireland where returning merchant ships made their landfall. François Thurot's brief appearance in the Irish Sea in 1759 had caused panic in Liverpool which was virtually defenceless. Thurot however was soon caught in the Irish Sea and killed in the fierce action that followed. Liverpool had entered a period of rapid growth which had begun during the Seven Years War and continued when the war ended. Her docks were expanded and many more ships were fitted out for the slave trade and for commerce with the West Indies and North America. Glasgow, the other port on the west coast of importance, also prospered, although her merchants became alarmed at the turn of events in the American colonies before 1775 and tried to recover their debts by importing large quantities of tobacco.[32] This helped to bolster Glasgow's commerce during the war of American Independence.

During the peace which separated the Seven Years War from the War of American Independence the composition of the merchant body began to change. Whereas the West India merchants had been a disparate group, dominated by a small number of rich planters and merchants, from 1769 they formed an organized and more cohesive body. The Committee of West India merchants was formed in London, an action that was mirrored by the creation of a similar body in Bristol, and this became the spokesman for the West India interest. It was the first step towards a reorganization of British commerce into geographical areas, each of which was dominated by a committee of merchants. This was a great advantage to the Admiralty and later the Board encouraged other groups to form their own committees. It was of particular importance in the War of

American Independence because from 1778 British naval superiority was first threatened and then directly challenged. In 1779 Spain entered the war against Britain, and Holland followed suit in 1780 after Britain had interfered – as Holland claimed – with her rights to carry French goods. The combined attack on British commerce and naval power had important results. Although the French government devoted its naval resources to the main battle fleets, French privateers also put to sea to raid British commerce and American privateers used French ports as bases. However, British trade was spared the form of squadron attack that had been mounted by Saint-Pol in the War of Spanish Succession, and many French merchants were reluctant to invest in privateers because they could make more profit from trade. The result was that for British commerce, the war can be divided into two parts divided by 1778 the year in which France declared war. Before then the Admiralty had the naval resources to provide convoys on a similar basis to earlier wars. All the major trades were served by regular convoys, and the Admiralty could afford the comparative luxury of supplying a convoy for about thirty ships to and from the Baltic – a strategic advantage in view of the importance for the navy of receiving regular supplies of naval stores. After 1778 the navy was forced for a time to follow a more defensive strategy in the English Channel where the combined French and Spanish squadrons were more powerful than the British. The consequence for trade was that the Admiralty faced the dilemma last confronted during the War of the League of Augsburg – the danger that the Mediterranean and Iberian commerce was at risk if not escorted by a battle fleet to the Mediterranean, but that Britain was defenceless if this was done. Convoys became fewer and increased in size: Baltic convoys were usually over a hundred, and the trade in naval stores is the only one which increased during the war. The larger convoys to Portugal and the Mediterranean lost more ships because they were vulnerable to raids from French and Spanish ports along the Bay of Biscay as well as from Spanish ports. This is demonstrated by the figures for British commerce during this war *(see table p. 65)*.

Trade with southern Europe fell steeply from 1778 and did not recover until the end of the war. So too did the Newfoundland fishery whose imports of wine and fruit from Portugal were included in the Customs returns for southern Europe and not British North America. Shipping at ports in the English Channel also declined during the war. Weymouth, whose shipping had grown at about twice the rate for outports until 1770, reflects this collapse. Her

Table 2.3 OFFICIAL VALUES OF IMPORTS AND OF EXPORTS AND RE-EXPORTS COMBINED FOR GREAT BRITAIN

(£000)

	N. Europe*		S. Europe		Asia		Africa		British N. America		United States		British West Indies		Foreign W. Indies and S. America	
1775	3,427	5,444	2,148	3,809	1,092	1,041	67	1,786	136	659	1,953	197	3,628	1,717	59	25
1776	3,076	4,873	2,249	3,398	1,468	726	100	471	119	830	106	56	3,301	1,605	53	20
1777	3,712	4,019	2,103	2,782	1,834	786	63	239	120	1,653	14	59	2,792	1,257	49	3
1778	2,910	4,296	1,429	2,258	1,526	1,200	82	154	132	1,030	18	38	3,011	1,151	53	7
1779	3,671	4,324	667	1,633	716	703	34	159	135	842	24	351	2,831	1,167	16	18
1780	4,278	4,270	817	922	971	1,116	22	196	120	837	20	829	2,606	1,752	34	127
1781	4,243	3,870	685	840	2,526	595	26	313	119	536	100	855	1,859	1,024	33	31
1782	3,763	4,400	717	1,262	626	1,468	68	352	223	702	38	267	2,506	1,272	100	229
1783	4,704	3,665	1,216	2,050	1,301	701	48	788	150	732	170	1,003	2,892	1,797	29	61

* Left-hand column is imports; right-hand column exports.
Source: Mitchell and Deane, *Abstract of British historical statistics*, pp 310–11.

tonnage for 1769 was over 6,000; by 1782 it was no more than 2,855.[33] Subsequently it recovered and by 1786 had reached 4,787 tons, still lower than the figure for 1769. Exeter, to the west, was less fortunate. Her decline could not be reversed for the Norwich clothers maintained their supremacy and drove Exeter from the markets of Germany and Holland, All that remained was a commerce in wines with Spain, Portugal and the Canaries. This was not sufficient to merit special convoys and therefore Exeter trade joined the main Mediterranean convoys off Topsham and returned with them at the end of the season.

Bristol shipping was again defended by a naval vessel, although the Society of Merchant Venturers was less active in asking for convoys and was eclipsed by the new West India Association towards the end of the war. The Admiralty's policy was to offer a 20-gun sloop as a coasting convoy to any port that would provide a crew, and Bristol accepted the offer. George Berkeley offered to command the vessel and raise the crew at his own expense. The Society helped by increasing the government bounty but insisted that the Corporation should share the cost and that the sailors should not be pressed into the navy.[34] The escort's duty was to see Bristol ships safely to another British port and not, as in previous wars, to escort overseas commerce on the first 150 leagues of the voyage. In 1779 when four Bristol ships sailed for Canada they were instructed by the Admiralty to meet the main convoy at Portsmouth – a request to join the convoy in the Scillies was rejected as impractical. A new threat to Bristol in this war was the occasional appearance of privateers in St George's Channel. In 1781 the Society was asked by the Committee of Trade of the Port of Lancaster to support a petition for cruisers to be stationed in the channel to protect the returning West India trade. At times there was friction between naval captains and the Society. In 1781 and 1782 there were complaints that masters had not asked for sailing instructions and that coasting convoys would not be provided if numbers were low. But these were exceptions, and at the end of the war the Society recommended that two escort commanders, Cunningham and Hawker, should be made post captains as a reward for protecting the city's trade.[35]

Liverpool's shipping was not protected in the same way. In the earlier wars her growing trade had been largely immune from privateering attack; masters of French privateers considered navigation in the Irish Sea dangerous without a pilot and did not enter, though some cruised off Tory Island to intercept shipping to the ports on the west coast of Britain. In the War of American Independence a number of American privateering captains pretended to be British and obtained pilots who were forced to navigate their ships in the Irish Sea where the privateers took a number of prizes. Many American masters became familiar with these waters during peace time trade and were able to gain some support from the Irish. John Paul Jones' appearance in the Irish Sea caused panic in Liverpool, though he did little damage to the city's trade. In any case, the Admiralty could do little to help. Resources were strained by the anti-British alliance and only occasionally could a warship be spared for local defence. Trade at the port declined as the following figures show:

Table 2.4 LIVERPOOL SHIPPING

	(000 tons)	
	Inwards	Outwards
1775	86.4	76.7
1776	74.1	68.5
1777	70.8	71.3
1778	76.3	63.4
1779	57.1	64.8
1780	58.8	61.6
1781	58.9	65.5
1782	66.3	64.5
1783	96.1	105.1

Source: F. E. Hyde, *Liverpool and the Mersey; an economic history of a port 1700–1970*, (Newton Abbot 1971), p 236.

There were two main reasons for this decline: difficulties of carrying on the West India slave trade – an area which had contributed much to the port's prosperity after 1760 – and the collapse of commerce with America.[36] In neither case can the Admiralty be held responsible for this temporary decline, as the Liverpool ships could sail to the African coast in comparative safety without convoy and could join the West India convoys for the return voyage. The most dangerous part of this triangular voyage was the closing stage of the Middle Passage, as the slavers approached the West Indian islands. French privateers constantly cruised to windward of the principal landfalls and only the most strongly armed slaver could beat them off. However, the slave ships took varying lengths of time to load their human cargoes and never left the African coast together; moreover, they went to trading posts which were widely separated. Under these circumstances it was impossible to organize a convoy system for the slave trade, in this or any other war before the commerce was abolished. The fall in

Liverpool's trade was only temporary; within a year of the ending of hostilities over 122,000 tons of shipping entered the port – a record – and the figure continued to rise until the war with Revolutionary France.

Glasgow's commerce suffered a similar decline. At one time it was believed that the closing of the Virginia and Maryland tobacco trade had catastrophic results for Glasgow, but it is now known that this view was exaggerated.[37] Some merchants lost heavily in 1775 because they could not collect their outstanding debts but others had foreseen the political crisis and were able to import large stocks of tobacco. Some was also imported from the West Indies during the war, no doubt via St Eustatius, which was frequented by American merchants while it remained neutral. Some Glasgow ships carried Irish provisions from Cork to the West Indies which provided freight for the outward voyage. The Admiralty did not have enough frigates to provide an escort from the Clyde to Cork for these ships, although they were safe once they arrived there as they joined the main West India convoys which also loaded provisions at this port. If the Glasgow ships returned from a British Caribbean island they sailed under convoy protection for most of the voyage; if they went to a neutral island they returned independently. Before the French declaration of war in 1778, American privateers cruised between the Mull of Kintyre and Belfast Lough. The frigate *Arethusa* was sent to the area in July 1777 in order to protect trade.[38] The Admiralty refused to supply an escort; many warships were in West Indian and American waters and none were available for this duty. In 1778 even one of the two armed vessels intended for coastal protection was withdrawn because of the war with France and the Lord Provost of Glasgow, Hugh Wylie, and the city's merchants complained that the remaining guardship, a slow collier, was inadequate and that the Clyde was 'infested with privateers'. It was not until 1781 that the frigate *Seaford* was sent to the Clyde, but it remained under Admiralty orders and Wylie could not order a convoy or cruise – unlike at Bristol where the Master of the Society of Merchant Venturers had been given this right. From June to July 1777 the threat to Glasgow shipping was so severe that merchants subscribed £3,000 for fitting out three armed vessels, but they were not kept in service long. In 1779 merchants began to arm their ships with carronades which gave protection in close action. This stopped privateers boarding Glasgow ships but gave the latter no protection in long range action. Measures of this sort gave some protection to West India commerce which became the mainstay of Glasgow's wartime economy. It is significant however that Alexander Spiers, one of the most influential merchants of Glasgow, asked for wine to be shipped from Oporto on a neutral ship.[39] Trade between Glasgow and Portugal was obviously dangerous for British shipping.

Every trade suffered to some degree in this war though only 3,386 ships were lost; this was about the same as in the War of the League of Augsburg when the merchant fleet was only half as large.[40] Even Liverpool and Glasgow lost ships, though they had been largely immune during the wars of the mid-eighteenth century. During the War of American Independence fewer escorts were available to defend the overseas and coastal shipping and it is likely that the majority of losses occurred during a comparatively short time, between the entry of France into the war in 1778 and 1782. It is difficult to assess the scale of losses year by year; there was no outcry in parliament against the Admiralty on this score which suggests that losses were kept within reasonable bounds. Some merchants no doubt tried to make greater profits as wartime prices of imported commodities rose. These men sent their ships independently as runners and ordered them to return to London and east coast ports round the north of Scotland. This was dangerous in winter, and many ships were wrecked on the islands off the west coast of Scotland most of which were so remote from civilization that it took weeks and sometimes months for news of their loss to reach owners and underwriters in London.[41]

After the war, commerce quickly recovered and by 1795 had again reached a record level even though war had once again broken out with France. London continued to dominate British commerce and the rise in the number of vessels entering this port, especially in the second half of the eighteenth century, is indicative of the enormous growth in the nation's trade:

Table 2.5 VESSELS ENTERED INWARDS AT THE PORT OF LONDON

	Number of coastwise vessels	Average tonnage per vessel	Number of vessels from foreign ports	Average tonnage of vessels
1700	5,562	50	—	—
1702	—	—	1,335	118
1750	6,396	80	—	—
1751	—	—	1,682	139
1795	11,964	100	2,832	205

Source: J. Bird, *The major seaports in the United Kingdom*, (1969), p 340.

This posed serious problems for the Admiralty which had a greater number of merchant ships to protect than in any previous war. The figures for the number of British ships entered and cleared from ports in Great Britain in 1792 demonstrates the scale of this task:

Table 2.6 NUMBER OF BRITISH SHIPS ENTERED AND CLEARED AT PORTS IN GREAT BRITAIN, 1792

		Entered	Cleared	Average tonnage
Long distance trades				
Asia		28	36	707
West Indies, British and Foreign		705	603	233
United States		202	223	221
British North America		219	383	147
Africa, excluding Egypt		77	250	202
	TOTAL	1,231	1,495	
Southern Europe and Mediterranean				
Spain, Portugal, Atlantic Islands, Malta and Gibraltar		975	615	126
Italy and Austria		138	215	143
Turkey, Levant, Egypt		38	48	224
	TOTAL	1,151	878	
Short sea trades				
Russia, Scandinavia, Baltic and Germany		2,746	1,367	186
Holland and Flanders		1,603	1,734	117
	TOTAL	4,349	3,101	
France		1,413	1,317	73
Greenland and Southern Whale Fisheries		160	135	270
Foreign trade total		8,304	6,926	
'Foreign coasting trade':				
Ireland		4,194	6,354	75
Channel Islands and Isle of Man		532	611	47
	TOTAL	4,726	6,965	
Total entrances and clearances		13,033	13,891	

Source: C. N. Parkinson (ed), *The trade winds; a study of British overseas trade during the French wars 1793–1815*, (1948), p 73.

During the course of the war, in spite of heavy losses, the numbers of merchant ships used in British trade and owned by British and colonial merchants increased, largely as a result of the purchase of prize vessels and an efficient building programme (Table 2.7).

Table 2.7

| | 1792 | | 1814 | |
	Ships	1,000 tons	Ships	1,000 tons
Great Britain	12,776	1,187	19,585	2,329
Ireland etc.	1,558	250	1,665	84
Colonies	1,745	103	2,868	203
TOTAL	16,079	1,540	24,418	2,616

Source: *ibid*, p 83.

The key to this undoubted success lies in three factors: the Admiralty's convoy policy, a lack of effective French privateering and squadronal *guerre de course* and the ability of British merchants to continue trading with French controlled territory during the course of these wars through neutral agents and forged papers. A Convoy Act was passed in 1798, which made convoys compulsory for all ships engaged in foreign trade, with certain exceptions.[42] These were the East Indiamen, Hudson's Bay Company ships and vessels bound for Irish ports, as well as any ship fast and well armed enough to sail independently as a 'runner'. It should be emphasized that the key to this successful system of commerce defence lay in the efficiency of the Board of Admiralty in arranging convoys on such a scale as the above figures indicate, and in the close and amicable relationships between the Board and merchants in London and the outports. Whereas at the beginning of the period the Board had arranged convoys with chartered companies, by the time war broke out in 1792 there existed in London and the major outports committees of merchants which controlled all the important parts of British commerce. Moreover, Lloyds was the unchallenged leader in British marine insurance and the centre of a commercial intelligence system without equal in Britain or indeed the world, and the Admiralty and the Secretary of Lloyds co-operated closely throughout this period of the two French wars to co-ordinate commercial policy. It is for this reason that the Admiralty was able to organize a system of convoys that on occasion protected huge convoys of up to a thousand ships from the Baltic – an area of trade that was of enormous strategic importance. When it became necessary for ships to sail under false colours, use false names and papers, the naval escort commanders were able to turn a blind eye and concentrate on keeping privateers at bay. Some of these commodities were carried on Norwegian ships, a trend already apparent in the wars of the mid-eighteenth century and a factor which helps to account for the rise in the tonnage of Norwegian merchant shipping.[43] Outports trade was protected in the same way as in previous wars; cruisers were stationed at ports when necessary and coastal convoys provided to take ships to points where they could safely join convoys. Another feature of relations between the Admiralty and the outports is the co-operation on matters of convoy discipline, a factor which had caused trouble in previous wars. The Admiralty and Lloyds co-operated to bring offenders to trial and this helped to ensure that those vessels which sailed with convoys arrived safely at their destinations with them.[44]

When it came to assembling convoys, the principle difficulty was the size of some of them. Convoys could not be assembled in the Thames; the river was crowded in the first half of the century and seriously congested thereafter. Convoys placed a heavy burden on dock facilities by, concentrating the arrival and departure of shipping for overseas markets, overburdening the legal quays and stretching the resources of lighters and dock labour. The construction of additional docks and wharfs never kept pace with demand either in London or the outports where overcrowding was also a serious problem. The only solution was for convoys to assemble outside the Thames at places where there was good holding ground, adequate sea room for the ships expected and where defence could be provided against enemy warships and privateers. It was also important that these places had good communications with London so that the Admiralty could delay the sailing of a convoy if the Board received news of enemy warships in the offing or if additional merchant or warships were to join the convoy.

Two sites were chosen, the buoys of the Nore and Portsmouth Road. Both met these requirements and were used throughout the period; commerce for Quebec, Hudson Bay, the Baltic, Archangel and northern Europe assembled at the Nore, the remaining convoys off Portsmouth. Although the Nore was outside the protection offered by the Thames it was fairly close to the Medway and the principal naval dockyards. Warships, frigates and sloops regularly sailed in the area and their presence helped to deter French privateers and warships from trying to attack the convoy as it assembled or from attempting to cut out any of the ships from the anchorage. The largest convoys that assembled there were those bound for the Baltic; they ranged from twenty or thirty at the beginning of the period to over a thousand by the end, although not all of these joined the convoy at the Nore. The first task of the convoy commander when the vessels were assembled was to have their masters come on board his ship to receive sailing instructions. These were printed forms which described the signals for ships in the convoy and instructions for sailing discipline. Additional instructions were sometimes given when the escort commander considered them necessary. The system of signalling, by flags and pennants during the day, and by cannon fire and lights or flares at night, was clumsy and open to misunderstanding. Escort vessels, whether naval or merchant, spent as much of their time trying to keep the convoy together as driving off privateers. It was essential that masters of merchant ships received these instructions. Not only did it ensure that they could understand the signals, but it was established in law during the eighteenth century that no owner of a vessel could claim for loss under a policy 'to sail with convoy and arrive' unless the master had received a copy of the printed instructions.[45]

Once this formality had been completed – a lengthy business when the convoy was large – the escort commander gave the signal to unmoor and the ships moved slowly from the anchorage. Once under weigh it became extremely difficult in confined coastal waters to avoid accidents between merchant ships. Many were undermanned – it was hard for owners to obtain prime seamen in wartime when so many were pressed into naval service – and merchantmen were slow by naval standards, and were usually clumsily sailed. When ships were damaged they left the convoy and made for the nearest port where they were repaired and where new insurance was arranged for their subsequent voyage. The Baltic convoys, after leaving the Nore, usually made their way along the east coast to Hull, where they were joined by more ships. Hull was the main outport engaged in Baltic commerce; it imported materials for the extensive shipbuilding industry that was established on the north-east coast in the eighteenth century. Large quantities of Swedish iron and steel and later, Russian iron, were imported for the Sheffield cutlers. Hull also served as the main export centre for Yorkshire woollens many of which found a market in the Baltic.

From Hull the convoy sailed for the Skagerrak. It passed close to the Dogger Bank which was a favourite cruising ground for French privateers who attacked the fishing fleets. The Admiralty tried to ensure that the convoys entered the Baltic in early spring, as soon as the ice had melted and navigation became safe. As the ships entered the Skagerrak privateers were often sighted, their captains tried to cut out stragglers and generally took their prizes to Bergen. For most of the period the duties of the escort commander ceased when he had accompanied his convoy as far as the Sound, for once within the Baltic they were generally safe. In the Great Northern War and the Napoleonic War the Baltic powers were hostile to Britain and ships had to be escorted within the Baltic as well, for there was a danger that Russian, Swedish or Danish warships might attack British commerce.

The greatest danger was in the years 1808–12 when British shipping could not pass safely through the Sound. Although it provided the easiest passage into the Baltic, it was controlled by the guns of Elsinore Castle and privateer galleys and other craft based at Copenhagen harried commerce. Instead, convoys had to pass through the Great Belt where navigation was hazardous and slow. Shoals within the Belt forced ships to make frequent changes of direction and each time had to wait for favourable winds before continuing. In consequence it was not unusual for ships to take up to six weeks to pass through the Belt, and because convoys were arriving from Britain approximately every fortnight, warships were stationed in the passage to provide local protection.[46] These were exceptional circumstances however. For most of the period the ships were able to sail unmolested from the Sound to Riga for hemp and iron, to Stockholm for pitch and tar, to Danzig and Pillau for oak and deals and to a number of other ports for a variety of naval stores. For the return voyage, convoys were assembled between 1808 and 1812 in Hanö Bay where masters could obtain supplies of fresh water. At other times the ships passed through the Sound and gathered at Gothenburg.

This port also served as an assembly point for the Hanö Bay convoys, for a number of ships traded at Christiansand and Arendal in southern Norway for small and medium masts and spars and met the returning convoys off Gothenburg. This port was the pivot for the organization of much of the Baltic commerce. Vingå Sound, off Gothenburg, provided a rendezvous where ships could rejoin a convoy into the Baltic if they had been separated from it by stress of weather, and the Admiralty used the port as the administrative centre to which consular reports could be sent from Elsinore and other Baltic ports.[47] Commanders of Baltic squadrons were informed in this way of the movement of enemy or hostile shipping and of the intentions of Baltic powers towards Britain and so could co-ordinate arrangements for protecting trade. Escort commanders tried to get convoys away from Hanö Bay by 1 October, because during this month ice began to form in the Baltic and winter storms in the North Sea made navigation dangerous for the heavily laden ships. When trade was interrupted in the Baltic, it was sometimes necessary to send the convoys later. In 1811 the last convoy returned from the Baltic in November with disastrous results. It was struck by a storm and three large warships were lost: *St George* 98, *Defence* 74 and *Hero* 74, together with 2,000 men.[48] During the period 1808–12 when the Admiralty had to allow the widespread use of forged papers and when neutral ships were used in large numbers to carry naval stores, escort commanders were obliged to keep a careful watch on all ships in the returning convoys. Licences were issued to the masters of neutral vessels to allow them to trade in Britain, but there was always the risk that they would use the opportunity to carry their cargoes to French or other foreign ports where they would fetch higher prices. The Admiralty decided that the test for a ship in convoy was whether it arrived at a British port or whether a master, if his ship was separated from the convoy by stress of weather, made for Leith to await a coasting convoy. Any merchant ship which was taken with naval stores that was not sailing to a British port was automatically declared a good prize in an Admiralty court.[49]

Ships bound for Archangel also sailed from the Nore. This commerce had originated in 1553, but only a few merchants traded there, even after the ending of the Muscovy Company's monopoly in 1698. Thereafter commerce grew under the stimulus of Peter the Great and by the mid-eighteenth century a small group of merchants pursued a moderate, though widely fluctuating trade in timber and iron.[50] Many of these ships were large – 600 or 700 tons was normal – and by the 1780s some were over 1,000 tons. These were escorted by frigates who saw them in safety across the North Sea, where there was a danger from Dunkirk and Boulogne privateers, and along part of the Norwegian coast. The principal danger for most of this period was the difficult navigation. It was dangerous to sail near the Lofoten Islands and in the grey northern seas, visibility was generally poor. During the years of Napoleon's blockade, British trade with Archangel increased considerably. This was because the port was too far north for the Russian government to control effectively and British goods poured in to the port. However, the war also brought French and Danish privateers to the area, and the Admiralty tried to protect commerce by stationing cruisers off the North Cape. This was especially dangerous in 1813, after the United States had declared war in 1812, and three American ships took at least twenty British merchantmen.[51] Once past this cape, merchantmen had to avoid the strong inshore current, and navigate without the use of the compass, which was frequently inaccurate. Visibility was also bad for several days at a time, but masters had to approach the Murman coast to sight Cape Sviatoi Nos, which marked the entrance to the White Sea. The return voyage was equally perilous, and in 1809 several ships were taken from a convoy by a privateer before the Admiralty, alerted by Lloyds to the danger, sent additional protection.

Other ships which passed through these waters to the north of Scotland were those bound for Hudson Bay and, from 1760, for Canada. Both were escorted from the Nore by one or two frigates; although they sailed at approximately the same time they never sailed as a single convoy. Both had to enter northern waters as ice melted and be clear before the water froze again. The Hudson's Bay Company ships, of which there were never more than half a dozen, were escorted to a position 100 leagues west of the Orkneys by a ship which then returned to Britain. On their return, the company's ships were met at the Orkneys by a frigate and escorted to the Nore. In the case of the Quebec trade, the ships sailed under the protection of a frigate as far as the Gulf of St Lawrence. At that point the merchantmen proceeded independently and the escort cruised in the Gulf to protect the fishery; in the autumn the convoy reformed in the Gulf and sailed back to Britain. Sometimes the trade, which was never large and was completely controlled by London merchants, was escorted through the English Channel, at other times the ships sailed independently round the north of Scotland. Other trades which sailed from the Nore were those for ports in northern Europe, principally Hamburg and the Texel. Hamburg became the centre for lucrative smuggling on a grand scale after 1808 and ships in those years sailed with the Baltic convoys to Heligoland where the goods were unloaded before being run ashore on to the north German coast. At other times the commerce with European ports was carried by convoys that sailed on a regular basis. During the wars of the League of Augsburg and the Spanish Succession this pattern was frequently interrupted by rumours of French privateers in the North Sea and the English Channel.

The rest of the commerce from London and the east coast ports sailed from Portsmouth. The principal convoys were those to the West Indies, and the East Indiamen and slave ships frequently accompanied them for as far as they shared a common course. Portsmouth convoys were often delayed by the prevailing westerly winds which made it hard for the escort commander to get all the merchantmen into the Channel before the wind changed. Once under weigh, convoys called at Portland, Torbay, Plymouth and Falmouth for any additional merchantmen. It was essential that the sailing instructions should include a rendezvous where convoys could reassemble if scattered by storms, for this part of the voyage was the most perilous in view of the presence of French privateers. Captain Lynn of the *Roebuck* committed a serious misdemeanour when he temporarily abandoned his West India convoy in December 1758. His mast had been broken below the crosstrees in a gale, and instead of making temporary repairs he put in to Hamoaze dockyard to have a new mast fitted. The Board's comment was brief and to the point: 'Let him know there are so many ways to make the mast serviceable notwithstanding his having discovered it to be sprung 'tis no excuse for having left so considerable a convoy exposed'.[52]

Once clear of the English Channel the West India convoys usually steered for Cork to load provisions for transport to the Caribbean, especially in years when trade with the northern colonies was interrupted. At Cork the convoys were joined by ships from Bristol, Liverpool and the other western ports. The purchase and loading of these provisions took several weeks and when it had been completed the convoy set sail on a course for Madeira which took them well clear of the Spanish and Portuguese coast. Funchal, the principal port, had no harbour and ships lay at their anchors offshore. This was always hazardous, for the wind frequently changed and ships had to ride out a storm or cut their cables and put to sea. The loss of anchors and cables was a normal hazard of the voyage, but masters of merchant ships usually loaded wine, partly to use on the voyage and partly for sale in the Caribbean or England.

From Madeira the convoys continued sailing west-south-west to keep in the prevailing trade winds and turned to the west in approximately the latitude of Barbados. Navigation was crude and frequently inaccurate. Masters of merchant ships possessed some charts but had no instruments other than a compass, backstaff or quadrant, log line and hour glass. Consequently, masters sailing independently tried to measure elapsed distance by means of the log line and hour glass and tried to check this by measuring latitude. This took little account of drift or the effect of currents. Many naval captains were little better. From 1755 it was possible to estimate Greenwich time, and hence longitude, from Tobias Mayer's lunar tables, which were printed in the *Nautical Almanac* from 1767, but this required a knowledge of mathematics which few captains possessed.[53] Another method of measuring longitude, which became generally available about the same time, was to use a chronometer. John Harrison's K4 had demonstrated, on a voyage to Jamaica on the *Deptford* in 1761, that it was possible to make accurate measurements of longitude, but the Admiralty was slow to adopt it. Consequently, all convoys to the West Indies during this period approached their landfall on Barbados from some distance away and sailed down the line of latitude to the island. It had the merit that it recognized the shortcomings of the traditional methods and made it unlikely that a convoy would pass Barbados. However, it is seldom appreciated how inaccurate this method could be. The British measurement of the log line was to allow 49 or 50 feet to a glass of 30 seconds, but at times the knots were carelessly made. Those on the *Winchester*'s line in 1755 were too close together and resulted in an inaccuracy of approximately 300 miles on the voyage from Madeira to Barbados. Admiral Frankland commented bitterly to the Board of Admiralty about the '. . . ignorant, erroneous and . . . obstinate method of marking their log line.'[54] The main disadvantage of this method was that it forced all convoys to approach the West Indies along the same line of latitude and French privateers were able to wait on this for the convoys to approach. For the masters of merchant ships it had the advantage that few changes of direction were required and the ship could be sailed fairly well with the small wartime crews. Captain Surman, on whose ship William Hickey sailed to Jamaica in 1755 commented: 'I find some benefit arises from a badly manned ship, for had my ship been properly provided with hands I should, from the threatening appearance of the sky an hour ago, have now been under double or close reefed topsails, thereby losing time and distance, whereas here we are with everything set, and fine weather.'[55] There remained the problem of sickness on these voyages. Ships usually carried some poultry, sheep and cattle or pigs to provide fresh meat on the voyage, but these were for the captain and passengers. The crews were fed on salt meat, dried peas and biscuit, with wine, beer and water to drink. During the voyage it was usually supplemented by fish: albacore, boneta and dolphin, though any appearance of scurvy weakened the efficiency of crews that were already under strength.

All convoys called at Barbados, though masters of merchantmen disliked the practice; the island lay far to the south of the course to Antigua and Jamaica and ships frequently lost anchors and cables in the roadstead. When sailing from Barbados to Antigua, the next port of call, the convoy had to pass the French island of Martinique which was one of the main privateering and naval bases. Antigua was the administrative centre of the Leeward Islands command, and produced large quantities of sugar. Many ships left the convoy there and the remainder sailed first to the other British islands in the Leewards chain: Nevis, Montserrat and St Kitts, and thence to Jamaica. This was the most dangerous part of the voyage, for convoys had to pass close to the island of Hispaniola. The western half was Spanish and the eastern half French, until Toussaint l'Ouverture's revolution in the 1790s, and considerable numbers of privateers cruised off Cape Beata, because it lay on the line of latitude along which most ships made their final approach to Jamaica. Sometimes escort commanders tried to use an alternative route which was less hazardous: in 1757 Admiral Cotes sailed south from St Kitts to latitude 15°30′N and passed a short distance to the south of Dominica. He then sailed west until he estimated that he was opposite the eastern end of Jamaica and then turned north. This demanded high standards of navigation, for it was extremely difficult to beat against the prevailing easterly trade winds if he had sailed too far west, and the method was too difficult for any masters of merchant ships to adopt. Another way of defending British shipping as it was approachin Jamaica was to station cruisers off the south coast of Hispaniola between Port Louis and Cape Alta Vela. These met the convoys and rounded up any merchantmen that had been separated from, or had deliberately left, the convoys.

This proved a suitable method of protecting the West India commerce for, although the number of islands under British rule varied from war to war, it provided a means of escorting ships to the principal islands. British commerce to the American colonies – states after 1783 – followed a similar course, although the convoys crossed the Atlantic further north and did not pass through the Caribbean. The trade winds in the north Atlantic imposed this pattern on British commerce. The system had a further advantage. It enabled the Admiralty to send East Indiamen and slave ships with these large West India convoys which were always well protected by warships sailing to join Caribbean squadrons. The convoys took these other ships safely through the dangerous European waters and when their courses diverged, left them to continue independently. However, it also left the slavers to make the approach to Barbados independently, although they might be met by a warship cruising off the island and escorted there in safety.

The remaining trade, with Portugal and the Mediterranean, was also protected by convoys. In the War of the League of Augsburg the danger facing these convoys was emphasized by the loss of the Smyrna convoy and thereafter the Admiralty made every effort to provide adequate protection. Convoys for the Portugal trade saw ships safely to Viana, Oporto and Lisbon and whenever necessary waited until ships had passed over sand bars and into the safety of a port before proceeding. Cruisers were also posted off Viana to meet the Newfoundland fishing fleet when it arrived in October or November. The Mediterranean convoys were escorted first to Gibraltar, after its capture in 1704, and then to destinations within the Mediterranean, by a system of smaller convoys. In this way ships were escorted to Leghorn, Genoa, Smyrna and Zante and the landfalls and straits along the route were patrolled by cruisers. At the beginning of the period there was a threat of capture by Barbary pirates, but their power waned in the course of the eighteenth century, and ships equipped with Mediterranean passes were ensured a safe passage.

The most striking feature of convoy organization in the period from 1689 to 1815 is the gradual increase in the efficiency of the Board of Admiralty and the growth of the number of escorts available for commerce defence. In the War of the League of Augsburg the Admiralty lacked experience in organizing convoys and was short of small naval vessels to protect trade against privateers. This made heavy losses of merchant ships inevitable, but after 1694 the position was made worse by the decision of the French administration to use warships for commerce raiding. These small raiding squadrons did enormous damage, but after 1713 the policy was not adopted again. During the course of the eighteenth century the Admiralty became more proficient at organizing commerce defence and except for periods of crisis as during the War of American Independence and the Napoleonic War there were no serious losses of British shipping, and convoys were generally organized to the satisfaction of merchants, though they usually exaggerated the threat to trade and thereby the numbers of escorts required. Another feature of the period is the replacement of chartered companies by independent groups of merchants. This symbolized the growth of British trade and the desire of merchants outside these companies to throw off the restrictions that prevented them from participating effectively. There was a similar movement in the outports. By the end of the period a committee or society had been created for every trade and the Admiralty was able to consult groups of merchants, as well as Lloyds underwriters, on the best methods of commerce defence and thereby create a comprehensive policy. The introduction of compulsory convoys for most sections of British commerce thus reflects this new organization of British trade and the improvement in the Admiralty's administrative efficiency.

3

Marine Insurance

IT IS NO exaggeration to say that without marine insurance, British commerce would not have been able to survive the shocks of war in the way that it did, and the steady progress which Britain's commerce demonstrates in this period would have been seriously hampered. As will be seen in this chapter, Britain had a number of advantages in respect of the insurance market: financial institutions which, on the whole, were relatively stable and a wide variety of trades over which to spread risks. The inexperienced and dishonest seldom stayed long in marine insurance; they were initially attracted by high premiums, but usually paid the penalty by losing their capital and the merchants quickly learned whom to trust. Their losses enabled the more fortunate to survive the attack on commerce, though few came through the wars unscathed, and at times there were spectacular disasters, such as the loss of the Smyrna fleet in 1693. In the main however, the progress of marine insurance can be measured in two ways, first in the definition of legal principles by Lord Mansfield in a series of important cases, and second through the growth of insurance in London and the outports, and the measure of control adopted by those who participated in it. This is a feature of much of economic and political activity in this period: the co-ordination through committees which act as spokesmen and co-operate with executive boards such as the Board of Admiralty in time of war.

The early history of marine insurance is not yet fully understood, but it is certain that it was first used in Venice in the fifteenth century when it was at the height of its fame. The underlying feature was the co-operation between merchants to share risks, and this remained in use for three hundred years. Even in fifteenth-century Venice the main prerequisites for marine insurance were already in existence. Risks were shared among a comparatively large number of vessels and spread across a variety of voyages. In addition commerce was protected by a powerful navy. This kept losses within reasonable limits and the shared cost was a comparatively light burden for the merchants. So well established was the practice of marine insurance that the policies became standardized and the risks understood. The dominance of Italy in European commerce in the fifteenth and early sixteenth centuries ensured that Italian methods and practice of marine insurance came to be adopted elsewhere. In England there was at first comparatively little marine insurance, though the practice was widely adopted in the more commercially advanced parts of Europe, and in 1575 Richard Candeler tried to establish a monopoly of marine underwriting in London. He was granted a patent giving him the right of 'making and registering policies and instruments of insurance' in England. This raised a storm of protest. There was a widespread fear that he would exploit the patent, and not, as he claimed, merely bring the underwriting under proper control. The Lord Mayor was forced to set up a commission to investigate the complaints and established a scale of reasonable charges, though the patent was not revoked. It had little effect on marine insurance; merchants continued to share risks among themselves.

Whatever the practical result of Candeler's actions, the fact remained that marine insurance in England in the 1570s lacked any form of control; policies had no legal definition and underwriters acted without any accepted code of practice. The result was that marine insurance was open to exploitation and in times of crisis was unable to provide the security which it was intended to provide. The attempt to bring underwriting under central control, to standardize policies and procedures, and make it easier for merchants to obtain redress in case of grievance – all of which should have been possible through Candeler's insurance office – was commendable. The weakness was Candeler's lack of experience and the likelihood that he wanted to exploit rather than alleviate this weakness. He certainly lacked an up-to-date knowledge of each English trade and the merchants who arranged insurance among themselves at least possessed an adequate working knowledge of their own branches of commerce.

The outcome of the Candeler patent was the creation in 1601 of a Court of Assurances to hear insurance disputes. Until this cases had been heard in Common Law and Admiralty courts, but the method was not completely satisfactory. However the new court proved little better. Its main disadvantage was that although it had been created to provide a quicker verdict in disputes, its hearings were limited to policies registered with the Office of Assurances. This automatically excluded many cases, and the court lost importance as the Office of Assurances declined. It was finally abolished in 1688, and by then much business was in the hands of private underwriters. There were other attempts to establish offices of marine insurance: in 1662 a group led by Colonel John Russell, William Brereton and Sir William Killigrew had petitioned for a patent to create a Marine Insurance Corporation, and a similar proposal was made in 1673 by Colonel Dymock. Neither proposal was successful.

By the outbreak of war in 1689 marine insurance was well established in London, but during the war underwriting suffered a major setback. In 1693 the huge Smyrna convoy of approximately four hundred ships was attacked by Tourville's fleet in Lagos Bay and suffered heavy losses. This precipitated a wave of bankruptcies in London among underwriters and merchants, but it taught the merchant body an important lesson. Those who were broken by the disaster had overreached their financial resources. Some were honest men who in a crisis lacked liquid assets to cover their debts, some were speculators who hoped to profit from high wartime prices of Mediterranean goods and had failed to insure their venture adequately. Others were the inexperienced, greedy or dishonest who had entered underwriting in the belief that high wartime premiums would always cover losses. Those who survived the Smyrna disaster through luck, financial expertise, honesty and experience, formed the basis for the more stable institutions that followed.

This contributed to the commercial prosperity that followed the decline of the French *guerre de course* towards the end of the War of Spanish Succession. These years also saw the growth of fire and life insurance companies, notably the Amicable Society for a Perpetual Assurance Office, chartered in 1706, and which continued to conduct business until 1866 when it was absorbed by the Norwich Union. This provided a form of life insurance by which varying and increasing amounts of money were divided among the members who died each year. Membership was limited to 2,000; each paid a membership fee and a net annual premium of £5. The company guaranteed a minimum benefit of £125 in 1757 and £150 in 1770.[1] From 1710, largely because of a growing interest in speculative ventures, insurance became less stable, and an increasing number of wager policies were issued. These ranged from policies on the lives of famous men to others which provided a sum of money on marriage and those which insured against the birth of children. Most were made on the tontine principle, that is the net premium income was divided among participants from time to time after expenses had been deducted. This was saving, not insurance. The premiums were not levied on an actuarial basis, policies were usually little more than a form of gambling and, most important of all, those who paid the premiums seldom had any interest in the subject insured.

Speculation was not checked in the peacetime recovery after 1714, though fire and life insurance was by now well established and marine insurance put on a more secure basis. In 1717 there was a new development. On 12 August a subscription was opened in Mercers Hall 'for raising the sum of one million sterling, as a fund for insuring ships and merchandize at sea'. This was an attempt to put marine insurance on a joint stock basis and create a fund that was large enough to cushion underwriting against any losses. To some extent this foreshadows the 'bubble' ventures of 1719 and 1720, but the immediate result was the use of the Royal Exchange to sell the shares. The Mercers Hall Company, as it was known at first, was not a wild speculation but a serious attempt to establish marine insurance on a secure foundation. The 262 shareholders included many eminent London businessmen: Sir John Williams and Sir Randolph Knipe were city aldermen and assistants (that is directors) of the Levant Company; Sir Justus Beck was a financier and director of the Bank of England from 1712 to 1745 and William Dunster was an assistant and later deputy governor of the Levant Company between 1722 and 1746. The organizer was a lawyer, Case Billingsley, and he probably originated the scheme. He had already held discussions with the Solicitor-General, especially on the form and content of the petition and joint charter, and persuaded private underwriters to subscribe. Owing to the size of the subscription it took five months before the books could be closed and the petition was presented to the King for a charter on 25 January 1718.

Inevitably this aroused opposition from underwriters and brokers in London and the outports who had not subscribed, and they counter-petitioned to have the charter rejected. The Mercers Hall Company argued that marine insurance needed a more stable organization to ensure that compensation would be paid, and that its subscription ensured that the scheme had adequate financial support. The company also argued that it would be able to provide cheaper insurance, and that the creation of a single office would end the existing uncertainty and delay when a merchant suffered a loss and had to sue every underwriter separately. This was an exaggeration, though occasionally it could happen. Finally, they argued that since many merchants found it cheaper to insure in Amsterdam, the

British system was clearly in need of reorganization. In reply to this the opponents of the scheme claimed that existing arrangements for marine insurance in London were adequate and that rates were lower than anywhere else in Europe. They also pointed to the danger of creating a monopoly of marine insurance and claimed that those supporting the scheme were more concerned with stock jobbing than creating a sound financial organization. Both arguments contain an element of truth: the syndicate wanted to promote a successful company, but were prepared to speculate in stock as well. On the other hand, the London insurance market was stable, and it had established an international reputation and was attracting business to the city. But there was room for expansion.

The opponents also challenged the legality of the scheme and said that it could not be enforced. The syndicate issued a new and more enforceable subscription which was opened and completed in fourteen days. The matter rested there; the Law Officers' report was unfavourable, and the government decided not to grant the charter. This put the syndicate in a quandry; they had raised adequate working capital, and they possessed the commercial expertise, but they could not gain formal approval to practice underwriting. They next took the unusual step of buying the stock of two defunct companies, the Mines Royal and the Mineral and Battery Works. Both had been chartered in Elizabeth's reign and possessed the right of mining and manufacturing various metals. On the basis of these two charters which were still legally valid, the syndicate opened a new subscription to raise the joint stock capital to £1,152,000, on which 10 per cent was to be called. After seven months careful preparation, the company began to insure ships. The syndicate consulted counsel on the legality of using one of their charters for a new company selling marine insurance and probably obtained the King's approval as well. On 9 March 1719 the Mines Royal opened an office in the Royal Exchange for the sale of marine insurance.

The venture proved a great success; the company kept its premiums low and paid debts promptly. It underwrote about £1,300,000 of marine risks and paid its first dividend in October 1719 of $\frac{1}{2}$ per cent on par value, which represented 5 per cent on paid up capital as only 10 per cent had been called in. Although it was of doubtful legality, the company's shares rose in value and reached 100 per cent above par in the summer of 1719. This represented a peak; shares later fell to around 50 per cent above par and by the end of October had reached 16 per cent on the open market. This stimulated a general interest in insurance ventures and others were floated soon afterwards.

The most important was Ram's insurance, initiated by a gold-smith, Stephen Ram, and supported by a number of leading merchants. A rival subscription later merged with Ram's and a joint subscription was opened at the Marine Coffee House on 22 December 1719 for £2 million, with a call of £1 for each £100 of stock held by investors. Intense rivalry developed between Ram's Insurance – also called the New Insurance and Chetwynd's Insurance after its sponsor Lord Chetwynd – and the Mines Royal. Both petitioned for charters of incorporation and Ram's shares, quoted at a premium from mid-December, rose from 1½ on 16 December to an average of 3 per cent in early January. Other more speculative ventures were floated as well and their sponsors requested charters for them too. This not only increased rivalry for business but also for speculative risk capital. The wave of speculation which this created helped to launch the South Sea Company whose plans depended on a steady supply of risk capital to maintain the share prices. The apparent success of Law's schemes in Paris added fuel to public interest. The frenzy of stock jobbing, which distinguished the early months of 1720, did not last. In March 1720 the Attorney-General reported that the principle of using the charter granted for one purpose for insuring ships and merchandize was illegal, though he made no criticism of the way in which the insurance was carried on. He refused to commit himself on the delicate matter of a charter for the company, though he agreed that one was needed, and made no comment on the size of the concern which had attracted adverse criticism.

These were only recommendations however. The final decision was taken by the House of Commons Committee, which presented its report on 27 April. This condemned the misuse of charters and was also critical of company floatations which proposed to raise very large sums of money but only made small calls on subscribers. The Commons quickly accepted the Committee's proposals and drew up a bill 'to restrain the extravagent and unwarrantable practice of raising money by voluntary subscriptions, for carrying on projects dangerous to the trade and subjects of this Kingdom.' This was not the end of the matter, and it was not until after Walpole had returned to office that each company – Mines Royal and Ram's – was granted a charter on payment of £300,000 each to the King's Civil List. The Commons welcomed this proposal as a means of paying a substantial debt without taxing the country, and the bill received its royal assent on 9 June. Ironically it was tacked to the so-called Bubble Bill which attempted to limit speculative ventures. The final stage of the bubble can be told quickly. Values of stocks began to fall at the end of June.

They then levelled off and fell slowly for a month or two before collapsing in early September. The height of the financial crisis came in October, and the Royal Exchange Assurance found it extremely difficult to raise the money it had promised. Eventually it had to appeal to the government for a remission of the outstanding debt, and was able to ride out the crisis through the security of its business organization and the financial reconstruction effected by Walpole. The granting of charters to these two companies did not give them a monopoly of marine insurance. One unexpected result of the Bubble Act was that by forbidding the sale of insurance by partnerships, it left the field open to underwriters and brokers acting independently.

When the Bubble Act was passed in 1720 there was no recognized centre for marine insurance in London. Merchants wishing to insure ships and cargoes met brokers and underwriters on the floor of the Royal Exchange or at one of the nearby coffee houses, such as Garraways or the Jamaica Coffee House. No one coffee house predominated, though there was already some degree of specialization in the clientele that some attracted, and merchants went to coffee houses or walked on the floor of the Royal Exchange to hear up-to-date commercial news and gossip. Underwriters, who had to have accurate information to assess the risks of each trade and fix their rates, obtained information in the same way. Merchants, brokers and underwriters were avid for news, and information, much of it fragmentary and sometimes inaccurate, was published in the newspapers which every coffee house subscribed to. Public scepticism about much of the news that was published led in 1728 to a dispute between the coffee house keepers and the newspaper writers, and was publicly fought through two pamphlets: *The case of the coffee-men of London and Westminster. Or, an account of the impositions and abuses put upon them and the whole town, by the present set of news-writers* and *The case between the proprietors of news papers and the coffee-men of London and Westminster fairly stated.*[2] This dispute coincided with the attempt by Thomas Jamson, proprietor of Lloyds Coffee House, to produce a more accurate news sheet, but he was defeated by disunity among the coffee house keepers, many of whom refused to support him. Six years later *Lloyds List* appeared. This was a single sheet newspaper containing the current prices of annuities and stocks, together with details of the arrival and departure of ships at London and the major outports. The publication of *Lloyds List* demonstrated the growing importance of Lloyds Coffee House. From 1739, when war broke out with Spain, newspapers again assumed great importance as merchants and underwriters tried to keep themselves informed of the progress of the war and its effect on trade. *Lloyds List*, clearly the most reputable, was extensively pirated by the provincial press.

It ensured that at least the most important commercial information was widely disseminated, and merchants and underwriters were able to assess current risks from day to day. There were inevitably some variations in the way that underwriters interpreted the information, but they were never large, and a great deal depended on how well underwriters and merchants knew and trusted one another. At times of mounting crisis, as for example during 1755–6 before the outbreak of the Seven Years War, few underwriters were prepared to offer insurance on any terms, because of the risk that ships, insured at peacetime rates, might be arrested in French ports or taken at sea before they knew that war had broken out. As soon as war had been declared underwriters increased their rates. The only way that a merchant could have a reduction of these rates was for him to send his ship with a convoy. For this a reduction of between 5 and 10 per cent was usually given. During the wars of the mid-eighteenth century, London dominated the European market for marine insurance. Her trade was larger and more varied than any of her rivals', which enabled underwriters to spread their responsibilities through cross risks. London's financial institutions were also more stable than those of France, where the schemes of John Law had collapsed in the early 1720s. One broker, Nicholas Magens, asserted that 'It is notorious to all the mercantile world that as the English insurers pay more readily and generously than any others, most insurances are done in England'.[3] It was also well known that because of London's advantages and sound financial management, her insurance rates were lower. France could not compete successfully. Such underwriting as was undertaken in the major ports was the work of merchant-underwriters who formed societies known as 'chambres'. They resisted attempts at state intervention and fought the threat from two major companies: the Compagnie d'Assurance de Paris founded in 1750 and the Compagnie d'Assurance générale which dated from 1753.[4] Both collapsed through internal mismanagement. As a result, although insurance societies operated in all the major French ports in peacetime, as soon as war broke out the business was transferred to other ports in Holland, in Portugal and to London. War emphasized the weakness of French insurance. When war broke out between Britain and France in 1744 French underwriting collapsed. Most ports specialized in a few major trades: Bordeaux with the West Indies, Nantes in the slave trade, St Malo in the Newfoundland fisheries and Mediterranean trade. Under these conditions French underwriters could not spread their risks across a number of trades as London underwriters were able to do, and in general the French navy was too weak to protect even its coasting trade effectively. This forced premiums up.

Many French merchants insured their ventures in London during Anglo-French wars, a practice that was not considered unpatriotic to begin with, for it brought considerable business to London underwriters. When they were forced to pay heavy compensation to French merchants for losses inflicted by British warships public opinion changed and the practice was condemned. Some insurance companies found this business expensive; for example the London Assurance paid £18,000 compensation to French and Spanish merchants during the War of Austrian Succession.[5] In 1748, the final year of the war, Parliament passed an act forbidding the insuring of enemy ships, but it was of limited duration and expired at the end of the war. It was not until 1793 that similar legislation was passed again, although discussions were held on the subject at the opening of the Seven Years War and the War of American Independence. What seems to have dissuaded Parliamant from passing legislation on the subject in these two wars is the claim that the business was very profitable: premiums of 40 to 50 per cent were charged on voyages from Bordeaux to the West Indies.[6] Government fears that underwriters would seek to protect their risks by sending information on British naval dispositions to enemy ports appear to have been groundless.

When French merchants stopped using London underwriters, either because of high premiums or legislation, they were forced to transfer their trade to neutral vessels. The evidence of Dutch underwriting suggests that the Dutch preferred to carry French goods in their own ships rather than insure French goods in French ships. The insurance company of the city of Rotterdam, De Maatschappij van Assurantie, Discontering en Beleening der Stad Rotterdam, underwrote many voyages to and from French ports during the Seven Years War. The trade was harrassed by British warships and privateers until 1759 when a series of test cases in the Admiralty Court showed how far the British Admiralty was prepared to tolerate the trade.[7] Dutch marine insurance never seriously threatened London's supremacy, and was severely shaken by financial crises in Holland in 1763 and in 1772–3. In any case, marine insurance could be swiftly and easily arranged in London, and the London Assurance Company, for example, had a number of Huguenots among its shareholders and directors who had many family and religious connexions in

European ports. Even the British trade with Scandinavian ports was arranged through agents of British underwriters.

London underwriters also paid more generous compensation than their continental rivals. Until 1720 the London underwriters had deducted 15 per cent in case of loss, and this led merchants to insure the deduction as well. The practice was gradually abandoned; the London Assurance Company offered two types of policy, one to return 84 per cent and the other 98 per cent.[8] The trend thereafter was for the abatement to be steadily reduced on all policies to 1 or 2 per cent. Underwriting also developed in the outports, and as early as 1718 provincial underwriters had been powerful enough to mount a strong attack on the Mercers Hall petition for a charter. The practice in the outports was for merchant underwriters to organize insurance on a mutual basis. In Bristol they met in the Society of Merchant Venturers, in the outports they met in coffee houses. Provincial underwriters possessed considerable capital reserves, and at times they were prepared to co-operate with London underwriters where the venture was particularly large. In 1747 a prize was insured jointly at London, Exeter and Bristol for £150,000.[9] One common practice was for ships to be insured at one port and the cargo at another; this helped to spread the risk. Another feature of the provincial insurance market was for the rates to be based on London's, though slightly higher, for many risks were reinsured in London – in spite of a law of 1747 forbidding this. The generally higher provincial rates ensured that foreign merchants did not insure there and that the outport underwriters only insured their own risks.

There was no disaster comparable to the loss of the Smyrna convoy during the wars of the mid-eighteenth century, but the underwriters and Lloyds kept their reputations and their capital largely intact. The speculators who had entered the business avoided bankruptcy, but the newer and less experienced underwriters and brokers tarnished the reputation of Lloyds in the post-war years. In 1768 there was concern among the more stable element at Lloyds when a writer in the *London Chronicle* accused Lloyds of writing a number of wager policies: on John Wilkes' life for a year, for Wilkes to remain in prison, at 5 per cent; on John Wilkes being elected member for London, at 5 per cent to 15 per cent, and on 'Alderman B — d's life for one year', at 7 per cent.[11] The writer tried to blacken the reputation of the more respectable members by claiming that these policies had the backing of 'many of the principal underwriters, who are, in every other respect, useful members of society'. There seems to have been some truth in the charge; the following year the greater part of the reputable members of Lloyds broke away to form New Lloyds Coffee House and engaged Thomas Fielding, who had been a waiter at Lloyds' to be the proprietor. They took premises in Pope's Head Alley, close to the Royal Exchange, and ensured that they received up-to-date shipping news. By early 1769 the proprietors of New Lloyds Coffee House had persuaded the Post Office to extend the privileges of free postage and early delivery of ship news to them as well, and they also made arrangements with Lloyds agents at the outports. New Lloyds Coffee House was formally opened on 21 March, and there followed a battle between the New Lloyds and the Old Lloyds. By 1771 New Lloyds had won and had replaced the earlier house as the centre of marine underwriting. The battle between old and new was not simply a struggle between honest and dishonest underwriters. To some extent it was also a struggle between younger underwriters and their more conservative seniors. One of the latter was Thomas Braund, a former Portugal merchant who also had interests in the East India trade.[12] In 1769 he was a respected though by no means a leading figure at Lloyds, but when the break came he felt unable or unwilling to break with the institution where he had spent so much of his working life. Others stayed with him; Lloyds declined and finally closed in 1784 or 1785.

The transfer to New Lloyds did not result in any change in organization or practice of marine insurance, and the decision in 1779 to settle the terms of the policy should be seen as an attempt by conservative elements at New Lloyds to favour the assured rather than the underwriters. When war broke out again with France in 1778, underwriters again insured foreign risks at New Lloyds. The combination of French and American privateers and warships proved a severe threat to the convoys of British ships and losses were high. A number of the underwriters who had been attracted by the chance of high wartime profits became bankrupt by 1780 when a combined East and West India convoy, outward bound, was attacked by the Spanish fleet under Cordova and lost 55 of the 63 ships. This was not comparable to the Smyrna disaster, but British losses were high – £1,500,000 by one account. The following year the subscribers raised the question of ransom at a general meeting on 3 January. Many British ships captured by French and American privateers were ransomed rather than taken into port and sold because that had advantages for the captured as well as the captor. The latter did not risk losing his prize while it was being sent to a friendly port and did not need to put a prize crew on board, which weakened the strength of the privateer, an important consideration for American privateers far from their home ports. For the captain of the captured ship, ransom had the advantage that the ship could continue the voyage and remain in the hands of the owner. The disadvantage for the underwriter was that a system that had benefits for the privateer captain and the master of a merchant ship sometimes led to collusive capture, whereby the merchant ship fell into the hands of a privateer by prior arrangement and was subsequently ransomed. The advantage for the privateer and merchant ship owners was that the cargo was sold at a high price and the profits were split between the owners of both vessels. The underwriters also feared that, if ransom was always allowed, crews might abandon their ships without a fight – when a ship was ransomed, only one member of the crew was taken as surety and imprisoned; the remainder stayed free. The underwriters' stand was unreasonable. Few merchant ships could hope to resist even a small privateer, and although the practice of ransom led in some cases to abuse of the principles of underwriting, it did keep the vessels and their crews and cargoes out of French hands for the remainder of the voyage.

In the final wars of the period between 1793 and 1814, there was a steep rise in the value of insurance made on ships and their cargoes. John Janson, one of the best known underwriters, insured a total of £986,200 in 1808 alone, of which £286,550 was on the coastal and Irish trades.[13] By comparison, Braund, though not one of the most distinguished underwriters in the mid-eighteenth century, had only received £11,377 in premium payments in 1758.[14] No other commercial centre enjoyed commercial prosperity such as these figures indicate; the French marine insurance market always collapsed in war, the Dutch had not recovered from the crises in the 1760s and early 1770s and the American insurance offices were still small. The principal American ports: Boston, Salem, Newburyport, Nantucket, Beverly, Marblehead, Gloucester and New Bedford all had insurance offices or companies and some merchant-underwriters made fortunes from marine insurance. They underwrote the American coasting trade and commerce with Europe and the West Indies, though most of the voyages to and from Liverpool were insured there or in London. The size of this commerce and the prosperity it brought to Liverpool helped to create the Liverpool Underwriters' Association in January 1802 as a symbol of civic pride and economic success. At the same time, Lloyds continued to dominate the London insurance market, and co-operated closely with the Admiralty over the timing and organization of convoys. In 1798 these were made compulsory for all ships engaged in foreign trade, though it was possible to obtain licences to sail independently under certain conditions.[16]

Lloyds supported the Admiralty in enforcing convoy discipline and in cases where the masters of merchant ships had flagrantly disobeyed the orders of escort commanders, asked the Admiralty to initiate proceedings under the Convoy Act at Lloyds' expense. The Admiralty supplied Lloyds with convoy lists and the Admiralty's secretary on the Baltic station sent regular reports of naval and political developments between 1809 and 1811. Lloyds assisted the Admiralty by sending information it contained from returning merchant ships and sometimes this was in advance of official naval reports. This close co-operation between the Admiralty and the Secretary of Lloyds was of considerable importance to both. It enabled the Lloyds underwriters to assess the risks faced by different trades with considerable accuracy, and Lloyds rates reflected the day-to-day progress of the wars. Much of the information obtained by Lloyds in this way was of national importance and was publicized through *Lloyds List* in London and the outports. Only where the information was likely to be of value to the enemy were the details falsified, for it was known that copies of *Lloyds List* circulated abroad. Underwriters and brokers at Lloyds however had the advantage that they could read all incoming letters, though they remained the property of the master.

Subscribers to Lloyds were also able to assess risks in relation to individual ships by consulting the registers that were kept of all ships insured there. Too much should not be made of these registers, for many of the entries were inadequate and frequently inaccurate, but they were a serious attempt to provide information on the seaworthiness of ships that should be available to all brokers and underwriters. Underwriters realized that many of the ships that sailed were either overinsured or unseaworthy, or both, and it was hard to prove that a ship lost at sea had been lost through the owner's negligence, and it was not until the case of the *Mills Frigate* that this principle was established in law. The first register to be kept at Lloyds dates from about 1760, but underwriters supplemented their copies with information on the ships they insured regularly. In 1797 underwriters tried to improve the register by classifying each ship according to whether it was Thames-built or constructed at an outport or abroad and according to its age. This raised complaints from shipowners who claimed that these categories were unfair, but their criticism is unjustified. Nonetheless, the shipowners published their own register, and the two, known as the Red and Green Books, circulated side by side until they were amalgamated in 1823. Neither was wholly accurate; apart from errors, neither was apparently kept up-to-date.

These registers served as useful guides to brokers and underwriters when asked to insure a ship for the first time, but to an increasing extent underwriting came to be practised by underwriters, brokers and merchants who habitually worked in close co-operation on the basis of trust and probity. From the end of the eighteenth century the membership of Lloyds was tightly restricted to exclude undesirable elements and the institution gained an international reputation for security. The contrast with underwriting at the beginning of the period is striking. Then, the merchant seeking insurance first tried to discover who were the underwriters and brokers to be trusted by discussion on the floor of the Royal Exchange. By the end of the period a merchant could assume that a Lloyds broker or underwriter could be trusted. A further safeguard for the merchant was the practice whereby for up to a year brokers kept premiums due to underwriters with whom they regularly did business. Out of this income they settled petty claims on the underwriters' behalf and made an annual settlement with them. This ensured that there was always a reserve fund to safeguard merchants' claims if underwriters found themselves in financial difficulties.

The growth of marine insurance in the eighteenth century made this an essential safeguard. What is perhaps surprising is that over the whole period peacetime insurance premiums varied very little. Most of the London marine insurance records were destroyed in a fire in the Royal Exchange, but from the meagre records that have survived elsewhere, a pattern has emerged. In war there were naturally variations, and Baltic rates varied from around eight guineas – the rate quoted in Liverpool in May 1756 – to Janson's rates after 1800 which ranged from 20 to 40 per cent in 1808 when much of the Baltic was under French control.[18] In peacetime premiums on Caribbean trade varied according to season; the approach of the hurricane season pushed rates up, and return voyages were always higher than those from Britain. Other factors which influenced premiums were the condition of the ship, the competence of the master, enemy naval dispositions and knowledge of privateers. For example, in two consecutive months in 1804, February and March, Janson quoted between 5 and 10 per cent for voyages from Britain to the Caribbean: 5 per cent for Falmouth to Tobago, 6 per cent from the Clyde to Jamaica and the Clyde to St Thomas, also for London to Demerara and 8 per cent for London to Bermuda. Finally, Belfast to Jamaica was 10 per cent.[19] Where the risk was even greater, as from Santa Cruz to Copenhagen, the rate rose to 25 per cent.[20] By comparison, French rates during the War of American Independence were higher. The premium for a voyage from Bordeaux to the Caribbean quickly rose to 50 per cent, after which underwriters refused to insure. Those merchants who continued to trade had to carry the risk themselves, and one voyage was made in late 1778 with only 29 per cent of the risk insured.[21]

The security of British insurance, the strength of her navy and the protection given by the convoy system all helped to keep British rates down. Even so during the Napoleonic War premiums, which were normally 2 or 3 per cent, never fell below 7 per cent, and were usually much higher. The evidence available for other wars suggests that this was representative of the whole period. Whatever merchants may have thought about the value of marine insurance in peacetime, in war the majority seem to have insured their risks, though the costs were a heavy additional burden. Only a wealthy and confident man like Alderman William Beckford, planter and Jamaica merchant, was able to carry his own insurance by distributing the risks across a large number of voyages, and on one occasion he boasted publicly in the Commons that he never insured his risks.[22] Lesser men had to try and offset these rising costs against higher wartime prices in home and overseas markets. Dutch rates, at least during the Seven Years War when the country was neutral, were much lower. Rates of 1 and $2\frac{1}{2}$ per cent were common for most European voyages to and from Dutch ports.[23] Mediterranean voyages tended to be higher because of the risk from Barbary corsairs, and were around $4\frac{1}{2}$ per cent from a Dutch port to the western Mediterranean and up to 6 per cent to Smyrna in the east. Voyages to Batavia rose to 8 per cent, Canton was rated at about the same, and those to Surinam and St Eustatius were about 6 per cent. However, these rates only applied to Dutch ships and British merchants preferred to send their goods in ships with British masters. Insurance at Amsterdam or Rotterdam would have been very expensive in view of the uncertain risk, and a Frenchman, François Rigais, was asked to pay 30 per cent on a voyage from Morlaix to Cadiz in September 1744. Insurance on a Dutch vessel would have been around 3 per cent. British merchants would have had to use false papers and hire Dutch ships, and the security of the convoy system and the comparatively low rates offered in Britain made such subterfuges unnecessary.

An important feature of marine insurance in the wars as from the mid-eighteenth century is the attention given by Lord Mansfield.

Many of the risks insured were not clearly defined in law, nor were many features of the convoy system, and Lord Mansfield heard a series of test cases to establish legal rights and make it unnecessary for brokers and their clients to settle out of court. In 1748 it led to an attempt to codify the law relating to marine insurance, but this proved impossible for the subject was too complex, and it was not until 1906 that this was achieved in the Marine Insurance Act. The term 'convoy' was not defined until 1783, though it was widely accepted before then that ships insured to sail with convoy should do so.[24] It was also accepted that the commodore should not ask for any reward for his services. The case of the *John and Joan*, heard in 1744, showed what the law was prepared to accept.[25] Insured to sail from Flekkefjord to London with convoy, the master of the vessel ignored orders to join the convoy when it arrived, and later sailed independently. The following day, the *John and Jane* was taken by a privateer after a running fight. The court decided that the master had forfeited his insurance, a decision reinforced in the case of *Taylor v Woodness* in 1763, when a ship insured to sail with a convoy failed to join it at Spithead. It sailed later and was taken by a privateer.[26] This raises a point of considerable importance. When the owner of a ship intended to send it with a convoy, which was not made compulsory until the Convoy Acts of 1798 and 1803, he took insurance 'warrented to depart with convoy'.[27] In a number of test cases, successive chief justices defined exactly what this meant. In the first place, the ship had to join the convoy at the port where the convoy usually assembled, and was protected by insurance while sailing from her port of lading to join the convoy. Thus the master was not obliged until the convoy acts to join a coastal convoy while sailing to the assembly point at Portsmouth. This ruling became so well established that even when more coastal convoys were provided towards the end of the eighteenth century, and it became easier for the merchant to sail under protection to Portsmouth, many masters sailed independently and were insured. In the case of *Warwick v Scott* in November 1814, the *Pomona* was captured by a French privateer while sailing to join a Portsmouth convoy. The rules of the British Association Insurance Club, with which she was insured, stated that she was only insured while sailing with a convoy. The Association argued that she should have taken convoy at the Downs, but was overruled by Lord Ellenborough.[28]

The crucial test of whether a ship was sailing in convoy was whether the master had received a copy of the sailing instructions issued by the escort commander. These stated not only the rules of convoy discipline and signals for the voyage, but also rendezvous for the convoy to reassemble if it became dispersed. In the case *Webb v Thomson* in May 1797, the decision hinged on whether the master, Captain Hodser, had received sailing instructions before sailing from the West Indies for Portsmouth with a convoy. The case was complicated: the ship was wrecked and Captain Hodser drowned, so no concrete evidence was available.[29] It would be wrong to assume that if a ship failed to join a convoy as arranged that her master was necessarily negligent. It generally took two to three months to find a cargo and load a ship, and when, as a result of unforseen delays the ship failed to join a convoy, the owner carried the responsibility. At times the owner accepted cargo on the understanding that the ship would sail with convoy, although subsequently the ship was delayed and failed to do so. In *Magalhaens v Bushar*, the former, a merchant, sued the master because he had promised that the ship would sail with convoy but had failed to do this because of the delay in loading the cargo. The merchant claimed a sum equal to the rebate on insurance for sailing with convoy, but he failed to win his case.[30]

It was also necessary to define the nature of the escort vessel appointed to accompany the convoy. It came to be recognized in law that a convoy escort had to be appointed by the government, or by the commander of an overseas station acting on its behalf. A naval vessel which happened to be sailing along the same route as the convoy and which offered protection did not constitute a convoy, even though the ship's captain offered to provide protection and sailing instructions.[31] The case concerned the *Arundel*, which reached Bluefields Bay, Jamaica, too late to join the convoy for Britain, but was offered protection by the armed ships *Jason* and *Glorieux* while sailing to join the convoy. Although the *Arundel* subsequently joined the convoy, it was lost in a storm. The insurance 'to sail with convoy' was declared invalid, because the armed ships had not been appointed escorts by the commander of the Jamaica squadron. On the other hand, a naval vessel could be detached from an escorting squadron when it was impractical for the merchant vessel to sail to a general rendezvous to join the convoy. The merchant ship also had to be protected while in the vicinity of the port of lading. The Tortola trade posed such a problem, for ships sailing from this island to Britain could not beat to windward to join the Leeward Islands convoys which assembled at St Christopher's. In consequence, Tortola trade was escorted a short distance by a frigate detached from the main squadron and this was accepted as a convoy.[32] One further point was that a master of a merchant ship had to join a convoy appointed specifically for his trade – merely to join one sailing in the same direction was not sufficient.[33]

When the ship had sailed with convoy and the master had received a copy of the printed sailing instructions, it was considered that he had fulfilled the main requirement implied by the phrase 'warranted to sail with convoy' provided that he did not later try to leave the convoy without the permission of the escort commander. Sometimes merchant ships were damaged on their voyage and had to leave the convoy to be repaired in port. He was still covered by insurance while sailing there and was not obliged to join another convoy when setting sail again, for his destination even when convoys were normally provided for the trade of that port.[34] At times the policy was inadequately worded. When that happened the law followed the generally accepted custom, on the grounds that it was the underwriter's responsibility to know what was normal practice and assess the risks accordingly. One such difficulty in interpretation, which was also one of the first to be defined clearly, was the phrase 'warranted to sail with convoy'. This was generally understood, when the ships were sailing from Britain, to mean that ships would sail with convoys from the Downs, from where escorts were often provided to escort ships to Spithead. When there was no convoy in the Downs, it was customary for vessels to sail independently to Spithead to join a convoy for an overseas destination. It was recognized that the voyage from the Downs to Spithead was included in the policy 'warranted to sail with convoy' because it was the intention of the master who sailed independently from the Downs to join a convoy at Spithead and reach there before the convoy sailed. This was the decision of Chief Justice Holt in 1702, in a case heard in which an East Indiaman had been lost.[35]

Vessels sailing to Spithead to join a convoy often arrived too late. The master could not continue his voyage until he had informed the underwriters, cancelled his policy and reinsured the remainder of his voyage to sail independently – except when convoys were compulsory. The merchant reclaimed the cost of the cancelled policy. This decision arose from the case *Stevenson v Snow*, in which a ship was insured to sail with convoy from London to Halifax in Nova Scotia and reached Portsmouth. The underwriters had charged a premium of five guineas per 1 per cent, and at first refused to give any rebate on the cancelled policy. The jury agreed that the customary insurance for a voyage from London to Portsmouth at that time was $1\frac{1}{2}$ per cent. The verdict was that as only part of the voyage had been completed, a rebate should be made on the unexpired part of the policy. The judge pointed out, when making his verdict, that the amount of rebate would vary according to the circumstances of each case.[36] When ships sailed with convoys, the masters were obliged to remain with them for the whole of the voyage. Most ships did so, but some – usually privateers sailing to and from the Caribbean – took advantage of their speed to chase French ships when they came in sight and often rejoined the convoys later. Their masters usually claimed that bad visibility had prevented them remaining with the convoy and generally avoided losing their insurance because it was hard to prove that their action was deliberate. They were a menace to the safety of the convoy however, for if they fell into the hands of a French privateer or warship they revealed that a convoy was following. In the Seven Years War the case *Cook v Townson* provided the opportunity of clarifying the position.[37] The dispute concerned the privateer *George* which sailed with a convoy from Cork for Jamaica. During the voyage the *George* and two other privateers left the convoy one night and cruised nearby in the hope of taking a prize. The verdict was that the masters had voided their policies.

Sometimes ships were separated from their convoys by stress of weather and had to put into harbour for repair. This deviation from the course was unavoidable, and the policy remained valid. If closer examination showed that the vessel was so badly damaged by storm that she could not continue the voyage, the underwriters paid full compensation just as if the vessel had been lost at sea. This amounted to 98 per cent of the sum insured, less 2 per cent for expenses and $\frac{1}{2}$ per cent for prompt payment. In July 1745 the *George and Henry* had been badly damaged while sailing with convoy from Jamaica to London. When she was examined at Charleston, she was found to be too badly damaged and was broken up; her cargo was transferred to other ships to be sent to London.[38] One point about which underwriters had to be particularly careful was the risk that a ship might put to sea in an unsafe condition, and it was to guard against this that underwriters kept records of each ship that they insured. Apart from dishonest merchants who sent rotten ships to sea and insured them heavily, there were some owners who were unaware of the dangerous condition of their vessels. This was the case of the *Mills Frigate*, French-built, and bought as a prize in 1757.[39] After seven years service the vessel was extensively repaired and appeared sound. In spring 1746 it sailed to Nevis, and developed a leak during the voyage. Attempts were made to repair this before sailing for Britain, and a surveyor's report said that she needed caulking. This was done and the ship appeared sound. The day after she had sailed from Nevis with a cargo of sugar she sprang another leak and the captain sailed to St Christopher's for repair. The Vice-Admiralty court ordered another survey and it was discovered that the bolts holding the timbers together had rusted. The ship required a more expensive repair than her value merited, and the underwriters declared that the condition of the ship voided the insurance. It illustrates a problem with French-built ships which apparently contained more iron bolts and spikes than British. It raised special problems over the insurance of French-built ships which were taken as prizes and passed into British hands. Where the vessels had to be repaired, British owners disliked having to pay for work that they could not supervise; insurers on the other hand had to be certain that each ship was 'staunch and tight'.

Another problem for insurers was that of a vessel that had been taken by a privateer and then recaptured. This raised two issues: the payment of salvage to the recaptors and whether the owners were obliged to take their ship back – with a sum for compensation for damage – or whether they could abandon the ship and cargo to the underwriters and claim as for total loss. The amount of salvage was determined by the length of time that the ship had been in French hands. If the vessel was retaken by a British privateer within 24 hours, the salvage charge was one-eighth of the value of ship and cargo. Salvage charges rose by stages to half the value of the ship and cargo if the recapture took place more than 96 hours after the capture. When the vessel was retaken by a warship, the charge was one-eighth of the total value regardless of the amount of time the ship had been in enemy hands.[40]

When the merchant ship arrived safely in Britain and the owners claimed compensation for damages received during the voyage, the underwriters had to establish whether the damages had been caused by enemy action, or by storm. The case of the *David and Rebecca* in 1756 showed that when a ship was damaged by bad weather, recapture made little difference to what was otherwise a disastrous voyage.[41] The ship sailed from Newfoundland with a cargo of fish for Spain or Portugal 'without the Straits'. During the voyage the convoy ran into a storm which partly disabled the ship, and part of the cargo had to be jettisoned to lighten the vessel. The *David and Rebecca* became separated from the convoy and was captured by a French privateer. Later, it was retaken by a British ship and taken to Milford Haven. When they heard the news, the owners abandoned the ship to the underwriters. The latter disputed this, on the grounds that the ship had arrived safely in Britain. The verdict was that because of the total loss of the cargo, the storm damage and salvage charge, the owners had the right to be paid compensation as for total loss.

However, when the ship arrived safely and undamaged in Britain, the owners had no right to abandon her to the underwriters. The *Selby*, which sailed from Virginia to London in March 1759 with a cargo of tobacco was taken by a French privateer, the *Aurora* of Bayonne. The owner abandoned his interest to the agent, who offered to abandon the ship and cargo to the underwriters. They refused to accept this and were prepared to pay salvage charges and costs arising from the ship's capture. When the ship reached London, it was found that the ship and cargo were undamaged. Mansfield decided that the agent, to whom the owner had assigned his interest, had no right to abandon this to the underwriters and claim total loss, since both ship and cargo had arrived safely. The underwriters' duty was only to pay salvage and other charges.[42]

When a ship was taken into dock after a voyage, the underwriter had to be able to distinguish between wear and tear and storm damage, for merchants tried to get underwriters to pay for both. For this reason the respective obligations of owners and underwriters came to be carefully defined. In the case of *Vazeley and others v St Barbe* in 1786, a ship sailed from Viborg to Lynn and was damaged during the voyage.[43] At first the owners claimed partial loss, but changed this to total loss when they found that the ship was too badly damaged to be repaired. The underwriters offered to pay for partial loss, to cover the cost of repair to the damage caused by the storm. The court decided that a claim for partial loss could not be subsequently changed for total loss, and that no claim could be made for that if the vessel arrived safely. The court also held that the underwriters' offer to pay partial loss – the balance of the value of the ship to be made from parts salvaged when the ship was broken up – was fair. The inference was clear: wear and tear was the responsibility of the owners. In the same way, when cables were lost, the underwriters were only to pay for those which were broken or badly frayed when the ship was riding out a storm. Opinion was not unanimous however and one authority recommended that compensation should always be paid when cables were broken, because they were lost when the captain was trying to save his ship and cargo. The one serious difficulty was over the East India trade, where underwriters paid compensation on the value of cables in Britain, but the owners had to buy cables in India which were always more expensive.[44] In the Atlantic trades, cables were frequently lost at Madeira, where there was a heavy swell and frequent gales which forced captains to cut their cables and beat out to sea. Many were also lost at Antigua while convoys were assembling in English Harbour.

Another difficulty facing the underwriter, especially in wartime, was to establish whether the owner intended his ship to arrive. Many voyages were insured in London, and captains were instructed to send details of their cargo before returning from a foreign port so that insurance could be obtained. Normally in wartime these letters were carried in neutral ships, but sometimes they were delayed and the information did not reach the owners and underwriters until the ship had completed the voyage. This enabled unscrupulous merchants to delay insuring their ships until the convoy arrived and then insuring the ship if it did not arrive. Underwriters were only prepared to insure these risks at high premiums, and always expected to be given full details of each voyage in order to assess the risk. In 1747 the *Prosperous Esther* was insured at 60 per cent on a voyage from Virginia or Maryland to London because she was considered a 'missing ship'.[45] The underwriters' first consideration when a claim was made was whether the merchant had made an accurate statement, and they usually asked to see the bill of lading and customs house docket which provided the means of assessing when the ship sailed and when it was likely to arrive. It also established the total value of the cargo.

Underwriters were expected to possess a thorough knowledge of all trades in which they issued policies, and where disputes arose, they were usually because of a difference in interpretation of sections of the policy. Mansfield often used these disputes to define the meaning of each section of the policy more clearly. Occasionally an underwriter misunderstood merchants' terminology. One example is the capture of Fort Malborough by d'Estaing in 1760.[46] Before the fort was attacked, the governor of the trading post on the island of Sumatra realized that the risk existed and arranged insurance through his brother in London on goods to a value of £10,000. The policy was to run for one year from 16 October 1759.[47] Within the year the fort had been captured by d'Estaing and the governor of the fort claimed compensation. The underwriter claimed that he had been misled; Fort Malborough was not a fortress but only a fortified trading post which was virtually defenceless against attack by Europeans. He also considered that the governor had not informed him of the risk of a French attack and asked that the policy be declared void because relevant information was hidden from him. It became clear in the course of the hearing that although the East India Company's forts in India were strongly fortified and designed to resist attack by Europeans, the forts elsewhere were not, although they appeared formidable. Fort Malborough had only a small force of native troops and a few Europeans and its main defence was its position on a river where it was dangerous to sail without experienced pilots. Moreover, the governor of the fort was not a military commander but a merchant who organized the collection of the pepper harvest on the island. The attack on Sumatra by d'Estaing took him by surprise and he had little chance in the time between the capture of Nattal in the north and the attack on Fort Malborough to strengthen its defences. Mansfield's decision was that the condition of the fort and the role of the governor were common knowledge and it was the duty of the underwriter to be fully informed of such matters: 'It was not the duty of the proposer to tell the underwriter things he should know already'.[48]

This statement by Mansfield underlines one of the main tenets of marine insurance, to which he contributed so much during his time as Lord Chief Justice. He took every opportunity of defining the law relating to marine insurance so that underwriters, brokers and merchants should understand the risks and be able to assess them in terms which all understood. The clarity with which he enunciated legal principles enabled underwriters to undertake business which otherwise they might have been reluctant to accept. As to the practice of underwriting, so many of the records have been lost that it is hard to assess how individual brokers, merchants and underwriters organized their business under the stress of wartime conditions. Convoys provided the main defence for trade and Mansfield defined the risks relating to convoy organization; that was the combination which contributed much to the success of British trade in wartime.

4

The Northern States and Canada

THE MOST IMPRESSIVE aspect of the commerce between Britain and North America in the period from 1689 to 1815 is the steady, and at times spectacular increase. It was partly in response to the needs of a growing population and increased wealth on both sides of the north Atlantic; it can also be attributed to the successful exploitation of commercial opportunities by a vigorous commercial body, supported for most of the period by a powerful navy. Definitive figures of the value of British trade are still lacking, but it is possible to discern the trend from statistics for the value of British imports and exports for the eighteenth century drawn up by the late Elizabeth Schumpeter.[1] In simple economic terms, the average annual value of British exports to the American colonies rose from £259,000 for the five years 1701–5 to £1,225,000 in 1751–5 and by the closing years of the century had reached £5,722,000. This was only surpassed by British exports to Germany, stimulated by the war with Revolutionary France. British imports from North America told a similar story: at the beginning of the century the annual average for 1701–5 was £264,000, by 1751–5 it had risen to £952,000 and by the end of the century the American states were exporting goods to Britain annually to a total value, on average, of £1,685,000. Even at that figure, a comparatively low sum in terms of overall British trade, it was surpassed by British imports from the East and West Indies, Ireland, Germany, Russia and the Baltic. But the American states remained a major source of supply for the British market, and some commodities, notably cotton, were soon important for the British economy.

Further examination of this American trade shows that it can be divided into two parts. The northern colonies, from the modern states of Pennsylvania and New Jersey to the Canadian frontier were primarily importers of British manufactured goods and had few commodities that could be readily sold in Britain. The balance lay in Britain's favour, though the gap was narrowed by American 'invisible exports', notably shipping, which never appeared in the trade records. The south, from Maryland to Georgia, constituted primarily a plantation economy that produced a range of valuable commodities, notably rice and tobacco which found a ready market in Britain for home consumption and re-export. These southern colonies enjoyed a favourable balance in their trade with Britain and were able to trade directly with the European markets after the War of American Independence. The northern and southern colonies were linked by a coasting trade that was almost entirely in the hands of northern

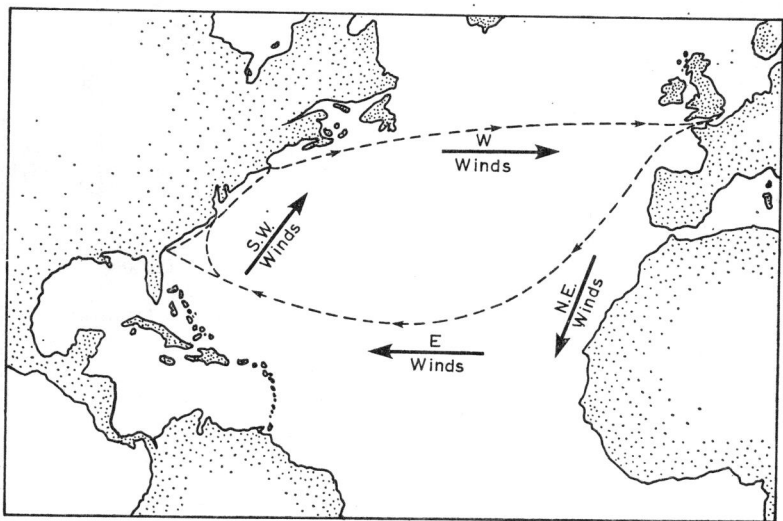

4   North American trade

merchants and to some extent became mutually dependent. But the differences between north and south make it necessary to discuss each area in turn: this chapter will examine the growth of the northern economy and the defence of its trade and a further chapter will study the south.

At the start of this period, the opening of the War of the League of Augsburg in 1689, the northern colonies consisted of a number of small settlements, concentrated, if one can use the term for such a small population, along the southern shore of Massachusetts Bay, at points on the lower Connecticut River and on Long Island Sound. The commerce, shipbuilding and fishing which formed the basis of

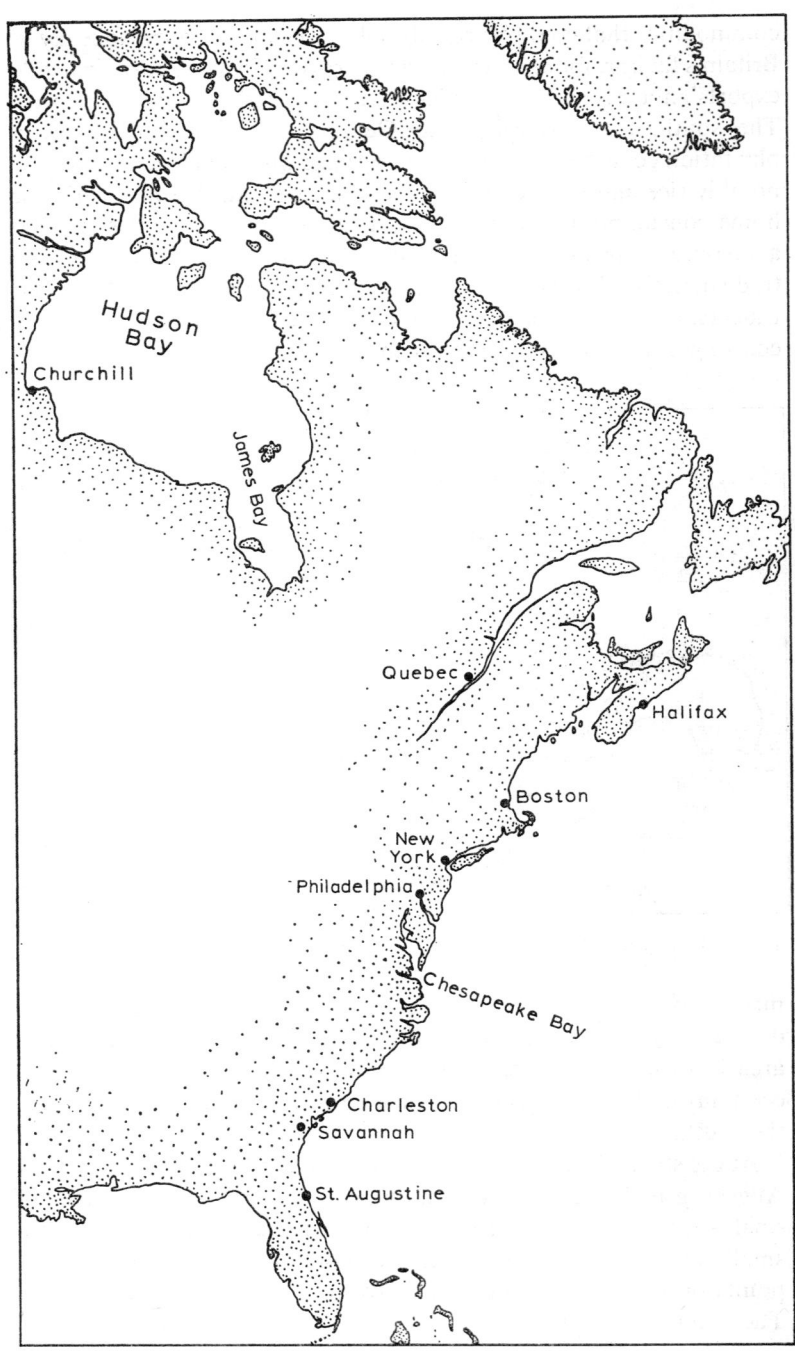

5   North American ports

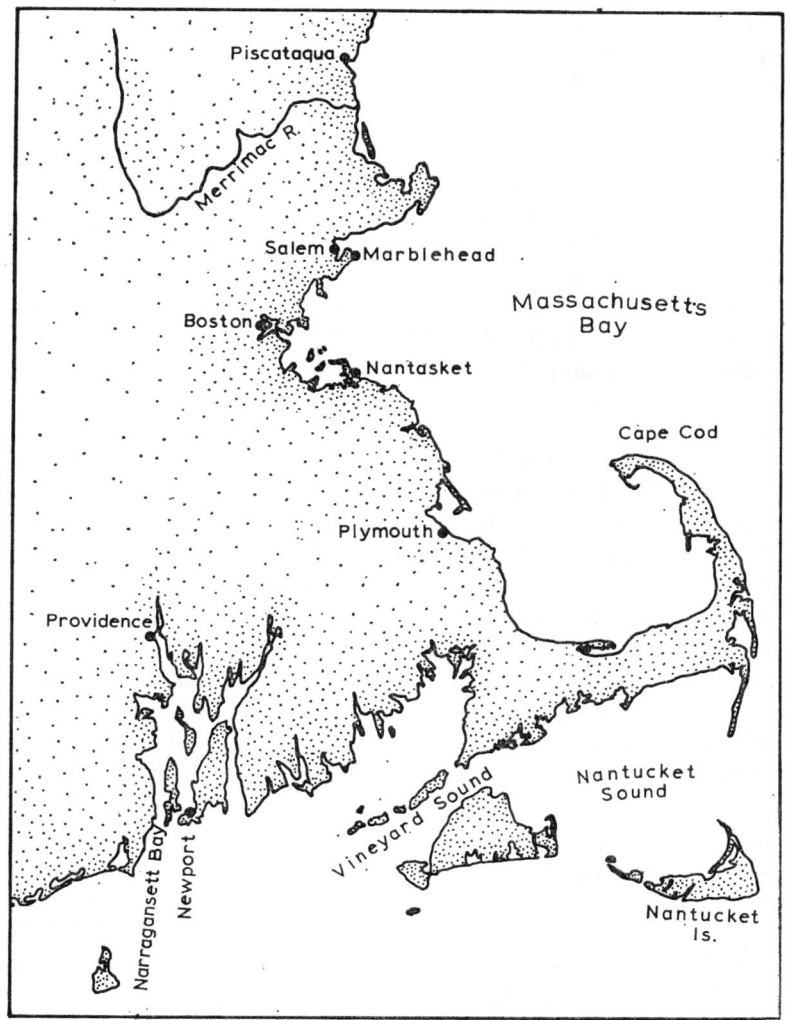

6   Massachusetts Bay

the coastal economy was centred on Boston, the principal port in the
northern colonies. After it in importance and size came other ports
on Massachusetts Bay: Salem and Marblehead, Piscataqua and
Plymouth, and to the west, Providence at the head of Narragansett
Bay. Further south were the ports of New York and Philadelphia.
Settlements in the interior faced a precarious existence; Indian
attacks and French raids were constantly feared after war had broken

out in 1689, and many of the marginal farmers moved to the security of the coast. Most of the inhabitants were engaged in agriculture: maize and wheat, beans, pumpkins and cattle rearing, though by the early eighteenth century some had turned to trade which was more profitable. Massachusetts Bay's main asset in this respect was the abundant supply of white pine, suitable for ship construction and supplying masts and spars. The northern forests continued to supply large pines for the rest of the period, and the area remained an important source of naval masts.

Shipbuilding played an important part in the colony's prosperity. It had developed in the years after the Great Migration, when the decline in the number of ships arriving in Massachusetts made many colonists believe they were becoming isolated.[2] By the 1690s shipbuilding was well established at Boston, North River and Salem, the lower Piscataqua River and the lower Merrimac River, and when the supplies of timber had been exhausted, shipwrights moved inland and established new yards. The Board of Admiralty and the Navy Board were pessimistic about the quality of ships built in these colonial yards and refused to buy anything but mast timber, on the grounds that colonial products were shoddy and expensive. This did not stop the colonists developing a thriving shipbuilding industry which supplied Massachusetts and other American colonies, and later, English merchants as well. With a stream of new ships coming off the slipways, Massachusetts merchants opened trade with the southern colonies and even with England, although many of these ships were small: around 50 tons in the inter-colonial trade and no more than 150 tons in commerce with England, where many of them were sold. Apart from this form of revenue, it was hard to know what these northern colonists could sell in England to pay for their imports of manufactured goods. The province lacked the raw materials that the English market demanded, but colonists gradually found that they could sell the products of the northern forests and fisheries in the West Indies and use this money to pay their English debts.

The provincial population gradually increased; so too did imports of English goods, for the mercantile system ensured that the demand could only be met by England, and after 1707 by Scotland as well. By the close of the seventeenth century Massachusetts and New York was paying for its English imports by exports to the Caribbean. Horses and corn were sent to work the plantation machinery and feed the workers, barrel staves and hoops made up the casks in which molasses and sugar were exported and joists, scantlings and shingles were sent to make the houses for the plantation owners and their servants. None of these could be sent to England, because English supplies were adequate, but they were essential to the West Indian economy and were soon joined by barrels of salted beef and butter and dried fish which formed the stable diet of the population. Some of these commodities were also sold in Portugal; the vessels which carried dried fish also took oak staves for wine casks. The income from the sale of these goods and of the ships was used to pay for the imports already mentioned.

Fishing was of particular importance. As early as 1641, Governor Winthrop had estimated the catch from the rich coastal fisheries as 300,000 cod.[3] By the final decade of the seventeenth century the New

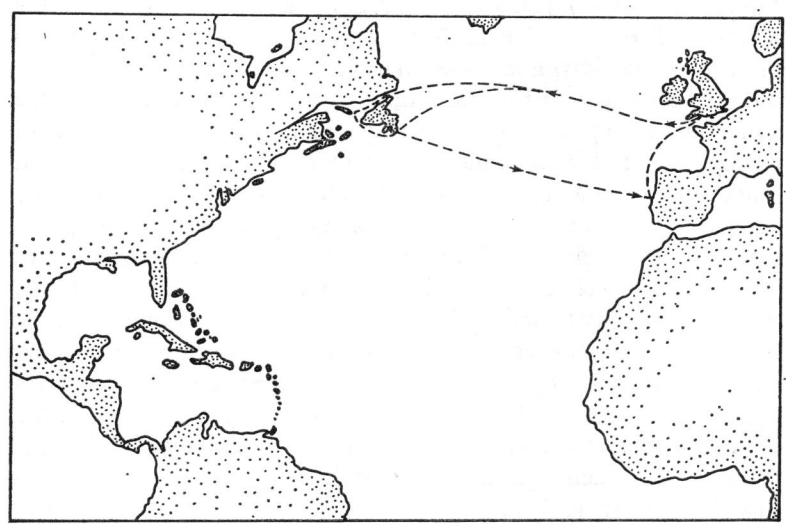

7 Newfoundland trade

England fishermen had extended their activities as far as the New-foundland Grand Banks, and whaling had begun from Marblehead. The Grand Banks and the shores of Newfoundland were already attracting many boats from south-west England and France. Cod, hake, mackerel and haddock caught by these New England fishermen were taken to the New England coast to be smoked and dried on stages or salted and packed green in casks for the Portuguese and Caribbean markets. Much of the salt used for this had been brought from the Island of Margarita, off the Venezuelan coast – the product of Caribbean trade – though the best came from the salt pans in the

Bay of Biscay – the famous Bay salt.[4] The best grades of fish were sent to Portugal, and broken and poor quality fish found a market in the Caribbean as food for slaves.

When England declared war in 1689 the fisheries and the colonies' Portuguese and Caribbean trades were put in danger. So too was commerce with England. Although at this point France did not possess a naval base in North America – the fortress of Louisbourg was built later – French privateers and letters of marque ships could, and did, prey on English and colonial shipping on both sides of the North Atlantic. English shipping was in serious and continual danger in English coastal waters from the many privateers operating from ports in France and the North Sea and off the American coast. Merchants who shipped goods from London and the outports to the markets of Boston, Salem, New York and elsewhere had to be protected by convoys and powerful business interests put considerable pressure on the Board of Admiralty to provide these, often at the risk of disrupting the Board's strategic planning. The large fleets of fishing and sack ships which sailed to the Newfoundland Grand Banks, the coastal fisheries and the Hudson Bay also had to be defended. As noted already, the Admiralty consulted groups of merchants in England and decided the best time for the convoys to sail. The dates were controlled in many cases by climatic conditions: the Hudson's Bay Company ships, for instance, could only be in the Bay during the ice-free period. Fishing boats were escorted from west country ports by naval escorts which then remained to patrol the fishing grounds and escort the fleet to Portugal at the end of the season in November. The disadvantage of the convoy system – the market was suddenly glutted by the arrival of the fish and prices fell sharply – led some fishing boat masters to leave Newfoundland in August and sail unescorted to Lisbon or Bilbao. This was a practice that the Admiralty tried hard to suppress, as it ran counter to the wishes of the majority of merchants for whom the convoys were provided, and merchants were informed that single ships would not be escorted by naval vessels off the Portuguese coast. Furthermore, if these ships were captured by Barbary corsairs, their crews would not be ransomed.[5] While the ships were in North American waters the escorts cruised to preserve order among them – the commodore was also appointed judge for fishing disputes – and keep the area clear of hostile French ships. They also to some degree helped to preserve the trade of the colonies. These also armed sloops which cruised off the principal harbours and landfalls, to which privateers were attracted. It gave a measure of local defence until the convoy returned to England or, in the case of Newfoundland vessels, to Portugal. This left the American coast undefended except for the American sloops, until the arrival of the fishing fleet the following year.

It may appear from the above that trade defence was well organized during the War of the League of Augsburg. In practice this was not true. In the early years of the period, especially between 1689 and 1697, the Admiralty was unprepared to fight a tactical war at sea and to organize a system of commerce defence. Too often the Admiralty was caught unprepared for war in the period 1689–1815, though the principles of commerce defence had been known as early as the Dutch wars. What was often lacking was a sufficient number of frigates and small line-of-battle ships that could be used for convoy escort duties and fleet reconnaissance. The French policy after 1696 of using naval forces in small raiding squadrons, though tactically disastrous in terms of maintaining battle strength, made this lack of small warships more evident. Consequently, English commercial losses could not be stemmed, yet merchants' clamourings for protection could be silenced only by diverting scarce naval resources. Neither strategic nor commercial needs could be fully met, and the resultant friction between the Admiralty and the mercantile interest in the House of Commons reached a high pitch in this war. Later, many more small escort vessels were built and in spite of an increase in the number of ships needing protection, a higher proportion was safeguarded and amicable relations established between Admiralty and merchants.

Compared with the trade with Europe, the commerce with North America was comparatively small, but it could not be ignored. In the intermittent warfare between 1689 and 1713 Customs returns indicate that the English imports from New England, measured at the official commodity values, were £31,254 in 1698, fluctuated between £22,210 (1706) and £49,635 (1708) during the wars and rose to £50,000–£60,000 in the peace that followed.[6] By comparison, English exports to this market were valued at £93,517 in 1698, rose to £127,279 in 1699 and fluctuated between £57,000 and £91,000 until 1707. In that year they reached £120,631 and maintained this new level until they increased again in the 1720s. Trade with the smaller colony at New York was even less: English imports in 1698 were £8,763 and exports £25,279; in 1713 these had reached £14,428 and £46,470 respectively. By comparison with Germany, one of the principal markets for English goods, for which the Customs returns show imports of £525,734 and exports of £694,349 in 1698, the North

American trade was derisory. Its importance however lay in its value as the major supplier of fish, corn and lumber to the English colonies in the Caribbean, a point that was harshly demonstrated in 1688 when the Island of Nevis faced famine when North American captains, fined for illegal activities, refused to trade there.[7] This commerce with the Caribbean and southern colonies, who were also supplied with provisions and lumber by New England ships, brought back rum, sugar, tobacco and cotton for the colonists and currency to meet English debts. In economic terms this trade was relatively insignificant, and its importance lies chiefly in the inter-colonial trade. Protection was apparently given grudgingly and was often inadequate.

Dominating this trade in the North Atlantic was the Newfoundland fishery. Long regarded as a nursery of seamen – a contemporary view that is no longer accepted – it employed a large number of men and ships from ports in south-west England, notably Poole, Exeter, Bristol and Dartmouth. It is impossible to obtain precise numbers for the ships involved but in 1700 the convoy returning from St John's, Newfoundland, consisted of 171 fishing ships and 43 sack ships; it was manned by 4,960 men and the vessels carried a total of 1,298 guns. In addition, there were 800 ships boats which had been used in the offshore fishery and 396 boatkeepers.[8] No section of the New England trade could employ so many men and ships. They were used on the fishery for manning the fishing boats and preparing the fish on shore, both activities being carried out simultaneously so that the best use could be made of the fishing season. The bulk of the provisions needed to support this unusually large fleet was carried separately by sack ships, which sailed first to Lisbon early in the summer to buy the high quality Bay salt required by the fishermen to cure their catch. These Newfoundland convoys also escorted merchant ships bound for New York and New England, although the convoys from St John's to Lisbon at the end of the fishing season were only joined by the New England fishing vessels sailing to a Portuguese market. Other vessels bound for England had to sail with a convoy for London or depart independently. Ships sailing to join the St John's convoy had first to brave the sea crossing between the New England coast and St John's – an area where French ships were often found, and were it not for the additional hazard of Barbary corsairs off the Portuguese coast many would not have thought the risk worth taking.

The commercial pressure exerted on behalf of the Newfoundland fisheries can be seen best in the memorial from the Board of Trade in January 1697. It asked for a squadron to protect the main fishing fleet, to consist of: two 80-gun ships, two 50s, two 32s, two 24s, two fireships, two bomb vessels, a further two 50-gun ships to escort the sack ships to Newfoundland, and a further two or three to see them safely to sea.[9] There is no record of the Admiralty's reply; the proposal was impractical, for it would have taken too many warships from the main theatre of operations in the North Sea and the English Channel – a risky move even in peacetime. The memorial indicates the frustration of the merchants. Convoy arrangements were at times badly mishandled by the Admiralty, although the Board was not always responsible for the delays. In the first year of the War of the League of Augsburg, the Newfoundland convoy had not sailed beyond Plymouth by early September, approximately six months after it was due to sail, and the merchants abandoned the fishery for that year.[10] This was a heavy penalty for the merchants, though there is no knowing on this occasion whether the delay was caused by Admiralty mismanagement or natural causes – adverse winds – or the threat of French naval and privateering forces. In another year, 1703, the sack ships were driven into Irish ports, by storms after sailing from England in July. They stayed there until September, and did not reach Newfoundland until October – one month after the main fishing fleet sailed from St John's for Lisbon.[11] The anger and frustration which this roused among the fishing interests was expressed most forcibly in a complaint voiced in the House of Commons on 29 January 1706. A member of parliament, almost certainly representing a fishing port, stated that because of the delays to the convoys, the French boats were able to reach the Grand Banks six to eight weeks earlier than the English, and held six-sevenths of the fishing grounds.[12] This was an exaggeration, intended to emphasize the financial penalties of delay, but it succeeded in inflaming opinion in the House of Commons, already critical of Admiralty inefficiency. On 12 January a committee of the House recommended that six fourth-rate warships should be appointed to escort sections of the fishing fleet to Newfoundland. The first would protect sack ships and sail for Portugal to buy salt by 10 February; the second would escort fishing boats and sail from the South Channel by 10 March; a third should meet northern fishing vessels in Milford Haven, and the last would protect a second group of sack ships, and leave by 20 May. All fishing vessels would leave Newfoundland by 20 November.[13] This too was no more than a recommendation to the Admiralty and it was unlikely that the Board would, or could, agree to it.

Commercial operations on the scale of the Newfoundland fisheries could command support in the Commons and protection at sea.

However, it was not the only North American shipping to be protected by convoy regularly. The mast ships were also escorted from Sheerness to the northern coast of New England, an area where there were many French fishermen and privateers, attracted by the rich offshore fishery. The mast ships, large, bluff bowed vessels constructed on the lines of a Dutch flyboat, carried strategic supplies which were of immense importance. The tall pines of New England forests were greater than any in the Baltic and supplied the masts for the largest line-of-battle ships. They had to be defended at all costs, for they were of equal value to the French. At times the mast ships were well armed and could help with their own defence. On 19 May 1690 the naval frigate *Rose*, captained by John George, sailed from Piscataqua with two mast ships for the Thames. When they met a French 30-gun privateer from St Malo on the 24th, one of the mast ships was well enough armed to help the *Rose* beat off the attack.[14] These convoys, sailing from Boston, Piscataqua and Nantasket may have helped merchant ships sailing in the same direction, but the escort captain was not under any obligation to protect them. Nor would the captain of a merchantman receive any sailing instructions which would have implied responsibility to protect the trade.

The trade for New England could sail with the Newfoundland convoys and proceed independently for the remainder of the voyage from the fishing grounds. Many merchant skippers probably considered the final stage of the voyage into Massachusetts Bay the most dangerous, partly on account of natural hazards and partly because privateers tended to cruise off the landfalls to the south. The perils of navigation in the Bay have been vividly described by S. E. Morrison:

> [The irregular bottom of Massachusetts Bay] gives the lead line no clue. With a northeast snowstorm obscuring Boston Light, a mistake of a quarter point fetched up many a good ship on Cohasset rocks or the Graves ... [Vessels] approach Boston or Salem only by the long détour of Vineyard Sound, Nantucket Sound, and the backside of the Cape [Cod] ... [Ships] were sometimes detained for weeks in Wood's Hole or Vine yard Haven, awaiting a chance to weather Monomoy and Pollock Rip ...[15]

These fearful hazards for skippers who had to rely on experience, on the log line and on a mariner's compass did however serve to keep away those with no local experience or pilots. At a time when the brilliant French naval commander, d'Iberville, was ravaging the Hudson's Bay Company trading forts and the shores of Newfoundland, the settlements on Massachusetts Bay were safe from swift sea raids. British naval vessels could not protect the inland settlements of the Bay Province from savage French and Indian attacks, or prevent the British forces in Nova Scotia from being driven out. The Canadian frontier was also kept in a state of panic by the Indian allies of Governor Frontenac.

This reign of terror, privateering and occasional piracy, had two unforseen results. The maritime attacks on Boston trade diverted commercial shipping away from Massachusetts Bay, Long Island Sound and the Delaware River. At the same time, war encouraged the wilder and more speculative element in colonial maritime society to promote privateering ventures against the French trade and fisheries in Canada. Both the diversion of commerce and the excitement of privateering stimulated economic growth in areas not fully developed, and provided New York in particular with the opportunities for exploiting the potentialities of its site. Standing on an island flanked by the Hudson and East rivers, New York possessed not only an extensive sheltered anchorage but also excellent communications with the interior by way of the Hudson River. It was the outlet for the Iroquois furs, bought by the Dutch at Albany. The Dutch were also helped in their Iroquois trade by the supply of trade goods at prices lower than the French had to pay.[16] By 1700 at least one observer had noted a new sense of prosperity about New York: Lord Bellomont, writing in 1700, credited New York province with 124 vessels to Boston's 194, although they were small, and only 6 were over 100 tons, compared with 25 at Boston.[17] By the end of the war in 1713 there were tentative attempts to open trade with Scotland (after the Act of Union) and with former Albany merchants in Amsterdam.[18]

South-west of New York another river port was also expanding. Philadelphia, founded as a Quaker settlement by William Penn in 1682 and with a population originally of Swedish, Dutch and English settlers, began to exploit the rich farmlands bordering the Delaware River. It proved to be no disadvantage that Delaware was 100 miles from the sea as seagoing ships could sail the whole distance to the town. The third port which expanded in this period, Newport, apparently prospered through successful privateering. This at any rate is the reason usually put forward, although privateering was seldom profitable for many elsewhere. Newporters claimed that the secret of their success was that they sent their young men to sea and lost fewer ships than Boston. The truth is more mundane. Newport had traded extensively with the Dutch at Curaçao and Surinam and with Caribbean pirates – all of whom paid high prices for Newport provisions and naval stores.[19] This illegal trade could not be hidden completely: Colonel Robert Quary, in a statement to the Board of

Trade in 1708 admitted it, but he made no admission of the link with pirates. The rapid growth of these towns in the troubled years of war between 1689 and 1713 cannot hide the fact that even by 1713 none of them could rival Boston, which for so long dominated the whole colonial trade of North America. Boston was the only colonial port that could stand comparison with English ports – though she was insignificant compared with London – and, by the same measure, other New England coastal towns were little more than insignificant outposts of civilization.

Table 4.1 ENGLISH MERCHANT SHIPPING, JANUARY 1702

	Number of vessels	Tonnage	Adjusted tonnage, less fishing and coasting vessels
London	560	84,882	71,977
Bristol	165	17,338	10,299
Boston, Mass.	—	—	6,443
Yarmouth	143	9,914	5,889
Liverpool	102	8,619	5,120
Hull	115	7,564	4,493
Exeter	121	7,107	4,222
Scarborough	100	6,860	4,075
Whitby	109	6,819	4,050

Source: Bailyn, *Massachusetts shipping*, p 20.

Boston people were more dependent on the sea and participated in more maritime ventures than the population of any other New England port. Of the total provincial population of perhaps 9,000, no fewer than 903 owned shares in vessels registered since 1689 during the period January 1699 to October 1714. Of these 903, over half – 544 – were Boston residents.[20] Three out of every ten adult males went to sea. Every aspect of Boston's maritime activity demonstrated her commercial dominance of North America. Between 1674 and 1714, 437 ships, a total of 30,075 tons, were launched from Boston yards. Her nearest competitor, Scituate, a small cluster of houses and shipyards south of Boston Bay built 159 vessels, of 7,621 tons. Salem constructed approximately the same number: 140 ships of 7,274 tons. Most were small coasters of around 50 tons. Boston's dominance is clear from a comparison of the average tonnage of these ships: Boston's is 68·7, Scituate's 47·8 and Salem's 51·9. Boston yards also constructed many larger vessels of around 150 tons for the trans-Atlantic trade. Although these ships were considered adequate by the English and American merchants who bought them, the Navy Board remained suspicious, though it conceeded that North America was potentially an alternative supply to the Baltic. During the War of the League of Augsburg, two London merchants, Sir Henry Ashurst and Sir Stephen Evance, tried to sell New England stores to the Navy Board, but the latter reported on 5 June 1796 that '. . . the plank, treenails and timber was infirm and not fit for the Navy, but of the rafters, pitch, tar and rosin [the report] spoke more favourably'.[21] The view was not shared by English merchants, many of whom bought colonial built ships. This trend is discernible as early as 1698, when 27.3 per cent of the London tonnage registered in Massachusetts had been built in Boston.[22] Between 1698 and 1714 a further 187 ships, weighing at least 20,601 tons were built in New England and sold to English merchants: 19,000 tons of this came from Massachusetts. Many of these were as large as vessels constructed in England: 14 built in Salem weighed on average 137·5 tons; Charleston's 31 vessels built for the English market had an average weight of 149 tons, and if one takes the 28 made for London merchants separately, the average rises to a remarkable 158·6 tons. New England ships were also sold to merchants in the Caribbean, Nova Scotia, the Madeira Islands and Newfoundland and of the 75,267 tons of shipping known to have been built in Massachusetts before 1715, 29·9 per cent was sold to merchants outside the province. The sale of these ships helped to pay for English goods imported into the province, and other province-built ships carried West Indian produce back from the Caribbean to help pay other debts.

When peace was restored in 1713, commercial prosperity quickly recovered. English merchants, freed from the menace of privateers, exported large quantities of goods to the northern colonies. News of the commercial prosperity of these northern ports encouraged English merchants to believe that the market could absorb more goods than in fact was possible, and when the market was flooded, there was a serious slump in 1714. Thereafter the economy gradually recovered as merchants ran down their stocks, limited their imports and paid off debts. By 1720 all the major northern towns: Boston, New York, Newport and Philadelphia were again flourishing.[23] There was also a movement of population into the rich hinterland of New York and Philadelphia as the Indian raids ended. The new inhabitants began to grow wheat on a large scale, and further cultivation was assisted by the immigration of new European settlers. Philadelphia became the centre of an export trade in fine quality flour, ground in mills at the port and shipped in barrels to ports throughout North America and the Caribbean. The vessels which left the wharves with cargoes of superfine Philadelphia flour also carried other commodities produced within the colony: lumber, horses, livestock, tobacco, general provisions, salt beef and pork, pipe staves and wool. This diversity of trade, supported by a commodity which was in demand throughout the northern colonies ensured the prosperity of Philadelphia for the rest of this period and beyond. This new wealth had created the merchants as a distinct class by 1720 and the fortunes of the leading families were laid by men such as Edward Shippen, Thomas Lloyd Junior, Thomas Masters, Richard Willing, Cadwallader Colden, William Fishbourn and Jonathan Dickinson, Philadelphia rivalled Boston, and her merchants developed trading links with the English outports, notably Bristol, where Philadelphia Quakers were welcomed by many merchants of the same religious persuasion. Philadelphia merchants also ventured into other aspects of commerce and Quakers shared, without apparant qualms, in the West African slave trade, pirate ventures and illegal trade.[24]

Elsewhere the rise in prosperity was less striking. New York also milled and exported flour – though lower in quality than Philadelphia's – and her merchants developed the fur trade with the Albany Dutch. Newport successfully challenged Boston's dominance of the northern colonies' carrying trade and managed to seize control of the coasting trade of southern New England. In the face of this mounting pressure, Boston merchants had a number of advantages: their efficient shipbuilding and fisheries, and the proximity of the new French outpost of Louisbourg. Boston merchants were able to profit from the needs of French soldiers and colonists through illegal trade with them and they also supplied provisions to the fishermen and by-boat keepers who came to Newfoundland every year. The French administration had appreciated the relatively defenceless position of Quebec after Sir Hovenden Walker's ill-fated expedition, and had constructed a fortress on Cape Breton Island to guard the mouth of the St Lawrence. It also replaced the fort at Port Royal in the Bay of Fundy, which Governor Quary of Massachusetts had feared as a privateering base and which was taken by a British naval and military expedition in 1708.[25] Boston could usually undercut French prices in Louisbourg, and at times there were also difficulties keeping the garrison supplied from metropolitan France. Provisions were also sold to French fishermen, though they were restricted to the fishery on the northern coasts of Newfoundland by the Treaty of Utrecht.

Illegal trade of this sort formed an essential part of the commercial expansion of the northern colonies. They were also helped by the suppression of piracy in the Caribbean and off the southern colonies. It made trade with these areas safer and more profitable, although occasionally ships were seized by high-handed Spanish coastguard vessels for carrying alleged Spanish goods. Trade with Spanish, French and Dutch colonies was profitable, and merchants found ways of breaking the Navigation Laws without bringing too much attention to themselves. Some used false papers to cover direct trade with French, Dutch or other colonies. Others smuggled goods ashore on to the islands; a number bribed venal customs officials, while yet more put in to foreign ports, claiming that their vessel had been damaged by storm, or was leaking, and needed repair. Goods were sold from the cargo to pay for the repairs. The excuses were legion, and the trade enormous and very profitable. Owners tried to prevent this, or shift the responsibility to their captains by expressly forbidding illegal trade in their written instructions, but many owners were secretly prepared to countenance and encourage such actions. Many seem to have considered that defrauding a European government of lawful revenue was in some way not morally wrong, and there were few merchants whose record in this respect is totally unblemished. In any case, smuggling was practised by the high and low alike. In England between 1723 and 1730 the port of London lost £100,000;[26] customs officers were beaten and abused, six were murdered; 251,320 lbs of tea and 625,924 gallons of brandy were seized and condemned; 2,000 people were prosecuted; 229 boats and other vessels were condemned, and there was widespread corruption among customs officers. One cannot blame the northern colonies for doing the same, and it helped to stimulate economic activity of a more legitimate nature.

The steady increase in trade produced a number of important changes in the northern colonies. Merchants in Philadelphia, Boston, New York, Newport and elsewhere were no longer concerned wholly with the provision trade or the export of draught animals or lumber. As the output of sugar and other commodities increased in the Caribbean, colonial merchants found that it was more necessary to take payment for their goods in sugar, molasses, coffee, cotton, logwood, mahogany, lignum vitae and other goods, as well as in some form of currency – usually Spanish. The largest single item imported into the northern colonies was molasses, and many distilleries were constructed in Boston and other ports to transform this into rum to sell to the Newfoundland fishermen, or barter in the slave and fur trades. Indeed, rum became so important in New England that it was used at times as a form of currency.

The other product of the colonial trade with the Caribbean, and one that had a direct bearing on English trade with the northern colonies, was negotiable currency: bills of exchange, or coins. These bills were used extensively as a means of paying colonial debts with British merchants. Unfortunately little is known about the growth of this currency market. What is certain is that the old, oft-repeated complaint that England drained the colonies of their silver to redress an adverse balance of trade and forced them to adopt paper currency can no longer be accepted. The colonies did lack adequate supplies of coin for normal transactions, especially in small denominations, and were forced to use a variety of coins, the majority of which were Spanish and entered the colonies as a result of Caribbean trade. Paper currency was only issued under special circumstances to meet extraordinary expenses, and in most colonies only became a problem during the Seven Years War and the War of American Independence, when colonial expenditure rose sharply. The coins used widely throughout the northern colonies and elsewhere in America were often poorly minted and were frequently clipped. They circulated at an exchange rate valued at weight rather than face value. At the same time, during this long period of peace, bills of exchange, payable in London and other commercial centres and backed by the name and personal reputation of noted merchants, came to be used increasingly as a convenient form of negotiable currency between colonial and English business houses. London was used as the main centre for collecting payment against these bills, though merchants trading extensively to European markets tended to negotiate bills in Amsterdam, which was more important, but deal only in European bills. The English merchant found the Royal Exchange an ideal place to negotiate the bills used in this trade. At the same time, the use of these bills in northern colonies emphasizes the colonies' position as a pivot between Britain and the Caribbean and demonstrates the way in which this part of the north Atlantic trading community worked.[27] At the same time it must be emphasized that it was English capital that enabled this trade to be extended, and the colonial merchant, whether he traded independently or as an agent for English houses, was helped a great deal by the English commercial practice of allowing up to nine months normal credit on normal transactions. At the same time, one must accept that the successful colonial merchant made his fortune because he used small, comparatively cheap vessels in a very efficient manner, peddling goods from island to island to find the best market, utilizing English credit to the best advantage, conducting business with reliable agents, many of them related to him by blood or marriage, and selling high quality colonial products which enjoyed a ready market. Luck, and a sound commercial judgement, was the basis of such good fortune.

When peace ended in 1739, the northern colonies were firmly set on the road to commercial prosperity. They enjoyed a flourishing and lucrative trade with the British West India colonies, probably traded illegally and extensively with Dutch, French, Spanish and Danish colonies and sent colonial produce and bills of exchange to London. In some cases, direct trade with European ports was allowed under the Navigation Acts, but this was generally in commodities which were produced in limited quantities, the main exception being fish, which had to be sent to a market quickly. The Customs returns demonstrate how much colonial trade had increased with England since 1713 and the way in which it had grown:

Table 4.2 AVERAGE YEARLY TRADE BETWEEN ENGLAND AND NEW ENGLAND AND NEW YORK 1711–5 AND 1736–40

| | New England | | New York | |
	Imports	Exports	Imports	Exports
1711–5	43.8	134.4	18.0	38.6
1736–40	61.6	228.1	18.1	114.0

(£000)

Source: Whitworth, *Trade of Great Britain*, pp 63 and 65

These were the only two colonies recognized by the Customs officials, and included the whole of North America to the north of the Delaware River. The figures do not show the commercial values of imports and exports, for the duties were levied at a fixed scale according to the Book of Rates, but the figures do show the rate of expansion that took place. Both New England and New York had increased their imports of English goods, the former by approximately £97,700 and the latter by around £75,400 – an impressive and rapid growth. It demonstrates also the continued commercial superiority of the area which today comprises the states of Connecticut, Providence, Massachusetts, New Hampshire, Vermont and Maine. At the same time it also shows that the merchants in both colonies had failed to discover commodities which they could export in bulk to pay directly for their imports. Of the two areas, New England had done better, sending spermaceti candles, whale oil and bone – the product of its whaling from Nantucket and elsewhere – masts, and some naval stores, production of which was encouraged by bounty. New England exports to England had thus shown a modest increase. New York, on the other hand, fared worse, and apart from furs from Albany and a little corn and flour, could produce little that could be sold in England. New York's exports to England remained virtually stagnant. Yet neither colony became bankrupt, and each was able to pay its debts. One reason was the steady increase in the volume of colonial shipbuilding sold to England – a form of invisible exports not shown in Customs returns. By 1730 about one ship in six in England had been built in America and by 1760 this had risen to one in four.[28] Since these colonies evidently did not become bankrupt, the trading figures are valuable as a form of index of economic activity within the colonies. Evidence of a steady increase too in the colonial population – New England's doubled every decade in the eighteenth century[29] – shows how this market for imported goods was increasing in the colonies.

This argument for the interdependent nature of the English and colonial economies is central to the whole question of naval defence of English trade, for it was vital to English merchants that not only should their own commerce with overseas colonies be protected, but also the intercolonial trade, because that produced the revenue to pay for imports to England. The outbreak of war in 1739 created a heavy responsibility for the Board of Admiralty. Within the limits of strategy, resources and the relative importance of different branches of trade, English and colonial shipping had to be defended against Spanish attack over a wide area. Fortunately for the Admiralty, Spain never launched a privateering attack on the scale of that of France, but English and colonial commerce in the Caribbean was threatened by Spanish coastguard vessels, naval warships and some privateers. The main danger to colonial trade came after 1744 when France also declared war against Britain and pressure on Caribbean trade rose considerably. In the north it was widely feared that French privateers based in the Caribbean would cruise along the American coast. From the point of view of merchants in New England and New York the main danger was from French maritime forces at Louisbourg on Cape Breton Island. This impressive fortress and fortified harbour, built in the Vauban style, sheltered privateers and warships and made it possible for them to mount a sustained attack on New England commerce and fishing. However, it is not clear whether this attack materialized in its full fury, for no reliable figures for English and colonial shipping losses exist. Contemporary estimates are usually wildly inaccurate: colonial reports and correspondence frequently refer to privateers cruising off the coast, but many were English merchant ships that had not been correctly identified. Similarly, reports of losses were exaggerated, for the same loss was reported more than once. Available evidence suggests that the fishing fleet was vulnerable to French attack and seems to have suffered heavy losses. In Massachusetts there was at one time 400 fishing boats, but a decline set in: at Marblehead the fleet shrank from 120 in 1747 to 55 in 1748.[30] This decline may not be attributable entirely to a French *guerre de commerce* based on Louisbourg, for that formidable fortress was in British hands from 1745 until its return to France in 1748. The decline in the fishing fleet was probably due to action by French fishing boats from the Biscay ports – La Rochelle, Bordeaux and Bayonne as well as St Malo – for these were usually larger and better armed than the New England vessels.[31]

Nonetheless, Louisbourg, until its capture in 1745, cast a baleful shadow over the merchants of New England. Many probably remembered the French and Indian attacks early in the eighteenth century, which had carried rapine and slaughter into the homes of many frontier people. Others wanted revenge and still more, perhaps because of their illegal trade in provisions with the fortress, knew that the garrison was close to mutiny. The awesome fortress was in fact built with poor materials – there had been widespread peculation and all the best materials had gone into the governor's house and one or two other buildings. The garrison and civilian population could never support itself, for corn would not ripen in the damp and foggy climate, and men gained their livelihood at sea. By 1745 the French population of Louisbourg, civil and military, was near to mutiny, for their supplies of food were low and the troops had not been paid for a considerable time. Leaders of the New England merchant community felt the time had come to strike a blow against France. The driving force came from Governor Shirley and a merchant, William Pepperrell, who was also a landowner and 'lumber king' of Kittery, Maine. They presented the attack against Louisbourg as a patriotic venture in a letter to the Admiralty and as a Puritan crusade to the New Englanders. The Massachusetts Assembly was persuaded to vote the money which it raised by issuing paper currency which the Assembly hoped to redeem from the profits of the venture. The New Englanders were united in their support. Colonial fishermen had found their markets for fish glutted by the French, and the northern coast, especially east of Piscataqua, was abandoned in the face of French and Indian raids.[32] The Admiralty was unenthusiastic, but Commodore Peter Warren, who was married to a Bostonian and was commodore of the Leeward Islands squadron, offered his support, although he doubted whether the New Englanders would succeed.[33] His small fleet of warships held the key to the whole campaign, for he provided an escort for the lobster boats which carried the Massachusetts army; he captured all but one of the French supply vessels – thus making the fall of Louisbourg inevitable – and he provided cannon for the siege.[34] The siege was comparatively short. The first landing was made at Gabarus Bay on 30 April and the fortress surrendered on 16 June, after the defences had been heavily pounded by the New England gunners. Generous terms were granted to the defenders. The triumph was unexpected, and Massachusetts' alone; New York had given no support, because her citizens had not shared the Bay Province's alarm. More important for relations between the colonial forces and the navy, was that the former had demonstrated that they could fight effectively.

The capture of Louisbourg had important consequences for the defence of English and colonial trade. It removed the threat – probably unrealistic – that the fortress might be used as a major privateering base against commerce. It destroyed the French fishery off the New England coast, worth, it was believed, about £980,000 a year and removed a dangerous rival in the European market for cod.[35] It also deprived the French of a valuable entrepôt in their Canadian and West Indian trade, and it shook the confidence of the Acadian Indians in their French overlords. This helped to lift the danger of a repetition of the savage French-Indian raids. Governor Shirley also considered that it gave the British government a hold over the colonies, 'if ever there should come a time when they should grow restive and disposed to shake off the dependency upon their mother country . . .'[36] At the same time, the capture of Louisbourg did not remove all threat to the northern colonies. D'Iberville's raids earlier in the century had demonstrated the crushing force of rapid mobility, and there was little that the Admiralty could do to prevent this. The only hope of the colonists was that the Admiralty would prevent a raiding force from setting sail or pursue the squadron and bring it to battle; such hopes were however seldom realized. The best defence of the Bay towns remained the hazards of navigation off the coast.

There remained the pressing need to defend English and colonial shipping while it crossed the north Atlantic and sailed along the coast of North America. The danger from French privateers remained: many cruised along the coast on their return from the Caribbean to France. Captain Nathaniel Uring had the misfortune to be taken off the coast of North America by a privateer. To his surprise he found that one of them had taken him prisoner before, when he was captain of a Falmouth packet.[37] No one could foresee the sudden appearance of these privateers and the only practical defence was to provide escorts for the convoys and cruisers to patrol the landfalls. In view of the Admiralty's shortage of suitable naval vessels, the colonies were expected to contribute to their own defence. The final solution, agreed between the Admiralty and the colonial assemblies was for colonies to hire two or three sloops and the Admiralty to send a 44-gun ship as escort to the convoys and cruise off the coast before leaving with the trade at the end of the summer.[38] The Admiralty could do no more. There were pressing demands for trade protection elsewhere, and the strategic need for frigates and sloops to attend the main battle squadrons overrode all other considerations. Some measure of protection was granted by sending Townsend with a squadron to Louisbourg, but in the face of mounting fears of a French attack in Nova Scotia, he felt unable to divide his force for any purpose short of a major encounter with a French squadron. He was fully justified in this view; d'Anville's raid on Nova Scotia, brilliantly planned and disastrously executed, was only defeated by insanitary conditions on the French ships, smallpox – which with typhus killed 8,000 men, including the commander-in-chief – and gales. The grand French plan to recapture Annapolis Royal and Louisbourg and ravage New England, caused near panic among the New Englanders, but came to nothing. Accordingly, during 1746 and 1747, the last two full years of the war, no special measures could be taken to protect the commerce of the northern colonies.

In any case, it was clear to the merchants of the northern colonies that the only hope of continued prosperity in the war was to maintain the same pattern of trade. Convoys from Boston, New York and Philadelphia would have defeated the main object of the northern merchants: the supply of commodities in relatively small quantities, at times when they were required, and when a cargo of a 50-ton vessel could if necessary be taken from island to island to fetch the best price. The infinite flexibility of this system would have been shattered by the organization of trade into convoys, which would have caused alternate glut and famine: a situation in which merchants could make little profit. Colonials trading to the Caribbean were accordingly forced to accept some measure of loss, and seek compensation through the higher profits of wartime trading – especially with neutral or enemy ports.

Under these circumstances, the cruising vessels played a major role in defending colonial trade. At the beginning of the period, command of them had been given to colonial governors for the period they were in colonial waters. This was only convenient while there was no

North American squadron, but by the mid-eighteenth century strategic requirements had made it necessary to create one, and cruising ships were placed under the orders of the commodore. Whatever the gain in efficiency in creating a unified command, it did not mean that the vessels could be assembled quickly to meet an anticipated attack; distance and the need to refit vessels from time to time ruled that out. In practice, it seems that a compromise was reached, by which commanders of naval vessels took their orders from their commander-in-chief, but the latter was guided by the wishes of the colonial governor and the principal merchants.

One practical disadvantage was that it left the colonial coastal waters undefended in the winter and spring, before the arrival of the convoy from England. Various means were tried for solving this problem. It was suggested that ships from Jamaica and the Leeward Islands should sail north in winter to avoid the risk of hurricanes. This was attractive on paper, but the practical difficulty was that after cruising in the warm waters of the Caribbean, many vessels needed resheathing to repair the ravages of the boring worm, *teredo navalis*. Few repair facilities existed in North America for this work to be carried out. Furthermore, when captains tried to take their ships to sea in winter they found the frost so severe that it was impossible for the seamen to climb aloft and handle sails, and there was a danger that hulls would be damaged by ice. When ropes froze in the blocks, square-rigged vessels could not be sailed effectively, and the only solution was to use schooners, which could be sailed by men standing on the decks.[39] Convoys delayed into winter experienced similar difficulties and one captain, Peter Warren, replying to Admiralty criticism that he had not granted adequate protection to a mast ship, claimed that he had performed a singular feat in bringing five out of six ships safely home in winter.[40] Captain Thomas Smith had the unfortunate experience of sailing to Newfoundland in November and losing all eleven ships in his convoy in a thick fog three days out from St John's.[41] He never saw any of them again during the remainder of the voyage, and the only English ship he did see was the *Elizabeth* bound from Jamaica to Glasgow with a cargo of indigo and sugar. Winter convoys were in any case to be avoided if possible; they wore out the ships, and the mountainous seas of the north Atlantic in winter frequently kept the crew wet and their bedding damp for much of the voyage. It was impossible to cook hot meals. The cargo was occasionally damaged and sometimes had to be thrown overboard to lighten the ship.

Stragglers from these convoys and coasters sometimes encountered

French privateers or letter-of-marque ships, especially off the favoured landfalls or points of departure, and French vessels were usually prepared to put up a stiff fight to make a capture or fight off a British naval attack. Captain Richard Spry of the *Comet* sloop, encountered a French privateer *Brador* (?) at the back of Nantucket Shoals early on the morning of 22 October 1744, while refitting rigging and mending sails.[42] Spry, who later rose to be commodore of the North American squadron in the Seven Years War, has left a graphic description of the action which followed:

[I] saw a sail bear down on me under English colours; I immediately made everything ready to engage and kept my men close, about 8 she brought up to within musket shot, and still kept her English colours up. I found she would come no nearer; hoisted my colours and fired two shots at her, which fortunately carried away his forestay and foretop-bowline (for notwithstanding his colours I knew him to be a French privateer), he then hauled down his English colours and hoisted French and gave me a broadside. I continued firing at least an hour, I damaged his rigging, so that he could not haul upon a wind. Then he sailed off, I followed and came up in the evening, and we continued firing at each other for four and a half hours; heard the captain order them to board us several times, but avoided this; ordered marines to fire at him, and a lucky shot passed through his speaking trumpet, then into his eye and lodged behind his ear; after which I formed a sensible difference in the working of the privateer. He struck about an hour later, badly damaged, six feet of water in the hold, thirty of his men killed, twenty more wounded. I never saw anything more shattered; had to lay by her two days to repair her. She is called the Brador, captain le Grass, bred in the Maltese service, a brisk active man, and if not luckily wounded would have sunk before she struck . . . We had none killed, and two wounded, and rigging and sails much destroyed.

Only naval vessels, stoutly manned, could beat off an attack of this sort, and the threat of French privateers put up insurance rates and made it more difficult for merchants to make a profit.

After the return of peace in 1748, normal conditions returned and it became noticeable that many important changes were taking place. Many New England farmers, who had been driven from their lands by the war, were attracted by the promise of good, cheap farming land near Philadelphia and in the Connecticut Valley. The latter was gradually filled with new settlers between 1720 and 1750. One area that did not develop in this way was New York colony, where vast tracts of land, often more than 100,000 acres, had been granted to favoured individuals.[43] These absentee landlords were unwilling to sell their lands, preferring to hold it while land values rose and were only prepared to lease the land on terms which for a long time were considered too high. It was only when land prices increased as the Connecticut Valley and Philadelphia colony began to fill up that colonists were prepared to pay the New York prices and that that colony received an influx of newcomers. This growth of the New York colony led to a rise in the volume of trade, partly to meet the needs of the expanding population, but also to export the growing surplus of agricultural commodities which this population produced. Other ports grew as well: Philadelphia developed a shipbuilding industry which rapidly increased the number of vessels available for carrying this new trade, and Rhode Island became the centre of an important slave trade with the Guinea coast, supplying labour to the expanding Carolina rice plantations. Boston however failed to maintain her relative importance in the colonial carrying trade and the trans-Atlantic commerce; her decline had set in after 1735 and by the period preceding the Seven Years War, she had been overtaken by Philadelphia and New York, and probably by Newport and some New England ports as well.

The Seven Years War was to confirm this trend. The constant factor in the growth of the North American colonies was the threat from the French in Acadia and along the St Lawrence, reiterated time and again in the wars from 1689. By the mid-1750s this threat had developed into the possibility that there existed a French plan to block any further expansion westward by the British colonies. French trading ports were opened along the Ohio, and French travellers had sailed up the broad waters of the Mississippi to create a tenuous French link between Canada and the Caribbean. It was not clear to the British government or the colonists whether the French possessed the means of strengthening these links, but it was evident that if the thirteen colonies were to continue to grow, this French policy had to be checked. In 1755 Britain and France each sent reinforcements to their respective colonies in North America: between January and March three French squadrons left Brest for the West Indies and Canada, and the British sent two regiments of regular troops to New York. At the same time, Boscawen was sent to Nova Scotia and a campaign was launched on land against French posts.

The effect of this campaign on the British colonies was twofold. In the first place the British victory freed the colonists from French and Indian raids and gradual encirclement. In the long term it also encouraged forces in the colonies to demand greater autonomy from Britain. At the same time, however, the use of New York as the headquarters for this elaborate and costly six years campaign, from Braddock's defeat to ultimate victory in 1760, brought considerable

prosperity. Most of this was in the form of Treasury bills for provisions and in some cases wages paid to the British forces while they
were in North America. Most of the major contracts for victualling,
clothing, transporting and paying the British soldiers were awarded
to British contractors – the Hessian troops were paid and maintained
on a separate account. These contractors, together with suppliers of
naval stores, armaments and munitions were among the most important merchants in London, and included Sir James Colebrooke. of the
firm of Messrs. Nesbitt, Colebrooke and Franks, and William Baker,
an alderman of the City of London, all of whom were provision
merchants. Men such as these were responsible for ensuring that the
supplies which they had contracted to supply to the British forces
reached them in good condition; many bought their provisions in
Ireland through subcontractors and shipped them under convoy to
North America. Other contractors who were suppliers of hemp,
cordage, sailcloth, timber and the whole range of what were popularly
called naval stores bought them in the Baltic and shipped them to
North America under the same system. In some cases however, it was
clearly in the interests of the contractors to obtain supplies in North
America, and it is in this context that the pre-war commercial links
between New York and London become significant. The farmlands
of New York and Delaware produced vast quantities of wheat, barley,
oats and meat – beef and pork. Under peacetime conditions these
were sent to the Caribbean to feed the white population, and the
trade supplied bills of exchange which were used for the purchase of
British manufactured goods: furniture, clothing and the range of
goods known in North America as 'dry goods'. The influx of
thousands of British soldiers to New York for the three expeditions
against Canada provided an alternative market for these commodities, and also offered the advantage of payment in Treasury bills
which were an acceptable medium of exchange on the London
market. These advantages were readily appreciated by colonial
merchants, and men such as Gerard Beekman made large profits
through judicious use of their knowledge of colonial markets. Not all
merchants were so fortunate. Thomas Hancock of Boston was owed
so much by the British government that he had to curtail his level of
business after a time until he could obtain payment.[44] Not all the
business was straightforward. British contractors wanted to buy
provisions at the lowest price, consistent with reasonable quality –
they had, after all, won their contracts by low tenders to the Navy
Board – and colonial merchants were prepared to seek the highest
price for their goods. At times, large quantities of provisions were

sent to traditional markets in the Caribbean – including French and Spanish islands – because wartime shortages there pushed prices up, and complaints were voiced in New York that the wheat needed to feed the British troops was being sold to feed the French in the Caribbean. Fluctuations in supply caused by the colonial exploitation of wartime shortages led contractors to rely heavily on naval convoys for protecting the supplies which they sent across the north Atlantic.

The convoy system appears to have worked well on the whole. There was no occasion when the expeditionary forces were unable to advance for lack of provisions or munitions: delays were caused by the leisurely preparation of expeditions in Britain or by geographical or military factors in North America, as in the painfully slow progress on Lake Champlain. There were of course many instances of acrimonious dispute between contractors and the Admiralty over the provision of convoy escorts.[45] One example is the series of letters between the Admiralty and the provision contractors Colebrooke and Nesbitt, and Baker, Kilby and Baker. In both cases the Admiralty and contractors had agreed sailing dates for the convoys to leave for North America, but when the time came for the ships to sail, they were forbidden to do so by an embargo. By then the contractors had hired ships, and the terms of the charter party did not allow them to sail without naval escort. There were also occasions when the Admiralty could not spare ships to be used for escorts, and when contractors could not send their ships to sea because they were not fully laden. The complications were endless, and since the contractors spent large sums of money on government service and were not repaid for many years, they tended to shift responsibility for any unforeseen costs on to the Admiralty. The inadequacies of the convoy system as it was applied to the northern colonies during this war – and the presence of these angry letters highlight these inadequacies – should not hide the fact that in general the system worked quite well. It certainly ensured the regular supply of provisions and stores to North America, and served to protect commercial goods as well.

This was an important factor, though usually ignored. The flow of Treasury bills to New York stimulated commerce to a considerable degree and helped to create a boom which lasted while British forces remained in North America. It has long been recognized that the withdrawal of British forces led to a depression in North America, and it is evident that colonial merchants, anticipating a long campaign, overstocked their warehouses. The Customs returns for British exports to and imports from New York reveals the extent to which this took place:

Table 4.3 ENGLISH TRADE WITH NEW YORK

	(£000)	
	Imports	Exports
1755	28	151
1756	24	250
1757	19	353
1758	14	356
1759	21	630
1760	21	480
1761	48	289
1762	58	288

Source: Customs returns printed in Whitworth, *State of the trade of Great Britain*, pp 59–67. The figures are for the period Christmas to Christmas each year.

While it must be recognized that this takes no account of the real values of imports and exports, nor of the value of services performed by New York merchants, which also helped redress the considerable deficit, it does reveal the extent to which the Seven Years War helped to launch the port of New York on a wave of prosperity. Once the initial effects of the post-1760 slump had worn off, the port was well placed to challenge the other centres of northern trade for a larger share of the inter-colonial and English commerce. During this period the other northern ports also benefited from the influx of Treasury bills as the contractors' debts were paid, though not to the same extent as the Customs figures show:

Table 4.4 ENGLISH TRADE WITH NEW ENGLAND AND PENNSYLVANIA

	(£000)			
	New England		Pennsylvania	
	Imports	Exports	Imports	Exports
1755	60	341	32	144
1756	47	384	20	200
1757	28	363	14	268
1758	30	466	14	357
1759	26	527	22	498
1760	38	600	23	708
1761	46	334	39	204
1762	42	247	38	206

Source: *ibid*.

The commercial expansion of the Seven Years War set the stage for the development of the northern ports in the period before 1775. The growth of commerce was built on two factors: a steady increase in the population of the northern colonies and an extension of British commercial credit which provided the means for this expansion to take place. A leading Newport merchant, Aaron Lopez, built up considerable trade through the judicious exploitation of a Bristol merchant, Henry Cruger, whose generosity in extending credit was apparently only matched by his inability to call in his debts. Lopez carefully avoided being called to account in a court of law, but seldom paid his debts to Cruger in full, in spite of the latter's letters.[46] Although the initial decline of New York had been sharp – British exports to North America dropped from £2,249,710 in April 1763 to £1,944 in July 1765 – the colonial ports gradually recovered and by 1775 New York's trade was double that of 1750.[47]

During the War of American Independence only New York remained in British hands. The other ports were closed to English trade and their merchants fitted out large numbers of privateers to cruise against English trade with Canada and Nova Scotia. The Customs returns show how the trade declined *(see table p. 133)*.

The evidence of these figures suggests that during the War of American Independence the only American colonial port that continued to receive English trade goods was New York. The hesitant reaction of merchants to the news from America is shown by the absence of any substantial exports after 1775, even though the port was the British headquarters and remained so until the end of the war. The imports, which begin on a very small scale in 1777 and 1778 and then rise steeply, are harder to explain. What seems to have happened is that the commodities imported from the port are prize goods, condemned in the Vice-Admiralty court in New York, and sent to Britain as the produce of the colony. It is unlikely that they are the results of legitimate trade. On the other hand, the Nova Scotia trade consisted almost entirely of masts and timber for the naval dockyards, and presumably included the masts shipped from the Bay of Fundy. The huge 1777 shipments to Britain represent the Admiralty's attempt to strengthen the navy and indicate the feverish construction and repair work in naval dockyards. On the other hand, the colony imported little; its population was small and scattered and its needs satisfied by a comparatively small flow of trade goods. Newfoundland appears from these figures to have passed through the worst part of the war comparatively unscathed. This is surprising in view of the reports of American privateers fitted out and sent to cruise against the fishery and the hostility of the French. One authority on this subject has stated '. . . the Newfoundland fishery suffered the same kind of ravaging expeditions, stimulated by orders from Congress "to Take, Burn, Sink or Destroy every English Vessel they should find Fishing on the Banks"'.[48] He adds '[until the summer of 1777] with the

Table 4.5 ENGLISH TRADE WITH THE NORTHERN COLONIES

(£000)

	Canada*		Newfoundland		New England		New York		Nova Scotia		Pennsylvania	
1775	472	74	123	50	72	116	1	187	56	2	1	176
1776	447	55	130	50	55	1	—	2	245	6	—	1
1777	586	66	122	46	—	—	57	8	934	8	7	—
1778	555	73	134	45	—	—	26	16	332	5	—	—
1779	521	61	88	66	—	—	349	15	227	2	—	—
1780	485	3	103	100	—	—	497	15	244	—	—	—

* Left-hand column is imports, right-hand column exports.   Source-: Customs 3/75–80, *passim*.

exception of St John's, every harbour from Cap Rouge to Bonavista was open to the enemy'. Yet until 1779 the Newfoundland imports remained high. What probably happened was that the American privateers were not interested in taking fishing boats, except in revenge. The Americans traditionally fished further south and under wartime conditions could not dispose of as much fish as they could catch in the offshore fishery. Privateers wanted goods that would fetch a good price in prize courts and therefore tended to attack the convoys returning from the West Indies, the supply ships sailing to North America and the trade with Nova Scotia and Canada. All these would provide goods that the Americans valued – Caribbean molasses that could be distilled into rum for the fur trade and for sale in the colonies; munitions, trade goods and furs that could be sold in the colonies or to the French. The British ships fishing on the Grand Banks were in any case protected by escorts and grouped relatively close together; attack was not very easy. After 1778 the position changed, for the French were anxious to disrupt the British fishery – the French fishing ports would benefit – although the French administration decided to leave Canada, Nova Scotia and Newfoundland in British hands. The fall in Newfoundland imports for 1779 represents caution on the part of the owners of sack ships and by-boats, who sent fewer ships to Newfoundland in the fear that they would be attacked. When the attacks failed to materialize the fishery began to recover, and the figures for 1780 were again fairly high. Exports to Newfoundland however tell a different story. After 1778 the volume became too great to be absorbed by the population of the island, much of which was in any case seasonal, and the figures seem to represent a smuggling trade to New England of the sort that becomes well documented during the embargo from December 1807 to March 1808. After 1779 the privateers had been swept from the seas off Newfoundland and the Gulf of St Lawrence and the way was open to any adventurous skipper to land a small cargo on the New England coast with the connivance of the local population. It was comparatively safe to do so, for the British warships were occupied patrolling the Gulf and Banks and the sloops were off the coast of Labrador. In the case of Canada, the final colony on the continent still in British hands, the import trade in furs remained unharmed by war. The rise in 1777 and 1778 represents the success of the North-West Company on the Saskatchewan, a forceful concern which was already proving a serious rival to the Hudson's Bay Company. On the other hand, the fear of an attack on Quebec remained, and many merchants feared that the town was defenceless; it is hardly surprising that few ventured to send their goods to Canada in 1780. The anxiety was well founded, for La Pérouse made a daring raid on the Hudson's Bay Company forts of Prince of Wales and York in 1782.[49]

The principal threat to British shipping that passed through North American waters came from the American privateers. Although it is impossible to know how many were fitted out in the colonies, it seems likely that the greatest proportion came from Massachusetts; it had a long history of hardy seamanship, and its sailors were skilled navigators of these coastal waters. The registration of Massachusetts privateers is as follows:

Table 4.6 REGISTRATION OF MASSACHUSETTS PRIVATEERS

	Privateers
1775	9
1776	97
1777	149
1778	167
1779	256
1780	218
1781	293
1782	287
1783	26

Source: G. W. Allen, *Massachusetts privateers of the Revolution*, (Massachusetts Historical Society 1927), pp 65–331.

If this is typical of American privateering, it would suggest that there was a close link between the numbers fitted out and the decline of British power in America. It is probably significant that after the French entry into the war in 1778 the numbers of vessels fitted out continued to rise and that 1781, the year of defeat at Yorktown, also saw the largest number of registrations. Whether these were successful is another matter; the experience of French *armateurs* was that privateering was financially risky and seldom gave large returns. With that in mind, one must assume that a mixture of patriotic fervour and moderate success kept the privateers at sea off the American coast and in the Caribbean, where Massachusetts vessels could pick up prizes from the inter-island trade. The defence against these was the organization of trade into convoys. All British ships destined for North America sailed to New York or Halifax, and naval and merchant ships could thus be combined to economize on escorts. Ships bound for Quebec were escorted into the Gulf and met there on their return by ships that for the rest of the season cruised to protect the fishery. It was a simple and economical means of using the small number of escorts available and appears to have been successful.

When peace was restored to America in 1783, American merchants found that they were barred from British markets in the Caribbean and elsewhere. The British government tried to replace the American colonies with Nova Scotia as the entrepôt and source of supplies of provisions, lumber, horses and fish that the West India plantations required. In the course of the 1780s it became clear that the plan would not work, and American merchants were allowed to trade with the British colonies in the West Indies through the system of free ports. Merchants had also discovered that the French, with whom some had begun to trade during the war, could not offer comparable terms to their former English correspondents, and the majority compounded their debts and reopened trade with England.

In 1793 when Britain and France were again at war, many Americans found themselves in an ambivalent position. There was much public support for France, but France lacked naval power and her outposts in North America, the small islands of St Pierre and Miquelon, which might have become privateering bases for raids on British shipping, were speedily taken by a British force in 1793 and their inhabitants transported to France.[50] Except for 1794, trade between England and the United States showed a continued prosperity, as the following figures show:

Table 4.7 EXPORTS (INCLUDING RE-EXPORTS) FROM
ENGLAND AND WALES TO AMERICA

	(£000) Average annual values
1766–70	1,825
1771–5	396
1776–80	264
1781–5	1,596
1786–90	2,106
1791–5	4,043
1796–1800	5,722

Source: E. B. Schumpeter, *English overseas trade statistics 1697–1808*, (1960), p 17.

There was comparatively little danger off the American coast, and in June 1794, for instance, two vessels, a 50-gun ship and a sloop of 12 were considered adequate.[51] The main burden for commerce defence in American coastal waters was laid on the commodore of the squadron at Halifax, who had to patrol the focal area off Newfoundland to protect the returning Caribbean and American convoys. The port in North America which benefited most from this surge of commerce was New York which by 1800 had surpassed even Philadelphia as the leading American port. It achieved this by gaining control of the export of southern staple commodities, by a rapid and spectacular increase in population, by a significant growth in upstate agricultural production and by a booming trade in provisions to the British and French West India colonies, as well as by developing new trade with China.[52] This growth of trade between Britain and North America, though spectacular, was interrupted and finally halted by the war which broke out in 1812. The embargo of 1807–8 was largely ignored by American merchants, and the war merely checked Anglo-American commerce for a time.

The importance of trade between England and the northern colonies is easy to overlook. Massachusetts, New York and Pennsylvania produced no crops of the importance of tobacco or cotton, but they did provide a market for British goods that was an important stimulus to British production, as well as building many of the ships used by English merchants. The War of American Independence proved no more than a temporary break in a commerce that had proved of considerable benefit to both American and English merchants and the wealth that this trade created helped establish Liverpool as the leading British outport by the mid-eighteenth century. On both sides of the Atlantic this commerce was characterized by vigour and determination and the convoy system was remarkably successful in safeguarding this prosperity.

5

The Southern States

EUROPEANS TRAVELLING to North America towards the end of the seventeenth century were struck by the contrast between the northern and southern colonies. In the north life was hard; the colonists had to wrest a living from the sea or raise crops in the short summers; harsh winters in this hostile environment bred a spirit of independence. In the south, behind the dismal pine barrens and sandhills that formed the coast, life was comparatively easy. Summers were warm and long, winters were mild. Tobacco, the 'sot weed' of contemporary speech, grew easily in the Tidewater region of Virginia and further south rice could be cultivated in the coastal swamps of the Carolinas.

Tobacco dominated the southern economy. As early as 1619 Virginia had sent 20,000 lbs to England and the figure continued to rise throughout the colonial period. By 1639 tobacco exports stood at 1,500,000 lbs, in 1702 they had reached 36,747,192, and in 1751 42,032,700 lbs.[1] In financial terms, this was the most important commodity imported into England from the American colonies, though a comparatively small quantity was consumed in England. Most was sent to northern Europe, and sales of tobacco in the continental markets contributed a great deal to England's prosperity. The wealth that this gave to Virginia and Maryland (also a tobacco producing colony, though on a far smaller scale), made these colonies an excellent market for English manufactured goods. This is demonstrated by the Customs records for the period. In 1697, the first year in which they were recorded, imports into England from Virginia and Maryland were valued at £227,756, while English exports to those colonies stood at £168,960.[2] No other colony in North America could match this.

This rich trade – tobacco to England and woollen goods, furniture, clothing and a variety of manufactured items in return – was in the hands of a fairly small number of English merchants. London men dominated the trade; they owned the ships, received the tobacco on consignment, insured the voyages and took their agents' fees on sales of tobacco and the purchase of commodities for the Virginia and Maryland planters. It was a system that had apparently grown up early in the seventeenth century, when London merchants helped planters finance the growing of tobacco.[3] In any case, no large, sea-going vessels were built in Virginia or Maryland, or were bought by the planters.

Within these colonies, population was meagre and was spread over a wide area; so too was tobacco production. Although Virginia was, by the 1690s, the most populous area in North America, there were still comparatively few plantations, and travellers to the colonies spoke of the country being 'ill peopled'. Emigration caused grave concern; Edward Randolph, reporting to the Board of Trade in 1696, expressed surprise that the population was still so sparse even after large numbers of white servants and others had been sent.[4] There were fewer colonists in Virginia and Maryland than in New England: about 113,000, including a maximum of 4,500 Negroes in New England, and only 92,952, including 10,000 slaves in Virginia and Maryland.[5] Slaves, introduced originally from Bermuda, held the key to colonial prosperity, for it was they who by the last decade of the seventeenth century, provided most of the labour force in the plantations.

In consequence, on the outbreak of war in 1689, Virginia and Maryland were in the unfortunate position of being unable to defend themselves effectively through lack of able-bodied men, while at the same time their rich trade attracted privateers. In the Dutch wars of the mid-seventeenth century, Dutch 'capers' had ravaged the Chesapeake and caused serious concern among English merchants. In 1689 the prospects of serious loss from French commerce raiders were, if anything, worse. There were two specific aspects that merited attention. The first was the threat from French privateers and war-ships to English shipping in English coastal waters and off the American coast. The second was the importation of slaves. Although not as important as the post-1713 trade, it was valuable because without a steady supply, tobacco production could not be expanded and might not even be maintained.[6] Many planters were already heavily in debt to English merchants who had financed their plantations and could not afford to allow tobacco production to fall.

On the question of French privateering, merchants and planters expressed grave concern for the safety of English ships sailing between England and the Chesapeake. In 1689, even before war was declared, merchants trading to Virginia and Maryland were still troubled by French attacks which were the aftermath of Bacon's Rebellion, and they petitioned the King for a convoy.[7] They claimed that the French had taken eleven of their ships, that the colonists were totally dependent on supplies of clothing and other goods from England and might try to manufacture their own if English supplies failed. The merchants added that every time a ship was taken the King lost between £5,000 and £10,000 in revenue. The King granted a convoy. The tobacco trade enjoyed royal support and when war broke out measures were taken to ensure that the trade continued unchecked. However a conflict soon appeared between the authorities and the merchants. The navy had to have seamen and looked to the merchant fleet to provide them. Accordingly, quotas were fixed: in 1690 London was allowed 400 men for the tobacco trade. The merchants, not unnaturally, protested that the numbers were far too small, and that they needed 1,000 or 1,200 men. The dispute could not be resolved easily; accurate figures for the numbers of ships used in the trade were lacking. The merchants went on to claim later that the annual tobacco fleet consisted of 'near one hundred and fifty vessels whereof about fifty are between four and five hundred tons, loaded with from seventy to eighty thousand hogheads of tobacco'. Merchants usually overstated their case, but on this occasion they were probably not exaggerating and their statement is of importance in assessing the effectiveness of the convoy system. Professor Davis has shown that between 1699 and 1701 – which were years of peace – an average of 15,000 tons of shipping was required for the import of tobacco.[8] Allowing for a modest increase in tobacco output in the 1690s and a generally higher level of trade in peacetime, the merchants' claim that 150 ships were engaged in the trade was probably fairly accurate. On that basis, so too was their claim for 1,000 or 1,200 men for these ships, for manning figures on trans-Atlantic voyages had not yet begun to fall and were probably around 9.8 tons per man, the figure for 1686.[9] That the navy too required seamen was undeniable and the clash between commerce and the navy illustrates one of the main problems facing the administration in wartime, how to strengthen the navy without seriously weakening the nation's trade.

The tobacco merchants' first priority was to petition the King for an embargo on shipping to Virginia and Maryland, and to force ships to sail either in convoys or fleets for mutual protection when this restriction was lifted. The justice of the merchants' claims was recognized: the quota for London ships engaged in the tobacco trade was raised from 400 to 800 in 1690, and to 1,000 plus 250 foreign seamen in 1691. In an effort to increase the available tonnage and ease restrictions on the trade, heavily armed and fast sailing vessels were given licences to sail without convoy and in 1690 the Privy Council ordered naval escorts for Chesapeake convoys to carry tobacco for the King's account at the rate of 10 tons of freight to each 100 tons of burthen. But the Privy Council did not fix the rates merchants were to pay, and this decision had the unfortunate effect of allowing naval commanders to compete with merchants for freighting tobacco. Partly for this reason, and partly because of heavy losses of merchant ships to French privateers, freight rates rose to the unprecedented level of £17 per ton, a figure never again reached in the colonial period.[10] When this happened it was not profitable to import tobacco. At this point one may say that the system designed to protect this valuable trade had failed, but the effect was only temporary and commerce revived as freight rates fell.

Was the convoy system to blame for these heavy shipping losses? Professor Price has claimed that outward bound convoys apparently had a better record than those returning to England and has estimated that an average of eight ships were taken each year from outward bound convoys. Losses from convoys returning to England he puts at sixteen: a total loss each year of twenty-four ships, representing about 120,000 or 130,000 lbs of tobacco.[11] In view of the merchants' claims that around 150 ships were employed in the tobacco trade, the loss of around twenty-four a year would have raised an outcry from merchants if these had been sailing in convoy. A more likely explanation of these losses would be that comparatively few were captured from convoys and the losses were mostly from 'runners' – ships sailing independently. In view of the merchants' earlier request for an embargo on independent voyages and the policy of licensing only faster and more heavily armed ships, this explanation too appears inadequate. What seems to have happened is that the greater part of the trade was controlled by London merchants and did sail in convoy. These merchants had every reason to use convoys. Their ships faced grave dangers from French privateers in the English Channel and only naval escorts could provide a measure of safety. Merchants in the outports were in a different position. Many found the convoy system unnecessarily cumbersome, especially when convoys were kept in harbour by rumours of French squadrons in the English Channel or a shortage of naval escorts, or were delayed by westerly winds in the English Channel, as frequently happened. On the other hand, voyages from western ports were quicker, less hazardous, because privateers seldom cruised in the Bristol Channel or Irish Sea, and more profitable when they could reach the market before the convoy.

In any case, it was extremely difficult for colonial governors to enforce the embargo on shipping and force all vessels to sail in convoy from the Chesapeake. Tobacco did not pass through a central port in Virginia or Maryland, but was loaded on board ships at wharves which were scattered over a wide area. Tobacco plantations had been laid out along river valleys which provided access for sea-going ships and planters erected their own wharves where ships were loaded. These plantations were often a long way from the seat of government and were not subject to effective control. In any case,

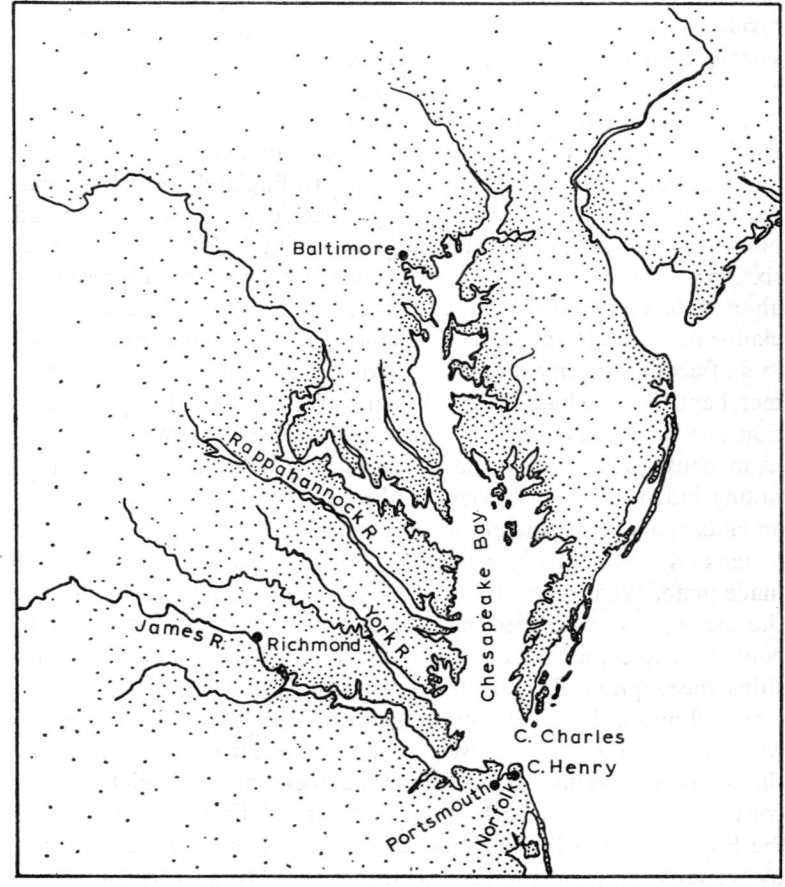

8   Chesapeake Bay

there were few customs officers to carry out the duties. These circumstances and the widespread development of small plantations producing a few hogsheads of tobacco a year encouraged outport merchants to trade illegally. It was easy enough for a ship to sail up the Rappahannock, York or James rivers and their tributaries, and load some hogsheads of tobacco at isolated wharves. It did not matter to the master of the ship that no customs clearances had been issued for these hogsheads. The tobacco could be unloaded at one of the centres of tobacco smuggling such as the Isle of Man and be run ashore to the mainland from there. Liverpool merchants in particular became adept at circumventing customs duties by shipping large quantities of damaged tobacco on which they paid no duty, and for which there was apparently a good market in England.[12] Scottish merchants were also able to trade illegally in the Chesapeake before the Act of Union in 1707, and this forms a prelude to the influence of Glasgow later in the century. The outport merchants thus enjoyed many advantages over their London rivals, and it is hardly surprising that much of the tobacco imported into Britain was carried in their ships to Bristol, Liverpool, Lancaster and Glasgow. On the other hand, because they arrived off the British coast unprotected, they probably lost a greater proportion of their vessels than London merchants, though they gained some protection off the American coast from cruising warships.

Official policy for commerce defence was to employ either two escorts for each convoy or one escort or a guard ship, the latter remaining on the station to protect 'runners' and the sloops and schooners engaged in the colonial trade. The use of naval vessels in this way reflected the administration's strategic dilemma. To protect convoys adequately against privateers at least two escorts were needed, one to lead the convoy and chase away privateers and the other to protect the flanks and rear. This safeguarded the convoys but left the single 'runners' and the important inter-colonial trade unprotected. To defend these, permanent guard ships were needed to patrol the coast and Chesapeake Bay. The administration could not spare more than two ships to protect the trade. The provision of single ships to escort convoys and a guard ship in the Chesapeake proved unsatisfactory in the early 1690s and thereafter convoys were given two escorts when they could be spared. This at least had the merit of defending the bulk of the trade and of placating the London merchants who possessed important political influence. It left unprotected the outport and colonial trade. The latter was important because Virginia and Maryland relied in large measure on supplies of corn and barrels of beef and pork from further north, especially New York and Pennsylvania. In addition to the French privateers who formed the main threat to commerce in wartime, there were still pirates cruising in colonial waters. Many were colonials and sailed in ships fitted out in ports in the northern colonies, often with official knowledge if not of support. Although the greater part of these raided Spanish shipping or sailed to the Indian Ocean, they occasionally seized provisions from colonial ships. At times they traded illegally with the inhabitants of Charleston, at this period a small, struggling community, and Spanish coins found their way into commercial life. The guard ships were intended to check their depredations on shipping and also the illegal commerce, but were severely handicapped because pirate vessels were generally faster and of shallower draught. They retreated into isolated bays and shallow inlets in the Carolinas and the Caribbean where naval frigates could not follow them.

Even in the Chesapeake the guard ships had limited success. In 1691 the frigate *Dumbarton* was found to be unserviceable, probably through the action of the teredo worm and the lack of adequate careening and repair facilities for naval vessels. She was broken up and her guns transferred to the fort on Tindall's Point.[13] Two vessels sent as replacements, the sloop *Wolf* and *Henry Prize*, an old sixth rate, proved more of a nuisance than a help. Captain Purvis of the *Wolf* ran his vessel aground and Captain Finch of the *Henry Prize* was so timid that he took shelter under the guns of Tindall's Point whenever a strange sail was sighted. Captain Purvis was probably unlucky. Shifting channels in the Chesapeake made navigation hazardous, and an unsuspecting naval captain could easily be lured into shallow water. On the other hand Captain Purvis does not seem to have lacked courage. Nor did a former pirate, Pound, who arrived in the Chesapeake as captain of a fifth rate, the *Dover Prize*, in April 1691. News of his presence kept the Bay clear of pirates while he remained on the station, and it is likely that his vigorous action kept the coast clear of privateers as well.

In general, the Chesapeake trade was protected when it sailed in convoy. Those ships that sailed independently were defended in American waters by convoy escorts in the summer and, when they could be spared, by stationed ships in the spring and autumn. The available evidence suggests that this latter form of protection was not usually very effective and the losses in the tobacco trade already noted were mainly from single ships. After 1700 the position changed. There was an increase in the commerce of South Carolina and merchants asked for protection for this as well. The Admiralty could not spare any more ships to defend this trade, and although ships on the outward voyage were defended until they left the convoy off Charleston, they had to make their own way to the Chesapeake to join the tobacco convoys for the return voyage to England. The Customs value of Carolina trade shows that it was insignificant by comparison with the Chesapeake, but it had a value as an extension of that trade.

The number of ships sailing with these convoys varied from year to year. When the Virginia and Maryland trade is examined for the period after 1700 it becomes clear that not only did the volume of trade change from year to year, but there was also a close relation between the value of colonial exports one year and imports the next. The rise or fall of colonial exports was reflected by a corresponding rise or fall in imports:

Table 5.1 ENGLISH TRADE WITH VIRGINIA AND MARYLAND

	(£000)	
	Imports	Exports
1700	317	173
1701	236	200
1702	275	72
1703	145	197
1704	264	60
1705	117	174
1706	149	58
1707	208	238
1708	213	79
1709	262	80
1710	188	128
1711	273	92
1712	298	135
1713	206	76
1714	280	129

Source: Whitworth, *Trade of Great Britain*, p 69.

This shows the effect of the consignment system; London merchants, who dominated the English tobacco trade, were naturally unwilling to send large quantities of goods to Virginia and Maryland planters unless the shipments had already been covered by tobacco imports.[14] This was elementary commercial practice and true of war and peace equally, but the concentration of each year's trade into one major convoy in wartime exaggerated the effect of crop variations on London prices. Once the convoy had arrived, there was little chance that more could reach London, and merchants could fix the price accordingly. In peacetime a measure of uncertainty existed for a longer time and prices fluctuated accordingly. This inflexible system created serious difficulties whenever convoys were delayed, for it upset not only the English trade with these colonies but also the re-export trade. In the same way, fear that the convoy might be intercepted by a French squadron caused panic among an influential section of the London merchant community.

In the first year of the war the arrangements for escorting convoys proceeded smoothly. On 31 July 1702, 155 merchant ships set sail from the Capes of Virginia under the protection of five warships, two fourth rates and one fifth rate.[15] The voyage was uneventful and the convoy reached England in mid-September; the main body of shipping sailed up the English Channel with the fourth rate ships, and merchantmen for ports in the Bristol Channel and Irish Sea were escorted to St George's Channel by the *Bedford Galley*. The dominance of London in this trade is seen again in the proportion of the convoy that was bound there: 92 of the 155. By comparison, the outports were poorly represented: nineteen ships for Bristol, seven for Liverpool and most of the remainder were destined for ports along the south coast of England, the Bristol Channel or the Irish Sea: Falmouth, Bideford, Barnstable, Plymouth, Deal, Weymouth and other, smaller ports. London's clear lead is also seen in the higher tonnage of the ships bound there: 187.4 tons, compared with 164.7 for Bristol and 100.0 for Liverpool. The value of the commerce between England and the Chesapeake which this represents led the Board of Trade to emphasize to the Lord High Admiral that the trade deserved 'a most particular regard'. Later the same year the latter proposed a more elaborate convoy system whereby four fourth rate warships should be sent to the Chesapeake before the end of January 1703. These would protect shipping bound for the southern colonies, cruise off the coast and in the bay, and return with the trade by the end of July. Another convoy would leave England in August 1704 under two fourth rate warships and return the following year. The choice of this type of vessel for escort duty calls for some comment.

These ships carried fifty and sometimes sixty guns, and at the beginning of the eighteenth century were still regarded as capable of fighting in a line of battle. They were however too slow to catch privateers, and their value as escorts for these large, valuable but unwieldy convoys was that they stood a chance of beating off the small squadrons of warships which the French used for commerce raiding in this war. There remained a strategic weakness. In the event of meeting a French raiding squadron the warships could have offered little protection from the swarms of privateers which generally accompanied the squadrons, and which took the merchant ships while the escorts were fighting the warships. The best that can be said of these proposals is that they were gestures of support by the administration for a valuable section of English trade. In view of the general shortage of suitable naval vessels the administration could have done little more, and the suggestion of sending four warships to protect a convoy is unusual.

Inevitably, this proposal did not satisfy all the London merchants or planters – Micajah Perry, one of the leading Virginia merchants, strongly argued for a July convoy[16] – and Colonel Quary, a royal official in Virginia, complained in May 1704 that the tobacco trade was badly managed. His argument, briefly, was that the planters did not know whether there would be one or two convoys a year, and could not decide whether to sell their tobacco cheaply or pay heavy freight charges to send it with the first convoy, or wait for the second in the hope that prices would rise and freight charges fall. If the second convoy failed to arrive, the merchants suffered heavy losses, because their tobacco deteriorated. The outcome was a clash between merchants in London and the outports. The former received tobacco on consignment and, like the planters, favoured a single convoy which would ensure relatively stable prices. Merchants at the outports on the other hand wanted at least two convoys each year for they knew that their markets would be more easily glutted than London's and also feared that the colonists would try to raise their tobacco prices. It must be remembered that outport merchants bought their tobacco in the colonies and had to keep prices high in England in order to maintain their profits in view of the rise in wartime shipping and insurance costs. This conflict of interests could not be resolved easily and continued to rage for several years.

Before it was finally resolved, the administration was faced with a request for an extra convoy because forty merchant ships had been delayed in Virginia and had not returned with the rest of the trade. In an effort to accommodate the merchants, the Board of Trade recommended in February 1707 that a second convoy should be sent or that the embargo should be lifted to allow them to sail independently; a sensible solution to a problem that the merchants, and not the administration, had created. Before any arrangements could be made the Privy Council accepted Quary's proposals for a single annual convoy which should reach the Chesapeake in October, and remain there until May. This met with general approval; the first packed hogsheads which were not available before October and the main part of the crop was packed in the following two or three months.[17]

It gave merchants ample opportunity to load their ships and it had the further advantage that ships hulls suffered less damage from the teredo worm in the winter than summer, though it deprived the Admiralty of the opportunity of repairing or refitting the ships sent to the Chesapeake. In general the new arrangements seem to have worked well, and merchants and planters made no further requests for special protection. Annual imports of tobacco were in general fairly high, and differences from year to year were the result of crop variations rather than losses at sea:

Table 5.2 TOBACCO IMPORTS INTO ENGLAND

	(000,000 lbs)
1700	37.8
1701	38.2
1702	37.2
1703	20.1
1704	34.9
1705	—
1706	19.8
1707	28.0
1708	29.0
1709	35.5
1710	23.5
1711	28.1
1712	—
1713	12.3
1714	29.2

Source: E. B. Schumpeter, *English overseas trade statistics 1697–1808*, (1960) p 61.

This consistency in commerce protection is all the more remarkable in view of the great increase in convoy size after 1700. Before that date convoys contained, on average, about fifty ships, but in the period following there were often 150–200 ships in each one. By the standard of the early eighteenth century these were exceptionally large and posed special problems for the administration. It becomes clear why the Lord High Admiral proposed in 1703 that four fourth rate line-of-battle ships should act as escorts. There was also difficulties of controlling such a large body of ships at sea, and it is to the credit of escort commanders that they were able to bring so many of their charges safely to port. The increased size of the convoys is also a demonstration of the greater feeling of security that they gave to commerce, and many merchants who sent their ships independently before 1700 took advantage of the convoy system thereafter.

When the war ended in 1713, the problem of protecting the trade of the southern colonies remained, although the danger was no longer from French privateers. The threat was from pirates and the second decade of the eighteenth century witnessed a determined attempt by British and colonial administrations to bring them under control. In the main, the royal officials were successful, leading pirates were hunted down, colonial support checked and enough pirates hanged to discourage those who remained at liberty. The American coast was gradually made safe for British and colonial

9 British ports

commerce and such pirates that remained sailed to the pirate haven of Madagascar, there to prey on the defenceless native trade and occasional European Indiaman. The Board of Admiralty withdrew guard ships from the American coast and laid them up while Britain under Walpole's administration became more prosperous from successful trade.

In the long interval before Britain was again involved in a major war, the pattern of trade with the southern colonies of America began to change. London merchants continued to dominate but major changes took place at the outports. Many of the smaller ones, such as Bideford or Falmouth which had imported small quantities of tobacco directly from the colonies before 1713 now turned to London, Bristol or Liverpool for their supplies. The leading outports became entrepôts in the supply of British provincial markets and increased their imports by purchasing tobacco from new plantations, as these were established beyond the Tidewater. Most important of all, Glasgow whose merchants had traded illegally with the Chesapeake before the Act of Union, came to dominate this part of trade not already controlled by London merchants. The result was that London's share of the market failed to expand significantly, whereas the major outports steadily increased their trade. The expansion of the tobacco trade can be seen from the following figures:

Table 5.3 TOBACCO IMPORTS INTO ENGLAND AND WALES

	(000,000 lbs)
1713	12.3
1720	34.5
1730	35.1
1739	46.7

Source: Schumpeter, *English overseas trade*, p 62.

These figures indicate the trend in imports rather than the average increase decade by decade, but they are nonetheless valuable because they show how the general level rose. Customs returns show the same trend:

Table 5.4 BRITISH TRADE WITH VIRGINIA AND MARYLAND

	(£000)	
	Imports	Exports
1713	206	76
1720	331	111
1730	347	151
1739	445	217

Source: Whitworth, *Trade of Great Britain*, p 69.

Taken together these figures for the volume of tobacco imports and the official values of import and export trade demonstrate the enormous strides which the Chesapeake economy had made by the outbreak of war in 1739. It would be logical to assume that this had been achieved by a proportionate increase in the number of ships plying between the Chesapeake and Britain. Available evidence however suggests that this was not the case, and that the convoys of the war of 1739–48 were approximately the same size as those of the War of Spanish Succession. The evidence to explain this is sketchy, but points to a number of conclusions: the ratio of ship tonnage to size of crew increased although the average size of vessel declined; there was thus a rise in the efficiency of the trade, and the fall of tobacco prices forced men to seek to fill their ships in order to make a profit on the voyage.[18] This drive for greater efficiency came mainly from the outports, and is closely linked with the rise of Glasgow as a major tobacco importer. Between 1739 and 1748 it appears that the bulk of the crop produced on the major plantations was still consigned to London merchants, but that of the smaller plantation owners was frequently sold to supercargoes and agents of outports merchants. The main reason for this shift in attitudes is that as smaller plantations were established further inland in the Piedmont region, it became more difficult for the owners to dispose of their crops. London merchants were not anxious to deal in these small amounts and it was left to agents of the Glasgow merchants in particular to engross much of this trade. They established stores at points on the wagon roads, stocked them with Scottish linen, household goods, clothing and other items required by the planter, and sold or exchanged these for tobacco. The tobacco produced by these planters was assured of a market, although planters claimed that the agents drove prices down, and that therefore the agents of the Glasgow merchants were able to collect cargoes quickly and efficiently for shipment. The main advantage enjoyed by Glasgow in this trade was the ready supply of capital, much of it obtained on the London financial exchange by agents of the Scottish houses such as William Cuninghame & Company, and Cuninghame, Findlay & Company. The creation of the Ship Bank and other banks provided the link between London and the extensive Virginia credit network.[19]

In wartime the Glasgow merchants enjoyed special advantages. Up to the 1740s the rise of Glasgow was part of a general shift of the trade towards the north-west, but in wartime this assumed a new importance. Not only were voyage times significantly shorter than from London, usually by two or three weeks, but the route was safer

Few French privateers were sighted north of Ireland, at least on the outward route. This kept freight charges and insurance costs low and the rapid turn round in Virginia waters ensured that Glasgow not only maintained her position relative to the other ports but tended to outstrip Bristol and ports further south. The secure market for Glasgow tobacco to the French purchasing agency was a further advantage, for the French paid promptly, though at times their agents tried to drive the price down. In view of the relative security of the Glasgow trade, ships outward bound from Britain had no need either for an organized convoy or even for a stationed ship for their trade as did Bristol. In American waters the position was different. From the outset, the coastal waters attracted first Spanish and, after 1744, French privateers. All ships sailing from the Chesapeake therefore requested convoy, and Glasgow ships were given convoy for the first 100–150 leagues into the sea, or sailed with the main convoy for part of the voyage. The Spanish privateers that attacked British shipping off the Virginia Capes sailed either from St Augustine, a small, struggling community in Florida that was significant only in wartime, and Havana, Spain's principal naval base in the Caribbean. In 1742 a Spanish privateer from Havana took seven vessels off the Capes.[20] This Spanish threat to British trade with the Chesapeake does not seem to have disrupted trade, perhaps mainly because there were comparatively few Spanish privateers in American coastal waters and few off the British coast.

After 1744 there was an additional danger from French privateers and warships, both in American coastal waters and off the British Isles. This had serious consequences for the trade. In the first year of war with France, 1744, a St Malo privateer took twenty-one ships in the English Channel, many of them Virginiamen.[21] In 1745 three Bideford ships from Maryland were taken by French privateers; in July, several tobacco ships were taken by five privateers off the Virginia Capes; in August, news reached Annapolis of the capture of two more Bideford ships by privateers from San Sebastian and St Malo. The melancholy catalogue was completed for the year by the Brest squadron's capture on 12 June of twenty merchantmen bound for the Chesapeake. This did not include the loss of a number of other vessels, taken mostly by the St Malo privateers, *Sultana* and *Hermione*, which was reported in the December 1745 supplement to the *Gentleman's Magazine*. A vigorous defence of the trade in 1746 and 1747 kept losses down, but they rose again in 1748 almost to the level of 1744. In the spring privateers entered the Chesapeake, captured vessels at the mouths of rivers and even sailed within sight of Fort George on Point Comfort.[22] Insurance rates reflect the seriousness of this danger, rising in May 1744 from the peacetime rate of 3 or 4 per cent to 12 or 15 per cent for the outward voyage and 20 to 25 per cent for the passage home. The unprecedented losses in 1744 led London brokers to refuse to insure one ship bound for the Chesapeake and there was talk of rates of 40 or even 50 per cent at Bristol. Rates remained high in January 1745 when 20 per cent was asked for a return voyage and dangers in 1748 again pushed up the rate to 25 per cent for a home voyage.[23] The rise in freight rates, also rose to reflect these dangers; in 1744 £14 per ton was asked, compared with £6 to £8 per ton in peace and remained at £13 to £14 per ton.[24] News of shipping losses in this trade made dismal reading for merchants in London and the outports, but did not signify the total collapse of the trade, as the following figures show:

Table 5.5 TOBACCO IMPORTS AT THE SIX PRINCIPAL CENTRES

Year Ending Christmas	London	Bideford and Barnstable	Bristol	Liverpool	Whitehaven	Port Glasgow and Greenock
			(000 lbs)			
1739	30,516	2,801	3,799	4,310	3,942	4,713
1740	17,437	1,967	4,748	5,358	4,457	4,255
1741	40,025	2,125	2,927	5,468	5,413	6,434
1742	23,360	2,221	4,311	5,312	6,970	8,569
1743	36,254	3,541	3,840	6,129	9,443	9,148
1744	22,805	673	3,791	4,248	9,359	8,832
1745	24,373	1,624	3,243	5,770	7,073	11,173
1746	18,407	365	3,979	7,195	9,145	8,194
1747	28,189	1,341	3,256	9,380	9,266	10,021
1748	27,782	1,149	2,861	8,161	10,622	13,537

Source: J. M. Price, *France and the Chesapeake. A History of the French tobacco monopoly, 1674–1791, and of its relationship to the British and French American tobacco trades* (2 vols, Ann Arbor, Mich., 1973), i, 590.

In fact, the picture may have been less bleak than the above brief details indicate. Merchants were understandably nervous about the effects of privateering on trade and rumours were rife. Their reaction was to attempt to push a Convoy Act through Parliament, but on neither occasion, 1742 nor 1744, were they successful.[25] On the other hand, when one examines freight rates for Maryland to London for this war, they do not show the same degree of near panic that Middleton notes.

Table 5.6 FREIGHT RATES FROM MARYLAND TO LONDON

	Rate per ton (£)
1739	7
1740	9–10
1741	9
1742	9
1743	9
1744	9–12
1745	12–13
1746	13–14
1747	16
1748	7

Source: Shepherd and Walton, *Shipping*, pp 191–2.

The rate climbed steadily from the outbreak of war with France, but at no time reached the peak simultaneously with Middleton's figures, and fell, surprisingly, in the last year of the war. Perhaps the situation appeared in a different light in Maryland, though that is unlikely. Also, a rise of £8 per ton, though significant statistically, does not suggest that the defence of British trade had broken down; rather it reflects the normal wartime risks. The Chesapeake trade was not singled out for special mention by those who sought to push a convoys bill through Parliament, and it is fair to say that the fluctuations noted in the yearly imports reflect crop variations rather than excessive losses, which Professor Price estimates at around eight a year.[26] Indeed, the rise in freight rates may indicate little more than a shortage of shipping. When peace returned to the Chesapeake in 1748, some of the tobacco exports which had been shipped through Liverpool returned to Bristol ships, and Glasgow and Port Greenock had to fight to retain their lead over these out-ports. Surprisingly, the average tonnage of ships engaged in the trade went up: in 1749 and 1754–5 it was 106·5, almost double that of the early 1730s.[27] This suggests that the lowering of shipping costs made it economic to use larger ships again.

The outbreak of war in 1756 once again made convoys essential for the Chesapeake trade, and it is significant that an appeal to Pitt by tobacco merchants was supported by one of the leading Glasgow men, John Buchanan.[28] In many ways the convoys to and from the Chesapeake in the Seven Years War were similar to those of the preceding war. There were comparable numbers of merchant ships, and the Board of Admiralty tended to order convoys to leave the Chesapeake in the late summer, to avoid the heat of July. It was not possible to do this every year, and in 1762 the convoy sailed from the Chesapeake in March.[29] The war is remarkable for the lack of criticism of the convoy arrangements. There was no attempt to introduce another Convoy and Cruisers Act, and in the case of the Chesapeake trade it is likely that the convoys were very well managed. The problems of organizing this diverse trade were certainly no less than they had been in the previous war, and were probably worse. There had been a steady, though unspectacular growth of Maryland tobacco exports which though largely destined for the continental market had to be protected. There had also been a growth in the export of some items of naval stores from an area adjoining Virginia. Colonists living in the area of Albemarle Sound in modern North Carolina, were encouraged to produce tar and pitch by bounty payments. These exports, though small, were shipped from Norfolk because North Carolina had no ports suitable for sea-going vessels. Ships carrying these items joined the convoys which assembled at Hampton Roads. The naval commanders had the co-operation of merchants and customs officials in arranging the dates for return convoys, and by the time of the Seven Years War the collection of duties and the storage of tobacco in warehouses was conducted in a far more efficient manner. It was possible for a captain or supercargo to buy tobacco from a warehouse and have the guarantee that it conformed to a recognized grade; the crop note, given to the planter when he deposited the tobacco stated that. Moreover, the customs authorities extended the warehouse system to cover the greater part of the tobacco producing area. This not only ensured that more planters paid duty but helped to channel the trade into a smaller number of outlets. This helped the captain or supercargo wishing to buy tobacco to make up his cargo. The result was a more manageable and efficient system which benefited the customs officials, the planters and the captains. It had the further advantage that when the principal merchants and the captain of the escort vessel had agreed a sailing date for the return convoy, the remainder of the captains could be easily informed by posting a notice in these warehouses. This improvement in communications was extremely important. Even in the late 1750s the tobacco trade was spread over a number of harbours. Most important was Port Hampton, at the mouth of the James River. Yet, of a total convoy of around 120 – Governor Dinwiddie's estimate in 1755 – no more than forty left Port Hampton.[30] Maryland's share was likewise small; in 1760 twenty-two ships were cleared for London and Whitehaven under convoy and a year later fifteen cleared from Annapolis, the principal port.[31] The remainder of the merchant ships cleared from ports on the York and Rappahannock rivers.

Efficient convoy organization was of prime importance in this war. Escort captains had to take all the ships bound for Britain if possible, for single vessels frequently fell prey to French privateers or warships off the British Isles. The escort captain facing winter gales on the return voyage was under a further disadvantage. The voyage of Captain Adams of the fifth-rate *Diana* shows how arrangements could go astray. In the spring of 1762 Captain Adams prepared to return to England with a small convoy of sixteen ships.[32] When the time came for the convoy to sail from Hampton Roads it was discovered that three of the ships had been frozen into the ice in one river – the winter had been extraordinarily hard. Two more had been blown on shore in a gale, and only eleven were able to sail at the appointed date, 4 March. Six days out the convoy was hit by a gale and scattered. Captain Adams found he had to run before the wind because he was in danger of foundering. He lost contact with the ships in the night, and when day dawned was faced with the almost impossible task of collecting them together. At first he lay to under easy sail, but when none of the ships appeared he set sail for the Soundings. On the way he sighted a French privateer and gave chase. This proved a mistake, for while trying to come up with the French vessel he sprung his main topmast. He not only lost the chance of catching the privateer but limped home without being able to rejoin any of his charges. He was censured by the Admiralty, the Secretary noting on his report: 'Acquaint him the Lords are far from being satisfied . . . and that . . . he has incurred their displeasure.'

Captain Adams may have been unfortunate in springing his topmast, but the Admiralty's comment was just. It was the duty of every escort commander to protect the ships to which he issued sailing instructions, and he had to do his utmost at every point in the voyage to prevent their capture. Although he had no chance of restraining those captains who deliberately broke from his convoy during the night, he knew that French privateers swarmed off the main landfalls, and single ships were easy prey for them. Significantly, four French naval vessels that received news of the imminent danger of a convoy while cruising off the American coast made no attempt to intercept it at the start of its voyage, but crossed the Atlantic to wait for its arrival in British waters.[33] On the other hand the tobacco trade was so important that any attack on it that was successful would seriously alarm British merchants and threaten commercial support for the administration. With this in mind, the French government ordered four 30-gun frigates, *Sauvage, Licorne, Améthyste* and *Brume* to cruise off the coasts of Virginia and Carolina in 1758.[34] The main purpose of the cruise was to alarm merchants and force the British naval commander in North America to send vessels to protect the Chesapeake trade, thus diverting ships from the attack on Louisbourg. This had no effect on the Chesapeake trade, but there was a further proposal in January 1761 to send a warship and frigate to cruise off the coasts of Virginia and Carolina. Le Vassor de la Touche, commander of the frigate *Thétis*, claimed that a cruise would produce thirty prizes in under six weeks, and, more important, provisions for the French Leeward Islands.[35] This suggestion was not accepted, but it does show the dangers facing the commerce of the Chesapeake and South Carolina.

The two areas were in no way connected. Separating them was one of the most dangerous coastlines in the world, and it would have been unthinkable for the Admiralty to have ordered South Carolina trade to rendezvous with convoys in the Chesapeake. The names of the capes off North Carolina gave warning of the hazards to navigation: Cape Fear and Cape Lookout, and these and Cape Hatteras claimed many ships, especially in easterly gales. There were no harbours along the barren, sandy shore to which ships could run for shelter, and off the islands and at the mouths of rivers sand bars made it difficult for all but the smallest ships to cross save at high tide. Carolina trade bore little comparison with that of Virginia and Maryland, although by the outbreak of war with Spain in 1739 British imports from Carolina stood at £236,192 and exports at £94,445 at the official Customs rates.[36] Virginia and Maryland, by comparison, exported £444,654 of goods and received from Britain imports valued at £217,200.[37] Yet the Carolina trade was important politically, and had grown rapidly:

Table 5.7 BRITISH TRADE WITH CAROLINA

	(£000)	
	Imports	Exports
1713	32.4	23.9
1720	62.7	18.3
1730	151.7	64.8
1739	236.1	94.4

Source: Whitworth, *Trade of Great Britain*, p 53

In percentage terms, the rise had been more rapid than that of Virginia and Maryland, and by 1739 there was a political lobby of merchants interested in Carolina trade. Protection had first been granted in 1719 to defend commerce and prevent illegal trade between the inhabitants of Charleston and these pirates. Until the 1730s the colony's growth was hampered by fear of Indian attack. When this diminished colonists arrived in greater numbers and commerce rapidly expanded. Although described as 'Carolina' in contemporary records, the area from the Savannah River to the Chesapeake fell into two distinct areas. In the north the economy was based largely on naval stores: pitch, tar and white pine, production of which was encouraged by bounty, though the products went largely to shipyards in the northern colonies. In the south, deerskins, indigo and rice formed the main exports. The population of the Carolinas was small and scattered; Charleston was the only town of importance, and it developed as the entrepôt for the south. It lay at the confluence of two rivers, the Ashley and the Cooper, and these gave excellent communications with the interior. It suffered from two major disadvantages: an unhealthy climate and a sand bar at the harbour mouth. Merchants unloaded at least part of their cargo into lighters before venturing to cross this bar.

In war this proved specially hazardous; many vessels were captured by privateers while waiting off the bar, and the town's defence lay in the unwillingness of French captains to cross it. Within the harbour the only defence was a single fort, usually in a ruinous condition. Effective commercial defence relied on the presence of an energetic naval commander, who could be relied on to chase away all Spanish and French shipping. Unfortunately for Charleston, this was often lacking. When pirates menaced southern trade after the Treaty of Utrecht, the Admiralty gave intermittent protection. In 1719 the *Flamborough*, a sixth rate built in 1707, was sent, and this proved an excellent choice for the vessel was fast and of moderately shallow draught. It was ideal for chasing pirate schooners into the shallow bays and inlets where they habitually sheltered. Between 1719 and 1725 a 20-gun ship was constantly maintained on this station; in the next three years a sloop was also provided, although it had to cruise as far as the Chesapeake.[38] In 1729 two 20-gun ships were sent, but as the risk of piracy diminished this was cut to a single ship between 1730 and 1737.

The outbreak of war with Spain in 1739 emphasized once again the hazardous geographical position of Charleston. St Augustine was an ideal base from which to launch an attack on the port, and Spanish privateers were periodically sighted off the bar. In view of the popular fears for the safety of the port and its commerce – the overseas trade was entirely in British hands – the Admiralty sent two ships, the *Phoenix* and the *Tartar*. These were a compromise choice. The first was a fifth or sixth rate and the other an old fifth rate constructed in 1720.[39] They appeared powerful enough to beat off a small attacking force, but were not fast enough to chase privateers and take them. The protection of Charleston's trade seems to have left much to be desired. The climate was unhealthy – the stagnant rice fields were breeding grounds for malarial mosquitos – and merchants complained that one captain, Fanshawe of the *Phoenix* was grasping and had been attracted to the post by hopes of material gain. Few naval captains received praise from merchants. They tended to be mutually antagonistic over matters such as the need to recruit sailors for naval vessels and the timing of convoys, and were often divided by naval considerations of punctilio. In the case of Captain Fanshawe, the man was probably totally unsympathetic to the merchants' point of view, and acted with a wilful disregard for any but his own interests. He was accused of recruiting a total of 800 men to replace desertions and of pocketing the allowances of all who had deserted or died. Merchants even claimed that he showed pleasure when hearing of commercial losses, though this may have been in a moment of anger.[40] Whether or not the accusation was true, he made matters worse by failing to take any privateers, whereas two sloops fitted out by the province were successful. The hull of the *Phoenix* became so badly damaged by the teredo worm that it had to be resheathed, and the vessel was consequently out of service for six months. The crowning disaster, from the point of view of Charleston merchants was that the *Tartar* was recalled while the *Phoenix* was being resheathed, and that left the province defenceless except for two small provincial sloops. To heighten their attack on Captain Fanshawe, Carolina merchants insisted that Captain Townsend of the *Tartar* behaved with moderation and fully deserved their thanks. He 'behaved well before St Augustine' and took a privateer. Even he was not perfect, and three of four ships that he escorted from Charleston were taken 'within the usual limits of a convoy' and two hundred barrels of rice were sent into St Augustine.

When the Admiralty appointed another sixth rate, the *Rose* to defend Carolina trade in 1742, the captain was ordered to cruise as far as the Bahamas. This at least encouraged him to seek out Spanish privateers from St Augustine and the Caribbean, but left Charleston defenceless. On balance this was the better strategy for it answered merchants criticisms that naval commanders failed to seek out Spanish vessels and encouraged merchants to send their ships in the one or more annual convoys which could be properly protected. During the war the fortunes of the colony altered greatly. Under the stimulus of naval protection and colonial immigration, rice production was greatly expanded. Unfortunately for the planters the increase in wartime costs and the dangers of shipping rice to the Mediterranean market led to a decline in rice exports, for under these conditions, Carolina merchants could not compete with rice from Egypt and the Levant. A further complication was that although rice was an enumerated item, a concession of 1730 allowed it to be shipped direct to any market south of Cape Finisterre. These voyages were not protected by convoy, and therefore declined sharply in war. Under these conditions the market for rice declined steadily. By the mid-1740s there was serious overproduction, and the Customs records reflect this crisis:

Table 5.8 BRITISH TRADE WITH CAROLINA

	(£000)	
	Imports	Exports
1739	236.1	94.4
1740	266.5	181.8
1741	236.8	204.7
1742	154.6	127.0
1743	235.1	111.4
1744	192.6	79.1
1745	91.8	86.8
1746	76.9	102.8
1747	107.5	95.5
1748	167.3	160.2

Source: Whitworth, *Trade of Great Britain*, p 53.

This reflects the major fall in rice exports which was a serious blow to the colonial economy. Exports of rice, the staple product, increased from 71,000 barrels in 1739 to 91,000 the following year, but fell to 73,416 in 1743.[41] Fortunately for the South Carolina planters, the worst years of depression also produced satisfactory indigo and a large quantity of deerskins, both of which found a ready market in Britain. Unsold rice either rotted in warehouses or was sold in northern colonies, although even in this case, if Philadelphia was any guide, the rice trade seriously declined.[42] Worst hit were the inhabitants of Charleston, for they grew little corn, were heavily dependent on provisions from the northern colonies, and had little money to pay for them. It was small wonder that Governor Glen complained that coastal trade with Philadelphia and New York was 'draining us of all the little money and bills that we could gather from other places'.[43] This was not the Admiralty's fault, and indeed, there was no criticism of the naval defence of British colonial trade with Charleston.

Carolina's economy began to recover in 1747 as rice sales and prices rose. The period 1748–56 saw a return to prosperity for the region and also an attempt to stimulate colonization to the south in Georgia. Climatically this area was similar to South Carolina, and the main crop which could be grown was rice. Until 1750 large-scale production was impossible because the colonists were not allowed to own slaves.[44] When this restriction was lifted, the colony began to develop, but only along a narrow coastal strip near Savannah, for the area bordering the Savannah River was unhealthy. Silk production was also encouraged: 847 lbs had been raised in 1747 and by 1755 this had increased to 3,458 lbs. The harsh reality however was that it was never profitable, and only survived until the reduction of bounty payments in 1769. The economy was gradually developed in other ways as well: part of the Carolina deerskin trade had been won by 1740 and small quantities of tobacco, Indian corn and lumber were produced, though mainly for home consumption.

South Carolina also flourished in these peaceful years, and the Customs returns chart the colony's economic expansion: British imports from Carolina were valued at £167,305 in 1748 and rose to £325,525 in 1755.[45] On the other hand, British exports to Carolina increased very little, from £160,172 in 1748 to £187,887 in 1755. This indicates a slow growth in population. In 1755 the Cherokee purchase opened new land to European settlement, and during the Seven Years War the colony attracted settlers from other southern colonies. A thousand Acadians were also brought to Charleston in 1756.[46] By the outbreak of the Seven Years War, both colonies were expanding. Carolina's trade was important enough to claim naval protection though Georgia's was not, and the few ships that sailed to Savannah went with the Charleston convoys. Naval activities in North America interrupted the cycle of trade protection at the start of the war, because ships could not be spared to escort the Carolina trade. Charleston convoys should have left the port in November or December – but were delayed until the spring, and convoys were also seriously delayed from Britain.[47] The first arrived at Charleston in May and left in August.[48] In 1757 and 1758, convoys sailed from Britain in March and probably left Charleston in early summer.[49] This hampered trade, for it was important to ship rice before the heat of summer, and many vessels were forced to sail independently to avoid damage to their cargo.[50] Commerce was disrupted and gradually declined:

Table 5.9 BRITISH TRADE WITH CAROLINA AND GEORGIA

	(£000)			
	Carolina		Georgia	
	Imports	Exports	Imports	Exports
1756	222.9	181.8	7.2	0.5
1757	130.9	213.9	—	2.6
1758	150.5	181.0	—	10.2
1759	206.5	215.2	6.1	15.2
1760	162.8	218.1	12.2	—
1761	253.0	254.6	5.7	24.3
1762	181.7	194.2	6.5	23.8
1763	282.4	250.1	14.5	45.0

Source: Whitworth, *Trade of Great Britain*, pp 54 and 58

This fall in commerce should have signalled a decline in the price of rice comparable to that of the mid-1740s. Yet this did not happen. Wholesale commodity prices at Charleston, which had fallen to 2·2 shillings South Carolina currency per 100 lbs in 1746 never fell below 4·8 shillings in this war:

Table 5.10 WHOLESALE PRICES FOR RICE AT CHARLESTON

(Shillings per 100 lbs)	
1756	4.9
1757	4.8
1758	6.2
1759	9.4
1760	7.4
1761	5.5
1762	4.8
1763	6.5

Source: A. H. Cole, *Wholesale commodity prices in the United States 1700–1861* (Cambridge Mass. 1938), p 154

There are a number of possible explanations. The most likely is that the surplus from Carolina and the whole of the Georgia crop in 1757 and 1758 were sold to merchants from New England and Pennsylvania who were purchasing provisions for the Louisbourg expeditions.[51] Alternatively, though less likely, the rice could have been sold illicitly to the Spanish colony at St Augustine, or the colonists, anticipating a glut like that of the mid-1740s, could have reduced the size of their crop. At all events, the lack of exports from Georgia in 1757 and 1758 highlights the weakness of the colony. A further illustration is the voyage of the merchant ship *Venus* in 1758. She set sail from Spithead on 12 March in a convoy escorted by Captain Man of the *Penguin* frigate. She apparently spent almost a year in Savannah and returned, carrying a cargo of rice, to Britain with the convoy that left Charleston on 1 March 1759.[52] Only London merchants traded with Georgia until 1760 and ships like the *Venus* were protected for most of their voyage.[53]

Merchants trading with South Carolina faced more than the problem of declining trade in this war. Occasionally the town was struck by a whirlwind. On 4 May 1761, as a convoy was preparing to sail from Britain, a tornado hit Charleston. In one brief spell it had dismasted the frigate *Dolphin*, sunk five merchant ships and damaged many more.[54] Little warning was given of its approach and many were drowned as their small craft were crushed beneath a column of water. The noise was terrifying. The timely arrival of the *Success* frigate enabled a much reduced convoy to sail shortly afterwards, and the remainder followed a month later when the *Dolphin* had been repaired.

The other problem was desertion from naval vessels. Some seamen on these ships took the first opportunity of deserting in a foreign port; others were tempted to desert by offers of rewards – apparently up to £40 in South Carolina currency. Many merchants found that their crews were seriously depleted by desertion and sickness and tried to make up their numbers by encouraging naval seamen to desert. This short-sighted policy hampered trade, for it made it more difficult for the naval vessel to put to sea to attack commerce raiders and weakened the effectiveness of the ship as an escort on the return voyage to England. It remained a perennial problem for the Admiralty, and Captain Hale's experience in 1757 is a good example. When he careened the *Winchelsea* at Charleston, most of his crew deserted and hid in the woods. He was not allowed to impress seamen in a colonial port and tried to make up his crew by encouraging deserters to return. Any who did so were promptly imprisoned by the merchants for debt – merchants had presumably made an advance payment of wages to these men. Captain Hale then tried to get men from the workhouse, but realized that between obtaining their release on a writ of *habeas corpus* and setting sail, he would be responsible for their wages. He appealed to the Admiralty for support, though it is not known whether or not he was successful.

Even when the captains were able to complete their crews, there remained the problem of assembling the convoy. Merchants sometimes found it more difficult to complete and load their cargoes than they had anticipated, and in 1761 when the whirlwind struck Charleston the convoy was still in the port because it had been delayed.[55] When the convoy was finally assembled, and sailing instructions had been given to the masters, vessels edged across the bar and set sail for Britain. These convoys were in general smaller than for other trades: the Carolina and Georgia ones contained only about twenty five.[56] They were more manageable than those from the Chesapeake and there were few complaints either from merchants or escort commanders. There still remained the difficulty of Atlantic storms which scattered the convoys. The most disastrous convoy was that of 1758. It was escorted by two naval vessels, the *Winchelsea* and *Blandford*, both frigates, the latter having put into Charleston for repairs while sailing from the Caribbean.[57] The convoy, consisting of thirty-six ships, many of which were bound for Portugal, set sail from Charleston on 28 August. On 16 September, when the convoy was in latitude 41°1′ N and 53°16′ W it was scattered by a violent storm, which broke both the main and mizon masts of the *Winchelsea* and strained the *Blandford* so much that she shipped water at the rate of six feet an hour for several hours. The *Gloster* foundered, although her crew were saved, and extensive damage was suffered by all the ships. Within the next few days the *Winchelsea* was joined by two ships, both of which were dismasted, and ten were reunited with the *Blandford*. The misfortune did not end there. On 10 October, in latitude 50°48′ N and 16′W from Paris the *Winchelsea* and her two charges encountered the French 64-gun warship *Bizarre* and the frigate *Minnion*, 28 guns, returning from Quebec. All the British vessels were taken.[58] This episode, unfortunate though it was for the Carolina merchants, was not as serious as indicated by Professor Laughton. His estimate that thirty-four ships were taken with the *Winchelsea* is more important as a reflection of contemporary concern at the incident than the considered judgement of a historian. It is valuable nonetheless, for it indicates the extent to which contemporary views could exaggerate British losses. The Seven Years War shows the success of the British convoy system. In general trade suffered losses which were acceptable and when losses occurred, their importance tended to be exaggerated. When Britain was again at war, from 1776, conditions were very different.

The two years before fighting started witnessed attempts by the colonists and the British government to control trade. The Boston Port Act, designed to punish the Bostonians for their challenge to the government over the latter's plans to import tea at reduced duty, created widespread hostility. It showed itself as an attempt to stop all trade between Britain and the American colonies through a series of non-importation agreements. They were not without some support in the southern colonies, where merchants were attempting to reduce their debts to British merchant houses by payment in colonial currency; the practice had been strongly resisted by British merchants and the dispute was occasionally acrimonious. As events moved inexorably towards war, British merchants made great efforts to have their debts paid before hostilities commenced and there was a marked increase in imports of tobacco, though little was sent in return. When war broke out in 1775 it checked the tobacco trade but failed to halt it completely, as the following figures show:

Table 5.11 IMPORTS OF TOBACCO INTO BRITAIN

	(£000)
1775	526
1776	69
1777	9
1778	20
1779	43
1780	70
1781	55
1782	45
1783	152

Source: B. R. Mitchell and P. Deane, *Abstract of British historical statistics* (Cambridge 1971), p 288.

What seems to have happened is that for the first three years of war – 1775–7 – exports of tobacco steadily declined. The principal planters were also the leading figures in the rebellion and were able to effectively halt the export of all but a trickle of the commodity. After that, the need for money to pay for French military supplies forced a number to look for a means of disposing of their tobacco profitably. Much undoubtedly went to France, but some was sent to St Eustatius where it was bought and shipped to Europe. Some of the merchants frequenting that Dutch port were colonists from St Kitts and there is every reason to suppose that the tobacco which reached Britain did so by this roundabout route. This may even have been the intention of some Charleston merchants who wanted to pay British debts but were prevented by the war from sending the tobacco direct to Britain. In 1778 the British occupation of Savannah placed naval forces close to the American trade routes with the Caribbean and made it possible to intercept tobacco cargoes. In 1780 the campaign of Cornwallis made it possible to seize tobacco and ship it to Britain. When he retreated to Yorktown the volume of tobacco sent to Britain likewise fell and Britain had to fall back on supplies of prize tobacco. Florida also played an important role. The colony remained under British control and provided an opportunity for colonial merchants to send their goods to Britain by way of the colony if they wished. East Florida was not a major producer of agricultural commodities, but her trade with Britain remained after that of the other southern colonies had collapsed. It is doubtful however if all the tobacco received into British ports came in this way. Much more, of the little that reached Britain, came from the smuggling trade via St Eustatius or from prizes, or perhaps from collusive capture – a form of illegal wartime commerce that was relatively common in the Caribbean. The following figures show how Britain's official trade with her southern colonies declined:

Table 5.12 BRITISH TRADE WITH SOUTHERN COLONIES

	Carolina		(£000) Florida		Georgia		Virginia and Maryland	
1775	597	6	21	85	103	113	758	2
1776	13	—	30	174	12	—	73	—
1777	2	—	48	138	—	—	—	—
1778	1	—	48	64	—	—	—	—
1779	3	—	24	128	—	—	—	—
1780	—	237	16	64	2	92	—	—

Source: Customs 3/77–80 *passim*.

The relative success of the Florida trade during the war – figures for 1781–3 are not available – stands in marked contrast to that of the other colonies. It reflects the British policy of dispersal since 1778, which put troops in loyalist areas and ensured that merchants had reasonable security for the goods they consigned to Florida. The high figures for 1776 and 1777 reflect commercial optimism and hope that Florida might provide a 'back door' to the American market. The imports from the colony however did not justify exports on this level, and one may assume that from 1778 much of the market for British exports to this colony was from the British troops that had been stationed there since 1778, though some of the commodities undoubtedly found their way into the colonies further north. It goes some way to disproving the widely held belief of American historians that during the war all trade with the colonies ceased.[59] The ships which carried these goods did not sail directly to Florida. The Admiralty was very short of suitable vessels for escorting convoys because of the heavy demands for protecting supply convoys – victuallers, troop ships and the like – and concentrated on maintaining links between Britain and New York. That was the headquarters of the British military command and from there supply convoys, and merchant ships, were sent to Florida, Halifax and Savannah from 1778 and to Charleston from 1780. Where necessary troops were sent from New York to the West Indies, although generally the Caribbean was supplied directly from Britain and only naval stores were regularly sent from the northern colonies.

By the end of the war, the only American port remaining in British hands was New York; all the rest had been taken by American and French forces. Yorktown was lost in 1782, Augusta in 1781; Savannah was evacuated in 1782. During the war, efforts had been made by Americans and French to open up trade in American commodities, partly to pay for imports of war *matériel* and partly to try and replace the traditional British trade with something more in keeping with the aspirations of the American people. The attempts failed. France lacked the stable and prosperous financial institutions that were the hallmark of British commerce. French merchants were impoverished by war and could not afford to give the nine or even twelve months credit that British merchants usually gave. France could not dispose of American goods in a wider European market as British merchants were accustomed to doing, and when peace came many American merchants either paid their outstanding debts to British merchants in full or compounded for a sum that was mutually acceptable. When Americans regained the right to ship goods directly to the Caribbean in their own small vessels they regained the means of paying for British imports through the triangular trade: Britain, North America and the Caribbean. Not all the trade of the southern states flowed back to British merchants however. Tobacco, of which only a part had been consumed in Britain, never recovered fully, and the balance was sent directly to France, where it was bought by the state buying agency that had hitherto bought tobacco from Glasgow. In Carolina, cotton production had replaced rice as the main crop and by 1790 overtook West India cotton in the British market. The new factories of Manchester and south Lancashire had by then begun to create an almost inexhaustible market for cotton which the British Caribbean islands could not hope to satisfy.

After war broke out with France in 1793, Britain maintained her trade with America. This continued to flourish, except for embargoes and animosity over the British claim to stop American ships and search for deserters, until war broke out between the two countries in

1812. Although the ports were now neutral and British warships could not enter them with the same freedom as hitherto, convoys were regularly maintained. Much of the trade with the southern states sailed from London; much, too went from Liverpool, a flourishing successful port for the American trade which was many days closer to American ports than her rivals. Wherever possible these ships were sent in convoys, but the pattern of trade allowed many of the Liverpool ships to sail independently. They were relatively safe from privateers in British waters and were protected off the American coast by the escorts that brought the London convoys out. Commerce defence off the American coast was maintained from the British naval headquarters at Halifax, and all escorts came under the orders of the British admiral there while they were in North American waters. This measure of control enabled the commander-in-chief to deploy his forces to meet any expected attack or threat from cruising French privateers, but in general there does not seem to have been much to disturb the even tenor of commercial relations. There were occasional threats of a French attack, but they were directed towards the British naval base at Halifax. To supplement the escorts that cruised off the American coast the commander-in-chief, Rear-Admiral George Murray, also appointed a small force of cruisers to range along the American coast as far as the Chesapeake and sometimes beyond to protect British trade and intercept French supply ships returning from the Caribbean. In 1796 for example, Murray had four small vessels cruising off the Carolinas and Georgia for this purpose: *Thetis* 38, *Privoyante* 38, *Thisbe* 28 and *Bonitta* 16.[60] They helped to patrol the area of the Chesapeake, which continued to attract French warships as well as merchantmen. When war was declared in 1812, all British trade with the southern states ceased and in November the navy established a close blockade of the Chesapeake. Apart from a trade in flour with the New Englanders, who helped to feed the British troops in Nova Scotia and Canada, all American trade ceased and in its place many merchants fitted out privateers which attacked British convoys returning from the Caribbean. By then, however, the commander-in-chief at Halifax had established an effective control over British shipping as it passed through the waters off Newfoundland, one of the focal areas of trade in northern waters. Convoys passed through these waters with almost clockwork regularity, and on the first sign of danger, Admiral Sawyer ordered all merchant shipping to sail in convoy. Although the Halifax squadron was far too small and weak for the tasks it faced, it did much to protect the commerce that passed through these waters.

In retrospect, one may say that British trade with the southern colonies (states after 1783) remained one of the main features of the growth of British prosperity in the period 1689–1815. The tobacco trade of Maryland and Virginia overshadowed all others on the North American continent until 1775 and Britain was enriched not only by the revenue from the carrying trade but through the sales of British commodities that were sent in return. The rice trade, too, made a notable contribution to British trade and enriched the planters of Charleston, which became a flourishing and majestic city in the colonial period. When the tobacco trade was diverted to some extent into different channels, its place in the British economy was taken by cotton which from 1790 overtook West Indies supplies in volume. The Industrial Revolution would not have been possible on the scale it attained without these new supplies of cotton and the new prosperity of Britain in the dawn of the machine age owes much to this American trade. It also added much to the prosperity of the leading seaports on the west coast of Britain: Liverpool from the 1750s and Glasgow between 1707 and the outbreak of war in 1775 were primarily ports engaged in American trade, though Liverpool gained much from the African slave trade and commerce with the Caribbean. Both lay outside the main area of privateer attack, but for the other ports especially London, the convoy system was essential for their continued prosperity. The continued success of the American commerce demonstrates the effectiveness of this protection.

6

West Indies

BETWEEN 1689 and 1815 the West Indian colonies were consistently the most important British overseas possessions. The main export was sugar, consumed in increasing quantities in Britain and on the continent as the drinking of tea, coffee and chocolate gained in popularity. By the end of the eighteenth century, sugar had produced huge fortunes for the leading planters and merchants; men who occupied a similar position to the newly enriched and ostentatious nabobs. But apart from being the source of so much conspicuous wealth, sugar had no other value except domestic and for its by-product, rum. It played no part in the *matériel* of war, and rum was its contribution to the provisioning of the forces.

It was important as a source of wealth and vast sums were spent protecting the sugar colonies and their trade. Both were vulnerable to French and Spanish attack. The British sugar islands were scattered over more than a thousand square miles of sea and could do little to support each other in war even if they had wished to do so. Few did; most colonists saw no further than their own shores and their own personal interests. Communication between the islands was only practical from east to west; trade winds carried shipping easily from Barbados to the Leeward Islands and on to Jamaica in about eight days under normal conditions. From Jamaica to Barbados, the voyage took at least seven weeks. Those who tried to work east usually gave up after weeks of fruitless effort. The only practical way was to sail north from the Caribbean and steer at least into mid-Atlantic before sailing down to the appropriate line of latitude to make a landfall. Under such trying conditions, it is hardly surprising that each island demanded special consideration from government in time of war. Each colony felt it was uniquely threatened, generally without a shred of sound evidence, and the Admiralty divided its available forces between the Leeward Islands and Jamaica.

Caribbean wealth attracted international rivalry throughout the period, and the population grew slowly. To begin with there was a steady increase through white immigration as indentured servants and even petty criminals were sent to work in the developing plantations. In Barbados, the most populous island, there were about 22,000 inhabitants in 1660. But this could not be maintained. Disease, especially yellow fever and dysentery, carried off many and others doubtless escaped to healthier climates whenever they had the chance. For these reasons, a decline set in after 1660; by 1700 the

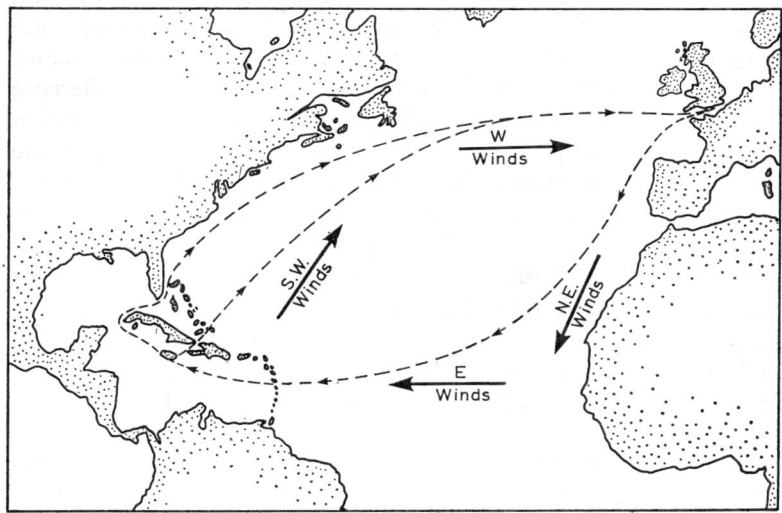

10   West India trade

white population had fallen to around 15,000.[1] Elsewhere in the Caribbean the white population was smaller and grew more slowly: Jamaica had around 3,000 white inhabitants in 1660; in 1680 it reached a peak of 12,000 before declining in the same way. Similarly in the Leeward Islands, the white population rose from about 8,000 in 1660 to a maximum of 11,000 in 1690. This was not adequate for an economy which demanded many agricultural workers and the colonists were forced increasingly to turn to slave labour, especially as it was evident that slaves could work more effectively in the Caribbean climate. From the start, the plantation economy was based largely on sugar, a crop introduced from Portuguese settlements in Brazil. To begin with, some tobacco was grown, but it quickly became the poor man's crop. The change in popular taste in Britain from the Caribbean to the Chesapeake leaf sounded the death knell for Caribbean tobacco.[2] The outcome of these agricultural developments was that most land under cultivation was used for sugar – as high as 80 per cent in Barbados – and the rest was used for cash crops: ginger, cotton, indigo and a little food. This provided the best return on what was frequently a considerable investment by seventeenth century standards. Food had to come from outside the colonies and to begin with, the demand was largely met from Ireland.

This created a trade that was large by contemporary standards: in 1697, the first year of official Customs returns and the last of war, Barbados exported sugar and other items to England with an official value of £196,532.[3] By comparison, in the same year, only Virginia and Maryland of the American colonies surpassed Barbados with exports valued at £227,756.[4] There was a significant difference between the American and Caribbean trades; the white population in the latter never provided a mass market for British goods in the way that the American colonies did, and the Caribbean trade was essentially one way. In consequence, throughout the period under review, the majority of British ships sailed out under ballast and only returned with a full cargo, if they were lucky. The small size of the islands was a further hindrance to efficient trade. The colonies' needs were easily met with a few cargoes of provisions and dry goods, and as commodities deteriorated rapidly in the humid climate, they had to be sold quickly. Merchant ships usually sailed from island to island seeking a market and information about the sugar crop, for they also had to obtain a cargo of sugar at the best rate for the return voyage.

How could the scattered merchant ships be protected effectively in war without at the same time ruining the market for British goods and sugar? This remained the central question throughout the period. The islands were too scattered for each to be given individual protection, though convoys were organized to protect trade in general. In the first year of the war, 1689, the Admiralty hired two ships to see that the West India and Virginia trades travelled safely to their destinations and back.[5] This was not the sole protection. Fortunately for the Jamaica planters, the Admiralty had already posted naval vessels to Port Royal to defend it against pirates. One ship, the *Assistance*, a fourth rate built in 1650, had sailed for England in March, eight months before France declared war. The other, the *Drake*, a sixth rate dating from 1652, remained until June 1690.[6] There was no regular convoy system at Jamaica until the 1690s,

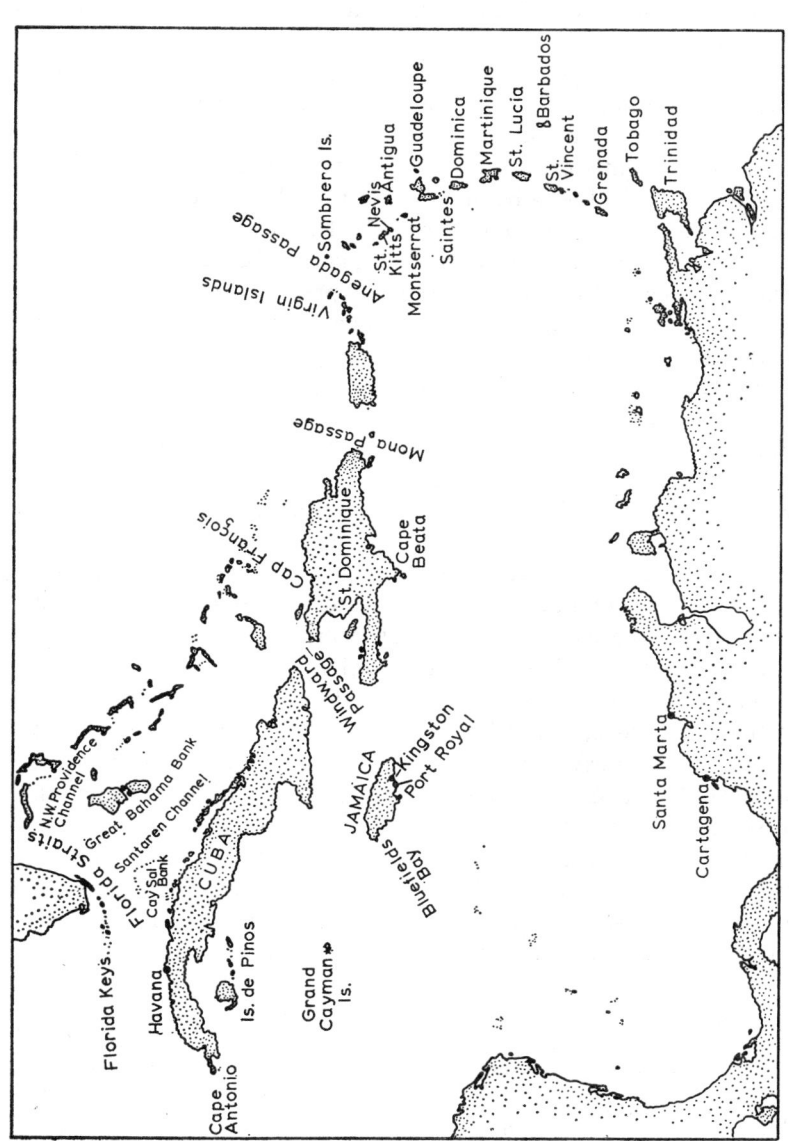

11 West India ports

though the King had ordered as early as 1671 that one should be instituted. The defence of trade rested with the commanders of the small squadrons that the Admiralty sent from England. Their main function was strategic: the capture of the French islands of Martinique and Guadeloupe. Commerce defence was limited to escorting ships out and home at the beginning and end of campaigns. These were disastrous and did little to raise English prestige. Captain Lawrence Wright's expedition of 1690 only succeeded in retaking St Kitts, which had been betrayed to the French the previous year. In the autumn of 1692, Commodore Wheeler was sent with a larger force, but this was also unsuccessful. Quarrels between naval commanders, local authorities and the army prevented united, energetic action.[7] In consequence, Martinique and Guadeloupe had become privateer bases by 1693, and threatened English communications and commerce from their position on the principal trade routes.

English security and trade in the Caribbean was further undermined by a series of slave revolts, the most serious of which occurred in Jamaica between 1673 and 1694. Savage punishment of the ringleaders, some of whom were burned alive, failed to crush them entirely and the fear of incipient revolt made local defence difficult and slowed sugar production. In consequence, privateering raids on the scattered plantations were always successful and the north coast of Jamaica was attacked so often that women and children were sent to Port Royal for safety. In 1692 the colony suffered another heavy blow. An earthquake destroyed most of Port Royal and wrecked one of the naval ships, the fifth rate *Swan*, though fortunately for the colonists the *Guernsey*, a fourth rate survived. Another of the same rate, the *Mordaunt* was sent as a replacement.[8] Little information survives about the trade which these measures were designed to protect, but it is clear that commerce declined. It had reached a peak in 1688, after suffering initially from the war, and had begun to recover when the earthquake occurred. This can be seen from the tonnage of shipping entering and leaving Port Royal harbour.

Table 6.1 TONNAGE OF VESSELS ARRIVING AT PORT ROYAL

	England	Ireland	Africa	North American colonies	Total (tons)
1688	5,785	750	765	2,410	9,710
1689	3,460	420	100	1,355	5,335
1690	2,590	160	250	1,165	4,165
1691	2,780	815	660	1,310	5,565

Source: Pawson and Buisseret, *Port Royal*, p 69.

Table 6.2 TONNAGE OF VESSELS CLEARING CUSTOMS AT PORT ROYAL

Year (March to March)	Vessels for England	Vessels for colonies	Total
1688	57	23	80
1689	45	9	54
1690	41	25	66
1691	55	13	68

Source: *ibid*.

The decline of 1689 and 1690 was not entirely due to war; there was a serious hurricane in 1690, and slaves were requisitioned to help build fortifications.[9] French privateers also took their toll. John Helyar, manager of the Bybrook plantation in Jamaica, was probably typical in losing 102 hogsheads of sugar in the first two years of war.

The first defence of English ships trading with the Caribbean lay in convoy. Runners – and this included all the ships from the North American colonies – had to keep clear of privateers or try and fight them. Losses to privateers were high, though precise figures are not available. Colonial vessels were small, averaging little over 25 tons as for instance those trading at Port Royal. They were also unarmed and carried a tiny crew. English vessels were larger on account of the Atlantic crossing, averaging about 120 tons in the Port Royal trade and they were usually over gunned. Even the little *Boneta* of 57 tons carried a crew of ten and four guns.[10] These ships at least stood a sporting chance of fighting off privateers, especially as many of the latter were small and carried a mixed armament and sometimes a large crew. Port Royal's example is probably typical of trade with the English colonies in the Caribbean, although Jamaica was not the principal sugar exporter. This was Barbados which in the 1680s and 1690s was troubled by soil exhaustion, insects, vermin and drought, and where efforts to increase output pushed up costs alarmingly. In 1691, in spite of these difficulties, sugar exports amounted to 9,190 tons, compared with Jamaica's 7,099.[11] War played its part in the decline of Barbados, though the problems already referred to were probably more important. In 1696 only 7,613 tons of sugar were sent to England and in 1697, the final year of the war, exports fell still further to 5,514 tons. Only after the war had ended did Barbados sugar exports improve to 15,587 tons. The scanty information on the progress of the sugar trade suggests that without adequate protection, commerce declined, though it is not clear whether the fall was due to losses to French privateers or because English merchants hesitated to risk their ships in the trade.

After 1697 there followed several years of peace. The pirate threat diminished after the royal offer of clemency in 1700, and sugar exports recovered. The renewal of war in 1702 rudely shattered this prosperity. The year was notable for the inglorious naval action off Santa Marta, in which Vice-Admiral Benbow fought a French squadron virtually single-handed. The gallant Benbow later died of his wounds, and two captains were subsequently court martialled and shot. The presence of the British force in the Caribbean helped to restrain French privateers to some degree and provided convoys for trade. Admiralty policy was once again to send a small squadron into the Caribbean each year and use it to escort merchant ships out and home. It did not prevent serious losses to English ships, and the merchants demanded more protection. Late in 1703 the Secretary of the Board of Trade and Plantations informed the Admiralty of merchants' requests for escorts. They were more elaborate than any yet provided.[12] Merchants trading to Barbados wanted two convoys each year, to return from the island at the beginning of May and the first of August. They specified the escort for the first convoy: two fourth rates, one fifth and one sixth. The merchants also wanted the convoys to return directly to England without sailing to the Leeward Islands and asked for a further two small frigates and a fourth rate to guard against Martinique privateers. Merchants trading to the Leeward Islands made a similar request: three warships to guard their trade and to return with the convoy after 60 days, and a fourth and two sixth rate ships to form a permanent guard. The Jamaican interest asked for even more ships: six warships to escort their convoy and ten or twelve more to protect the coast. When told that the Admiralty could not spare six escorts, the merchants and planters lowered their demands to four. These requests were totally unrealistic; they amounted in total to twenty-seven or twenty-nine warships and two small frigates. Even if they had been formed into two squadrons to guard Jamaica and the Leeward Islands, they would have amounted to twice the number the Admiralty had been prepared to send to the West Indies in the previous war. This large force was certainly justified by the value of sugar imports into England. In 1699–1701 the average annual value of these had amounted to £630,000.[13] It employed 7 per cent of English merchant tonnage and 11 per cent of English overseas trade in 1700.[14] Sugar was indeed the second most valuable import – linens occupied first place – but they formed a small part of the total of £5,849,000.

The trade had to be defended; the arrival in November of deputations from the Leeward Islands showed that opinion was being mobilized.[15] Meanwhile, reports began to arrive in London of privateers putting to sea from Martinique and Guadeloupe. A letter from Nevis in June 1703 reported eighteen and by 1704 there were apparently thirty, which had taken 163 prizes.[16] The Admiralty had no means of knowing how accurate these figures were, but they could not be ignored. Meanwhile, commerce continued to grow. In 1703 it was reported that the Jamaica convoy contained thirty-five ships, and it was claimed by merchants that an escort of two fourth rate ships was inadequate.[17] No doubt this was an example of the usual over cautious attitude displayed by merchants. The following year Sir William Matthew, Governor of the Leeward Islands, reported that about fifty ships would sail from there and 'a considerable number' from Barbados.[18] The Admiralty took steps to protect this trade. Vice-Admiral Whetstone, commander of the West Indies station, gave carefully worded orders to Captain Huntingdon before the latter sailed to England. The three escorts, *Dunkirk*, *Kingston* and *Greenwich* were to form a protective screen round the convoy and Captain Huntingdon was warned not to overpress the merchant ships by carrying too much sail 'they being deep and heavy ships'.[19]

It is small wonder that conscientious naval commanders took such care of Caribbean trade. Taken as a whole, it seems to have gone through a bad patch in the first decade of the eighteenth century, much as Jamaica had suffered in the last decade of the seventeenth.

Table 6.3 IMPORTS OF BROWN SUGAR INTO ENGLAND

(£000)	
1700	668
1701	599
1702	358
1703	565
1704	436
1705	—
1706	459
1707	533
1708	521
1709	546
1710	697
1711	505
1712	—
1713	700
1714	708

Source: Schumpeter, *English overseas trade*, p 48.

The value of imports of brown sugar fluctuated sharply from year to
year and the general impression is of a slump between 1702 and 1707
followed by a steady, unspectacular recovery – marred by poor
returns for 1711.

These figures, important as they are for an indication of Caribbean
trade, give no guide to the progress of individual islands. Customs
returns show that they did not always follow the trend already
indicated; local factors were more important.

Table 6.4 ENGLISH IMPORTS FROM THE CARIBBEAN

	Antigua	Barbados	(£000) Jamaica	Montserrat	Nevis	St Kitts
1700	88	366	238	42	44	44
1701	82	281	235	32	87	22
1702	91	114	149	32	74	15
1703	104	224	183	21	83	12
1704	66	137	184	24	74	5
1705	104	354	75	30	122	22
1706	30	303	162	13	17	12
1707	144	197	198	23	20	24
1708	71	252	214	12	25	20
1709	97	260	239	17	15	19
1710	172	230	214	25	96	44
1711	45	253	176	20	33	29
1712	96	196	254	28	46	30
1713	186	167	243	32	107	58
1714	131	307	274	15	64	52

Source: Whitworth, *Trade of Great Britain*, pp 47, 49, 57, 59, 61, 71.

These figures are not compatible with Mrs Schumpeter's. For one
thing, the Customs returns are for total imports from each island and
include indigo, logwood, cotton, and other items besides muscovado
sugar, which formed the bulk. These figures are also calculated from
an official table of rates and do not show market values. Nonetheless,
the Customs returns bring out two vital points: the dominance of two
islands, Jamaica and Barbados, and the enormous fluctuations in the
volume of trade at each. Protection of this commerce was extremely
difficult. Merchants had to sail from island to island to make up their
cargoes, for a glut or crop failure at one island was seldom if ever
general. Successful trading depended on inter-island commerce, with
all the attendant wartime risks. The Admiralty could not know how
large a convoy would return from the Caribbean or how valuable it
would be. Nor could the merchant community give any practical

advice. None could foresee accurately how large the sugar crop would be. Everyone connected with the trade hoped that good management of the plantations and the protection of shipping would produce a bumper crop and return large profits. Few plantations were successful; the exceptions were those managed by the owner or a close relation, and too many of these found an early grave through illness. Absentee landlords, for all their knowledge of plantation conditions, were poor advisors for the Admiralty in assessing yearly volume of trade.

There remained the merchants who sent out ships to the Caribbean. They at least provided a guide to the volume of trade – though not the value – for they knew approximately how many ships were sent. This proved a poor guide. Merchants were usually over anxious for the safety of their vessels and exaggerated the dangers from privateers. So too did colonial governors and agents, whose information was regularly passed to the Admiralty by the Board of Trade and Plantations. While the volume of trade remained fairly small by eighteenth century standards, it was generally possible to overcome these difficulties. It was no doubt annoying for the Admiralty that merchants trading to the Leeward Islands and Barbados refused to accept a single convoy for their return voyage, because Barbados sugar was ready for shipment later than that from the Leeward Islands. But while the English trade could be carried by thirty or forty ships it was generally possible to protect them with the small force available. Naval activity was usually limited to cruising off landfalls on the British islands in order to defend incoming trade and drive away French privateers. Occasionally warships were appointed to escort vessels trading with Spanish settlements. A request in December 1703 for convoys for provision ships from the northern colonies was apparently rejected.[20]

Until 1708 merchants seem to have been content with these arrangements. Early that year the avarice of Commodore Kerr raised an outcry in the House of Commons against the Admiralty's arrangements for convoy in the Caribbean. Kerr had demanded money from a merchant, Thomas Wood, in return for providing a convoy for three sloops sailing to the Spanish coast of South America.[21] Kerr was greedy and stupid. Demands for convoy money were politically sensitive – they had been firmly rejected in the seventeenth century – and his demand for £800 for the use of the fifth rate *Experiment* as an escort was exhorbitant and illegal. He made matters worse by demanding a share of £150 in the voyage, the money to be provided by Wood. Kerr was found guilty and cashiered. It was part of his duty to protect the trade between Jamaica, where he was commodore, and the Spanish colonies and he was not allowed to charge a fee. The trade was important and merchants and planters of Barbados and Jamaica had petitioned the Admiralty for protection for this trade in 1706 and 1707.[22]

This attack on Commodore Kerr in the House of Commons was the signal for other complaints to be raised about convoy arrangements. Another cause of merchants' anger was naval impressment. Disease – malaria, yellow fever, dysentery, dropsy, leprosy, yaws, hookworm and elephantiasis – killed and crippled scores of men, and losses from naval crews had to be made good if efficiency was to be maintained. On one occasion, in 1707, extra men were sent to the Caribbean.[23] Men were also impressed from merchant ships, a policy that was bitterly resented. It was often carried out in a high-handed manner, and merchants had to replace their losses by paying exhorbitant wages, encouraging naval desertion and even using French prisoners of war. Many times masters could not replace men lost in this way and had to set sail for England with weak crews. Such ships were sometimes lost at sea; the Florida Strait and the North Atlantic were especially perilous in autumn and early winter. To emphasize their point, merchants gave the House of Commons three examples of ships lost as the result of naval impressment in the Caribbean in 1704 and 1705: the *Roundburst Galley*, the *Somerset Frigate*, and the *Walthamstow Galley*.[24]

The Admiralty survived this attack on its convoy policy and during the rest of the war there were no more serious complaints. The Board provided convoys whenever possible for the three main sugar producing areas: Jamaica, the Leeward Islands and Barbados. Each merited special consideration and the annual convoys were still small enough to be protected by a single warship for their outward and return voyages. The method of convoy protection was simple and effective; dates were agreed for the return voyage before the convoys left Britain. When they had to be altered, merchants were informed in the Caribbean by customs officials, public notices and correspondence between merchants and planters. In Jamaica where there was a seasonal variation in the sugar crop – sugar ripened later in the north of the island – the convoy did not sail until late summer. Most of the sugar was carried from the plantation wharfs to Port Royal, and later to Kingston when that became the new administrative centre, by sugar droguers as the small coasters were called. At Port Royal and Kingston the sugar was transferred to the British and the colonial ships. Sugar from small, isolated plantations, especially in the north of the island, had to be collected by the ships that were to ship it overseas.

To suit the needs of all these ships – the Kingston and Port Royal trade and that which visited the north coast – Bluefields Bay was fixed as the assembly point for the returning convoy. It lay at the west of the island and ships wishing to join it were escorted there by frigates and small sloops from the naval squadron. When the convoy set sail, usually at the end of August, it generally steered a course through the Windward Passage. This provided a more easterly route than through the Florida Strait, and was generally quicker, though initially the convoy had to beat against the prevailing wind. It also took the convoy dangerously close to the French base at St Louis. Nonetheless, with a convoy of around twenty ships bound for Britain and a small number of colonial vessels that sought temporary protection the system worked well. It could not protect the slave ships that arrived and departed at different times from the main sugar fleet, but they were always better manned and armed and could beat off most privateers in the Caribbean. All these ships, sugar and slave alike, had to be clear of the Caribbean before the beginning of September when the hurricane season started. Those that did not faced serious risks and greatly increased rates for insurance.

To the east, the commerce of the Leeward Islands was concentrated at Antigua and Barbados, the main sugar producing islands. It was not convenient for merchant ships from St Kitts, Montserrat and Nevis to assemble at Antigua, for it lay to windward. Instead, ships gathered in Basseterre Road, St Kitts where there was adequate sea room and good holding ground. The ships could also be protected by naval vessels and shore batteries, and other ships patrolled the sea lanes between the islands to drive away privateers as the convoy was assembling. The organization of these convoys habitually raised difficulties. Barbados sugar was two months slower coming to market, because much of it was semi-processed by a method known as 'claying'. This whitened the sugar and raised its value. Muscovado from the rest of the Leeward Islands was ready for shipment by the end of July. Merchants were anxious to ship it to Britain as soon as possible in advance of the Jamaica convoy, which generally arrived later and whose sugar was always slightly more expensive on account of higher freight and insurance charges. This dispute led to wrangling between assemblies and naval authorities but as there were never enough escorts for an additional convoy, Barbados ships had to sail to Basseterre Road. When the convoy finally sailed from Barbados it had to run the gauntlet of the privateers from Martinique and

Guadeloupe. It was essential to weather these islands, for ships that passed to leeward were frequently becalmed and an easy prey for the small rowboat privateers that put off from the islands. When it proved difficult for the convoy to weather the islands, the ships stood off and on from them until the weather changed, as Captain Gordon was forced to do in 1707.[25]

In this way the commerce of the West Indian islands was successfully defended in the closing years of the war. In the years that followed the Peace of Utrecht the sugar output rose on every island except Barbados, where output was limited by soil exhaustion. Trade within the Caribbean also increased as merchants exploited the terms of the Asiento and traded extensively, and often illegally, with Spanish colonies. In the 1720s and 1730s relations between Britain and Spain became strained when Spanish authorities claimed that the Asiento was being abused. Logwood cutting in the Bay of Honduras was another source of friction. The coast was claimed by Spain, but the Spanish colonial authorities could not stop bands of British logwood cutters settling there. The wood was an important source of blue dye for the British woollen industry and merchants continued to ship it to Britain in spite of Spanish attempts to prevent the trade. Britain and Spain gradually drifted towards war as Spanish coastguards adopted a high-handed attitude towards Spanish goods they found on board British ships. War finally broke out in 1739 on the trumped up charge of Captain Jenkin's Ear. British merchants confidently expected to make enormous gains from the war, but the Admiralty was faced with many difficulties in protecting trade. It had increased greatly in value since 1713 and there were many more ships to protect.

Three sets of figures show how far the West Indies commerce had progressed: the total market value of British imports, the market value of imports of brown sugar and the Customs values of imports from each island.

Table 6.5 AVERAGE ANNUAL VALUES OF IMPORTS FROM THE WEST INDIES

	(£000)
1711–15	779
1736–40	1,326
1741–5	1,244
1746–50	1,344
1751–5	1,632
1756–60	1,937
1761–5	2,614

Source: Schumpeter, *English overseas trade*, p 18.

Table 6.6 ANNUAL VALUES OF IMPORTS OF BROWN SUGAR

	(£000)
1739	1,320
1740	981
1741	1,229
1742	1,014
1743	1,242
1744	1,115
1745	1,095
1746	1,098
1747	1,060
1748	1,435
1756	1,814
1757	755
1758	1,661
1759	1,814
1760	1,799
1761	2,126
1762	1,996
1763	2,422

Source: *ibid.*, pp 50–1.

Table 6.7 ENGLISH IMPORTS FROM THE CARIBBEAN

	Antigua	Barbados	(£000) Jamaica	Montserrat	Nevis	St Kitts
1739	292	198	706	39	68	263
1740	172	229	508	72	36	169
1741	204	298	581	55	56	210
1742	159	223	585	45	22	177
1743	217	259	580	66	56	226
1744	198	91	532	61	52	223
1745	189	166	358	49	49	213
1746	210	210	400	50	53	225
1747	99	132	522	31	23	134
1748	259	235	654	73	58	330
1756	256	222	806	70	69	242
1757	323	222	866	68	84	320
1758	327	221	897	68	71	241
1759	150	168	1,200	45	38	208
1760	159	224	1,034	76	46	292
1761	281	254	932	80	68	295
1762	249	255	853	57	42	246
1763	180	253	1,159	60	45	235

Source: Whitworth, *Trade of Great Britain*, pp 47–50, 57–62, 71–2.

These figures demonstrate above all the remarkable rise of Jamaica which increased its output of sugar by almost half between the outbreak of war in 1739 and the Peace of Paris in 1763. Even more striking is the fact that while Jamaica's output rose, that of the other islands remained almost static. Only tiny Montserrat increased its exports, while those of Antigua actually declined. When these figures are compared with returns for the first decade of the century the full magnitude of the change becomes clear. In 1714 Jamaica's exports were valued, at official Customs rates, at under £300,000. By 1739 they had risen to more than £700,000 and by the end of the Seven Years War stood at over £1,100,000. St Kitts presents another remarkable rise, though of a smaller magnitude, from under £60,000 in 1714 to more than £200,000 in 1763. Of the smaller islands, Antigua and Montserrat showed a modest gain, Barbados and Nevis declined. These figures give no more than the bare statistical outline to a remarkable economic change that was taking place in the Caribbean. It was also reflected in the increased power and prestige of the West Indies interest in Britain.

Early in the eighteenth century the group had been composed of comparatively minor figures, although there had been a consolidation of power on several islands and a plantation aristocracy had emerged. West Indies merchants and plantation owners living in London were summoned to give information on trade, and at times presented petitions and briefed members of parliament to present their views in the major commercial debates in the House. By the mid-century they, or at least the leaders of the interest, were easier to identify. They included such powerful figures as William Beckford, alderman of the City of London, West India merchant and plantation owner, William Baker, MP for Plympton and city alderman, Henry Lascelles of the West Indies firm of Lascelles and Maxwell, and Edward Manning, of the firm of Manning and Ord, who became a leader of the Mercantile or Kingston Party in the Jamaica Assembly, and ultimately Speaker. This was a powerful political group, linked by marriage and possessing in many cases large personal fortunes. No administration could afford to alienate it.

No doubt this was why trade between the Caribbean islands and the Spanish colonies was still encouraged during the war. For instance Admiral Vernon claimed he did not seize the merchants' treasure at Portobello in 1739 when he captured the town because he did not want to alienate commercial opinion there.[26] Commerce between the British and Spanish colonies was officially encouraged by Queen Anne's government; the Act forbidding trade with Spain only referred to Spain in Europe. In January 1740 Vernon was petitioned by the representatives of thirteen Kingston firms for convoys for this trade.[27] From the British point of view it was the ideal trade; it provided a good market for British goods which were probably cheaper than Spanish. Spanish merchants paid for the goods they bought in bullion which provided much of the coinage needed for commercial transactions in the West Indies, where there was a marked shortage of British currency. Spanish merchants also seem to have paid for the goods as they bought them – a great advantage to British merchants who usually sold on six or nine months credit. This does not mean that the trade was unrestricted. Vernon, while he was in the West Indies, expressly forbade the shipment of contraband and was able to regulate the commerce by the provision of convoys. It is significant that during the war of 1739–48 commerce between Jamaica and the Spanish colonies of Cuba and Cartagena continued to grow because it was protected, whereas trade between Barbados and the Spanish colonies fell because it was not defended. The warships which convoyed vessels to the South Keys of Cuba and Bastimientos near Cartagena tried to ensure that they did not carry contraband and the escort commander arrested any that he suspected of doing so. The commander-in-chief of the Jamaica squadron also benefited. Merchants saved a great deal of money in manning and arming their ships and the commanders-in-chief charged 5 per cent for this service. Although this practice was strictly forbidden by Admiralty instructions and was against tradition, it was hidden by the claim that it was a fee for carrying bullion – the proceeds of the trade – to Jamaica. The Admiralty considered the charge high for carrying freight, but the merchants seem to have accepted it until 1745 when the merchant Edward Manning quarrelled with Admiral Davers over whether Manning's sloops should be given a private convoy.

During this period there was some degree of co-operation between British, Dutch and French merchants in attacks on Spanish settlements. All three nations wanted to enlarge their share of Spanish trade. But in 1744 Anglo-French co-operation in this way stopped. Britain declared war on France, and planters and merchants on the French islands turned their attention to privateering. British trade was larger than it had been in the earlier wars and convoys contained more ships – as many as eighty in some cases. This put new strains on the naval protection of trade and one result was the introduction of a second convoy for Jamaica whose commerce had grown so much. Ships could now return to Britain either in May or in July or August.

This gave greater flexibility and benefited both merchants and planters.

The first sugar was generally ready for market in February. This came from southern plantations which were well sheltered from the cold northerly winds and had a good rainfall. Sugar from the north, which many considered better quality, came on the market a month later. It took planters many weeks to get their hogsheads of sugar, molasses and rum from the plantations to the coast. Rain sometimes made the island paths impassable and in 1745 and 1760 slave revolts seriously delayed the harvest. Merchants who took the first convoy knew that the first sugar to reach market fetched a good price; the most experienced took care to have their casks stowed on board last. The first to be unloaded always realized a higher price than the rest; the price fell steeply while the cargoes were being unloaded. On the other hand, the merchant who sent his sugar with the second convoy knew that it was probably of a higher quality and would realize a slightly better price. Sugar and its by-products dominated the Jamaican economy, and these were the considerations which regulated merchants' choice of convoy. In 1756 sugar, molasses and rum accounted for just over 82 per cent of Jamaican exports at Customs values. The proportion continued to rise in the next three years, reaching 88.5 per cent in 1759 and over 90 per cent in 1761, though this was due to a fall in the value of exports of pimento, logwood and other minor items. On the other hand, merchants valued these lesser imports for they could fill spaces in the hold with them. The most important was coffee, most of which was exported to European markets, for it carried a heavy duty in Britain and never challenged tea successfully. Other items included logwood, mahogany, cortex, lignum vitae and tortoiseshell from the hawk-billed turtles of the Grand Cayman Islands. Some ships carried Madeira wine, bought on the outward voyage and some West African products: gold dust, ivory and gum seneca – the by-products of the slave trade.

This growth of the Jamaica trade did not automatically raise the profits of planters and merchants. In fact, sugar prices had steadily fallen since the Peace of Utrecht, as demand failed to keep pace with production. The Molasses Act, designed to compel the northern colonies to purchase British sugar, had been largely unsuccessful.[28] From 1739 this downward trend was reversed. Profits rose, partly because more land was brought under cultivation, and also because from 1744 the French islands were unable to export all their sugar. Even under these more favourable conditions few merchants and planters made substantial profits. The concentration of sugar exports into two annual convoys depressed prices. The cost of provisions and dry goods for the plantation economy rose through increased freight and insurance charges. Some planters tried to avoid the worst effects of war by sending their sugar on 'runners' – well-armed ships sailing independently – often to outports such as Bristol and Liverpool that lay outside the area menaced by privateers. In this way they hoped to obtain higher prices for their sugar, for the cargoes reached port between or even before the convoys. There was in any case no obligation at this stage to sail in convoys.

Protection was given to these vessels in the Caribbean by an escort through the Windward Passage. Delays were common because of the prevailing contrary winds and to the north, coral reefs made the Crooked Island passage hazardous. To counter the risk from French and Spanish privateers, a sloop was normally sent as rear guard as far as latitude 23°N, after which it returned to Jamaica with the pilot. Once clear of the islands, merchant ships continued independently and escorts returned to Jamaica. These local convoys were especially useful for colonial shipping which faced few hazards for the rest of their voyage, and some naval vessels were almost continually employed in this way.[29] Most of the remaining ships left Jamaica with the second convoy in late summer. Delays were frequent, sometimes caused by merchants who could not get their ships ready in time, and sometimes by the navy. In 1757 Vice-Admiral Thomas Cotes was told that the winter rainfall had been heavier than usual and the crop would be delayed. It eventually sailed at the beginning of September in the hurricane season.[30] The harvest was again delayed in 1758 for the same reason, and in 1759 the threat of Bompar with a large squadron in the area prevented the convoy sailing and caused panic among the islanders, who feared invasion. Fortunately for Jamaica the attack failed to materialize. Sickness weakened the French fleet, and when it had sailed for France the second Jamaica convoy put to sea.

It would be wrong to assume that every ship left Jamaica before the hurricane season. Some stayed through the winter, either because they could not get a return cargo or because of a French naval threat which made it impossible for the commander-in-chief of the station to spare ships for a convoy. It was a serious risk for masters of merchant ships to take, as masters were often forced for reasons of economy to pay off their crews and could not be certain of obtaining another the following season. Disease, privateering and naval impressment claimed too many merchant sailors. There was also the serious hazard of storms and hurricanes, not because these struck the island every year but because of the enormous devastation they caused when they did. In October 1744 Jamaica was partially devastated by a storm that drove five of the naval warships ashore – only one was saved – and all the merchant ships. Contemporary records claim that at least seventy, many of them British vessels from outports, were lost in this way. Another naval vessel, awaiting repairs at Bluefields Bay, was also severely damaged.[31] Fortunately for Jamaica, such disasters were rare, but they emphasized the need for naval commanders to get the convoys away from the island before the hurricane season began in August.

As convoys increased in size it became more difficult to send them through the Windward Passage. The principal convoys had to sail through the slower and more hazardous route passing to the west of Cuba and enter the Atlantic via the Florida Straits. This was especially dangerous when convoys were delayed for they frequently met storms in the Straits and the North Atlantic. Under these circumstances, most merchants wisely insured their cargoes. London was the most popular centre for marine insurance, for rates were lower than in the Caribbean, and the market more stable. Planters and merchants accordingly sent copies of their bills of lading to consignees in London and the outports so that insurance could be arranged. This required that the bills should be sent about a fortnight before the convoy sailed, and the most suitable method was to send them on board a packet vessel or a neutral. Where neither of these was available, merchants and planters looked to the commander-in-chief of the station to provide a sloop. This placed an added burden on the squadron, for these vessels were needed for guarding shipping routes from privateers and scouting for signs of enemy activity. In 1761 Rear-Admiral Charles Holmes, commander of the Jamaica squadron, refused to supply a sloop. There followed an acrimonious debate in which Holmes refused to give way. He sent a full report to the Admiralty, for he knew that he would be bitterly attacked by the governor and legislature.[32] Ultimately the merchants and planters were forced to send their documents on board one of the convoy escorts. This was most unsatisfactory. It gave the consignee in Britain no time to arrange insurance. If the ship arrived safely with the convoy the consignee saved the insurance, but if it did not, he would only be able to arrange cover at an exhorbitant rate if at all. Under these circumstances, the only alternative was to arrange insurance in the West Indies, but this was more expensive and the underwriters less reliable.

The course which these convoys followed was only dangerous in wartime when the large size of the fleet made it difficult to control. There was not only the risk of collision but of running aground on one of the reefs that lay along the way. The first stage of the course, from Bluefield Bay to Cape Antonio, was relatively straightforward. Privateers were kept at bay by the extra sloops that accompanied the convoys as far as Cape Antonio. The prevailing wind and current carried the ships along at a good rate. Normally they passed well clear of the sand banks that formed the Grand Cayman Island, which were so low that '. . . four or five leagues off, it cannot be seen from a ship's quarter deck'.[33] The first hazard was the Island of Pinos east of Cape Antonio, where a northerly current set strongly against the reefs that surrounded the island. By keeping well clear of the Cape this was usually avoided and the convoy sailed on towards the Gulf Stream that carried the ships through the Florida Strait. This was the most dangerous part of the voyage, for no one in the convoy could navigate accurately and there were many sand banks and reefs to be passed. It was an age when masters of merchant ships had no means of measuring longitude, when attempts to compute the day's run by means of a log line were frequently inaccurate and when even experienced seamen mistook one Caribbean island for another.[34]

The escort commander had to get his convoy through the Strait as quickly as possible for in autumn the prevailing wind veered towards the north-east and east and drove ships towards the reefs bordering the Florida coast. To get his ships into the main part of the Gulf Stream after rounding Cape Antonio, an escort commander could either set a course for the Dry Tortugas or follow the Cuban coast as far as the Matanzas. The Dry Tortugas were a cluster of small, sandy reefs and cays that lay east of the Florida Keys, but they were low and barren and hard to identify, for tidal currents frequently changed their shape. From there the convoy followed the line of low coral reefs and islands which curved around the southern tip of Florida: a dangerous course, for the main current ran close to the reefs that formed these cays. Any change of wind drove vessels onto the reefs which all lay below the surface of the water.

The alternative route along the Cuban coast had fewer navigational hazards but was not used much during wars with Spain. Ships passed along the Cuban coast to seaward of the Coloradas, a chain of small islands on which ships were occasionally wrecked. When Britain and Spain were not at war, ships occasionally obtained provisions at settlements on the Cuban coast or put into Havana. When the two countries were at war. British crews stole what they needed from isolated plantations. From the Matanzas, the convoy sailed north east towards the Gulf of Florida. While sailing to the east to avoid the dangerous Florida Keys, the commander had also to avoid the Cay Sal and Great Bahama Banks, which lay at the south and east of the Strait. These were also ringed by coral reefs and seamen had to be particularly careful to avoid Cay Sal, on which the current set at high tide. The reefs at the eastern side of the Florida Strait did not lie in an unbroken line as they did to the west, though they were equally dangerous. The line was broken by two deep water channels in the south, the Santaren Channel from which a weak current flowed northward, and the North-West Providence Channel in the north. Escort commanders tried to steer a course through the middle of the Strait in daylight. Gales blew without warning from any direction between north-north-west and south-south-east and navigation was also hindered by strong land and sea breezes that could affect the whole width of the Strait. The passage of the Strait was further complicated by the action of many merchant captains who considered that they were safe once they had passed Havana and tried to sail ahead of the convoy to reach their market. Captain Hobbs had the unfortunate, and typical, experience in October 1758 of losing contact with ships on the Coloradas and off Havana and finding that the faster ships went ahead under a press of sails.[35] The bulk of the convoy was slowed by a lee current and he remained with them. When a south-south-east gale struck the convoy on 25 October he took the opportunity of sailing for the Florida Strait. To try and supervise the convoy he proceeded cautiously under double-reefed topsails. During the next few hours the wind increased and moved round to the south-west and Captain Hobbs was still in the Strait when night fell. Next morning he found that the convoy had split into two parts, only one of which was still in sight, a long way behind. These ships had disobeyed his earlier order to proceed through the Strait because they did not wish to attempt it at night when a south-east gale was blowing. Captain Hobbs sailed on to try and reach the rest of the convoy and left these behind. It was a hard decision to take, but his orders were to protect the greater part of the convoy and these were the ones that had drawn ahead during the night.

Within a day the convoy had passed through the Straits, but there remained other hazards: gales off the Carolina coast and Newfoundland Grand Banks, together with the risk of single privateers or warships returning to Spain and France. Captain Innes, sailing in 1761 with eighty ships, passed through the Florida Straits in sixteen days but was then delayed by storms for a fortnight. He lost seven ships from his convoy bound for Britain and three more were disabled. These made for South Carolina for repairs.[36] Occasionally naval vessels were disabled as well, and they later helped escort South Carolina convoys back to Britain after putting into Charleston for repairs. To prevent the loss of escorts and try to keep the convoy together under such difficult circumstances, escort commanders frequently employed large and better armed merchantmen as additional escorts. Captain Hobbs used no fewer than five in his voyage from Jamaica in 1758 and allocated them positions round the convoy to form a protective box. It was also a means of checking the faster vessels whose masters were tempted to sail ahead of the convoy, for these temporary escorts were placed under naval orders and discipline. Many were probably privateers. The front and rear of the convoy – the crucial positions if the convoy were attacked – were always filled by naval vessels. They helped to control the convoy if it encountered fog off the Grand Banks, for by firing guns intermittently the escort commander gave an audible signal of the course the ships should be taking. The greatest risk for an escort in these Atlantic crossings was of losing the convoy by chasing a suspected privateer. Such vessels were adept at leading escorts from their charges and doubling back to seize ships. It was a great temptation for an escort commander to try and catch such a vessel and win prize money, but the temptation had to be denied, and Admiralty instructions were very strict on such matters. Captain Faulkner lost his convoy of thirty-four ships in mid-Atlantic in this way in 1760 and the convoy of seventy which sailed from Jamaica in August 1757 under the protection of the *Humber*, 44, was first scattered in the Florida Straits and later dispersed in the Atlantic. The *Humber* finally reached Britain with only six ships.[37] This was no way to protect valuable convoys. Many of the vessels that became separated from their convoys in this way were taken by privateers in the Soundings or off the Irish coast as they made their landfall. Those that remained with their convoys were escorted in safety up the English Channel, to the Tuscar Rock or into the Bristol Channel. Local protection was also given by additional warships that were sent to patrol the approaches to the English Channel when convoys were expected. The allocation of these had to be arranged in advance, which was another reason why escort commanders were strongly ordered to keep to the sailing dates which had been agreed in England.

There remained one further problem. Many masters of merchant ships were strongly tempted to leave their convoy once they were in the English Channel. They knew that their cargo – including their personal venture – would fetch a better price if they reached port before the other ships and they would be covered by insurance if they were taken by a privateer. But when they were captured they gave warning that a convoy was approaching and jeopardized the safety of the other vessels. The Admiralty did all that it could to check this selfish behaviour – which often had the active support of merchants. In most cases it was powerless, as in the case of the *Ellis* privateer.[38] The *Ellis* broke away from a Jamaica convoy when it was approaching the English Channel. The escort commander, Captain Forrest, fired several warning shots but these were ignored. Normally this was the end of the matter, for the Admiralty could do no more than charge the owner of the vessel for the cost of powder and shot, but in this case the master was arrested. Possibly this was because his securities could be sued in the High Court of Admiralty, but it is also possible that the *Ellis* had been appointed a temporary escort and the master was arrested for disobeying orders of the convoy commander. It was in any case unusual and there is no means of knowing if the prosecution succeeded.

Convoys from the Leeward Islands faced similar difficulties though with an additional problem of collecting the trade for the voyage home. As in previous wars, the Admiralty refused to provide a separate convoy for Barbados trade, although the clayed sugar came to market later. During the war of 1739–48 the organization of these convoys continued in a similar manner to the earlier period. French Martinique and Guadeloupe privateers continued to harry British trade after 1744, and Antigua felt itself particularly threatened. There was bitter rivalry between the British islands, and a commander who failed to devote his whole resources to the defence of one was pilloried by others and accused of neglecting his duty. But between 1744 and 1748 there was no attempt to conquer any of the French islands, though there was a plan to seize the southern half of St Domingue to engross its trade.[39] In the Seven Years War the position changed. The British navy was so much stronger than the French that the Admiralty could consider the conquest of French islands.

Guadeloupe was captured in 1759 and Martinique three years later, at the second attempt. The reasons which lay behind this policy are interesting. The planters and merchants supported it because they were anxious to cripple their rivals: they believed that the French plantations were managed more efficiently and had a higher yield of sugar. They were unwilling to state this publicly, for that would encourage the opposition to claim that the war was being waged to suit narrow sectional interests. The administration and its supporters claimed that this policy of conquering the French islands prevented French attacks on British possessions in the Caribbean, brought benefit to the country through the import of French sugar and weakened France. The policy was justified; the weakness lay in its execution. Although the islands passed into British hands, the sugar was imported duty free, which drove down the price of British sugar, and the privateers were able to escape. Like pirates at the beginning of the century, they could use the small neutral islands as a base for their activities and the conquest of the French islands did little to check their activities. As a result, the burden of commerce defence became heavier as the war progressed. The conquest of Guadeloupe in 1759 added that island to the list requiring protection from privateers, who possessed the advantage of local knowledge. The commanders of the Leeward Islands squadron had to divide his force between convoys for the ships returning to Britain and cruising to protect the inter-island trade, and ships arriving independently from Britain and the northern colonies. He was hampered by the rivalry between islands under his command, each of which demanded protection and by the difficulty of deciding where cruisers should operate to protect incoming trade. Captain Middleton, later Lord Barham, initially criticized instructions that he should send his ships to cruise between 16° N and 19° N. At first, in December 1759, he claimed that the best method was to cruise between 16° N and 17° N, between these two lines of latitude.[40] He was also critical of the practice of sending cruisers back to Antigua to refit, a practice which he said wasted at least a fortnight. Within a few months, Middleton had modified his proposal and recommended that his ships sail between 16° N and 18° N and by the end of 1760 had extended the area as far as 18° 30′ N, which was close to the 19° N that he had earlier criticized.

There was a further difficulty which vexed the commodores. Privateers waited on lines of latitude to windward of the principal islands in the Leewards chain for merchant ships to arrive, and the navy attempted to counter this by sending cruisers to do the same. Unfortunately for the naval commanders, they found that the further the naval vessels cruised, the further the privateers moved to the east, and if the naval ships moved too far to the east, they left the immediate landfalls unprotected. This placed a heavy strain on the available forces, for they also had to provide local convoys for ships sailing from the islands, especially Barbados. Vessels also had to be posted to windward of French islands to intercept privateers returning with prize vessels.

The main function of the naval squadron, apart from expeditions against French islands, was the security of commerce. As the number of merchant ships increased, a more elaborate convoy system was developed to protect it. To begin with, Barbados ships were given some protection by ships which cruised between that island and Antigua. Gradually this was modified so that a naval vessel was sent to Barbados to escort the whole trade of the island to Antigua. The vessels assembled in Carlisle Bay, a spacious anchorage but with bad holding ground and sailed from there to English Harbour, calling off Guadeloupe, after its capture, to escort that island's trade as well. English Harbour was a most unsuitable assembly point for a large convoy. Though spacious and well-equipped – it was the main naval base in the Leeward Islands – it had a sand bar across the entrance, and heavily laden ships could not cross. To do so they had to be lightened, and this was clearly impossible for a convoy which by the Seven Years War at times numbered over 150.[41] In any case, ships which were lightened in this way became very leewardly, and in the face of adverse winds and currents sometimes took three weeks to cover the voyage from St John's Road in the north of the island, where guns or cargo were taken out, to English Harbour in the south. From Antigua the convoys sailed to St Kitts where they anchored safely in Basse Terre Road, a large bay on the leeward side of the island. Other ships from Nevis and Montserrat were brought here under naval escort, and in the final year of the war Martinique trade was integrated into this system as well. It is perhaps surprising that such an elaborate system was necessary to protect the Leeward Islands trade. The justification for it is the surprisingly large number of French privateers. In the War of Austrian Succession there were 2,500, according to the Marquis de Caylus, although in 1761 when the island was threatened by a British attack, the number had fallen to 1,200.[42] No other island had as many, for there was less trade and fewer sailors.

The convoys which were the target of these privateers generally left St Kitts in July. From that island they sailed north, passing to windward of the Dutch island of St Eustatius and finally left the Caribbean through the Anegada Passage between the island of Sombrero and the Virgin Islands. What is surprising is that there was no attempt to convoy the trade of Tortola, in the Virgin Islands, or of St Croix to the south, although additional protection was requested for them towards the end of the war. The reason for this neglect is that they lacked safe approaches and suitable anchorages for the large convoys and in any case lay outside the area usually threatened by privateers. In the final year of the war, it is possible that French privateers may have turned to these islands because the others were too well defended. The trade of these islands was in any case insignificant in comparison with that of the others: in 1758, for example, St Croix and Tortola exported goods valued, at the official rates, at £5,434 and £32,944 respectively. Antigua in the same year exported goods valued at £327,202.[43] What is remarkable about these islands is the proportion of their trade that was conducted with the outports rather than London.

Table 6.8 TRADE OF TORTOLA AND ST CROIX WITH OUTPORTS AND LONDON

| | From outports | | From London | |
	Tortola	St Croix	Tortola	St Croix
1758	32,944	5,434	nil	nil
1759	19,127	1,086	5,041	99
1760	25,980	nil	4,370	nil

Source: Customs 3/58, f 188, 3/59, ff 35, 152, 3/60, ff 34, 157

It appears that ships from Bristol, Liverpool and perhaps Glasgow, could sail independently because there was little risk from privateers in home waters or the Caribbean in this period. London merchants, on the other hand, realized that their ships were given little protection. The dominance of the outports in this minor Caribbean market emphasizes the importance of convoys for the London merchants, while showing how outport merchants were able to thrive by exploiting new opportunities for profitable trade.

Ships returning to Britain from the Leeward Islands generally made a faster crossing than from Jamaica, for they started further to the east, and were able to avoid the storms off the Carolina coast and the Grand Banks. Those ships returning independently to the outports relied on naval cruisers to keep the landfall of Tory Island off County Donegal free from privateers, for they generally made for there before entering the Irish Sea through the North Channel. The convoys set their course for the English Channel, and where necessary called off Cork for additional protection when French squadrons were known to be at sea. When war ended in 1763, Britain had demonstrated her naval supremacy by capturing the two chief French possessions in the Caribbean and Dominica, a neutral island that had been occupied by French colonists. In the Treaty of Paris, Britain's Caribbean gains were considerable. Although she restored Guadeloupe and Martinique to France – British merchants did not want French sugar to continue to pour into the British market – Britain gained Grenada, St Vincent, Dominica and Tobago. From Spain she gained certain rights of logwood cutting in the Bay of Honduras and Florida. Between the end of the Seven Years War and the outbreak of hostilities in America there was a further rise in the value of British trade and of West Indies trade in particular. The smaller islands gained from the French in 1763 were brought into the British commercial empire and made their contribution to this growing prosperity. Commerce also increased between British Caribbean islands and the American colonies. Indeed, the British planters came to rely even more heavily on supplies of American provisions, horses and lumber. By 1775 the two markets were closely linked, and the prosperity of many northern ports was based on West Indies sugar, rum, molasses – both British and French – and bills of credit to pay their British debts. The War of American Independence hit this trade hard, and imports of sugar fell sharply.

Table 6.9 IMPORTS OF SUGAR

	(000 lbs)
1775	1,940
1776	1,670
1777	1,336
1778	1,477
1779	1,442
1780	1,319
1781	1,027
1782	1,317
1783	1,499

Source: Schumpeter, *English overseas trade*, p 62.

Table 6.10 AVERAGE ANNUAL VALUES OF IMPORTS FROM THE WEST INDIES

	(£000)
1771–5	3,138
1776–80	2,751
1781–5	2,911

Source: *ibid.*, p 17.

There are two reasons for this decline in sugar imports: losses of British ships to American privateers, and the effect of intensive naval activity in the Caribbean from 1778. Early in the war between Britain and her rebellious colonies, the Continental Congress issued letters of marque to American privateers and large numbers were rapidly fitted out and put to sea. They quickly ranged along the length of the American coast and penetrated the Caribbean. One advantage that they enjoyed was that they were manned by young, eager and experienced seamen who had sailed in these waters and knew the focal points of trade. They knew exactly where to cruise to intercept British shipping, and were able to use French ports to dispose of their prizes and replenish their stores as other privateers were doing in mainland France. They could even increase their profits by combining privateering with trade, for there was a ready market for northern provisions in the French colonies, and many colonial traders were already familiar with the French markets.

The Admiralty found it exceedingly difficult to cope with this problem. There were so many privateers that the small naval resources could not cover every landfall and trade route. Furthermore, by 1775 there were more British islands to protect than in 1763; the Treaty of Paris had granted St Vincent, Grenada, Dominica and Tobago to the British crown. To make matters worse, most of these islands were in the Windward group, further south than the more traditional possessions of St Kitts, Antigua, Nevis and Montserrat, and to windward of Barbados. To try and protect all these islands under the special geographical conditions of the Caribbean strained the Admiralty resources to the limit. Commodores had somehow to overcome climatic conditions and shortage of naval vessels, for the navy was as usual unprepared for this conflict. Some attempt was made to combine the American and West Indies stations, so that vessels from the south could winter in the north, but Britain lacked adequate repair facilities in the colonies except at Halifax and New York, and these were too far from the Caribbean to contribute much to its defence. Sir Peter Parker, commodore of the Jamaica squadron, put the matter succinctly: 'The extent of this station and the various services expected from the King's ships are well known to their Lordships, and require perhaps more vessels than can conveniently be spared from England.'[44]

He proposed to buy sloops and other vessels to cruise against privateers, and suggested that one should be stationed in the Bay of Honduras – to protect the logwood cutters, who had been granted rights in 1763 – one at Turks Island, one in the River Mississippi and another armed vessel on Lakes Maurepas and Pontchartrain. He had already stationed one sloop, *Hornet* at Turks Island on the Moskito Shore and it also cruised for four weeks at a time at St George's Key besides acting as escort for ships passing through the Gulf of Florida. The principal difficulty that remained was that prolonged cruising made these vessels foul, and Parker warmly applauded the Admiralty scheme of sheathing some frigates with copper. Although the technical difficulties of fastening the thin copper sheets to the hull had not yet been overcome, a fact he did not appreciate, such vessels would have been useful in keeping the Caribbean clear of American sloops, schooners and other fast sailing craft.

The West Indies were of crucial importance to the French as well as the British and the Caribbean was the scene of a number of important naval actions. The French received around 30 per cent of their imports from this area and sent about 35 per cent of their exports to these colonies.[45] The first action of the Anglo-French conflict was in September 1778, when the Marquis de Bouillé took Dominica, a well fortified but weakly garrisoned British colony. More important strategically was Barrington's capture of St Lucia the following year, for the island lay to windward of the principal French naval base at Fort Royal, Martinique and could watch the movement of French shipping. Barrington's attack on the island and defence of his transports and squadron against the superior fleet of the Comte d'Estaing was masterly. After landing his troops, Barrington anchored his warships across the mouth of the harbour and successfully held off d'Estaing's attacks. Although d'Estaing later landed 7,000 troops, these too were unsuccessful in their attempts to dislodge the British. Possession of St Lucia was to prove of considerable value later in the war.

Barrington's success had been the more remarkable in view of his smaller squadron. This inferiority of numbers remained a problem in 1779 and it had one unforseen result. The strategic and commercial needs were bound to conflict, and although the British fleet had been strengthened by a force under Byron it remained smaller than the French. When it was necessary to convoy the Leeward Islands trade clear of the threat from d'Estaing, Byron had to strengthen the escort to the detriment of the more general defence of the Leeward Islands. D'Estaing seized the opportunity and took St Vincent on the 18 June. He followed this with an attack on Grenada on 2 July using his main fleet; he seized thirty merchant ships in the harbour and laid siege to the small British garrison of 125 regular soldiers and under 400 militia. Byron sailed to the island's defence as soon as he heard the news and attacked d'Estaing's squadron without waiting to organize his ships into line of battle. In the resultant melee some British ships were damaged and Byron withdrew to St Kitts to repair the damage.

D'Estaing continued his siege and the garrison capitulated on 6 July, an action that led to bitter resentment at what was considered Byron's 'abandoning' of the garrison, which put up a brave defence against overwhelming odds.

Shortly afterwards Admiral Sir George Rodney was appointed to command the West Indies squadrons. A testy and unsympathetic man, his first attempt to bring the French to battle, on 17 April 1780, failed because his subordinates did not appreciate that he wanted to mass his squadron against the French rear. His subsequent vindictive attack on his subordinates was unjust; he had failed to explain to them what he intended to do, and the signalling system was of little use in explaining unusual manoeuvres. He received a further setback when his squadron was badly damaged in a storm while returning to the Caribbean after wintering in North America. He found the Windward Islands had been devastated by a hurricane; over 6,000 people were killed in Barbados, plantations had been destroyed and the guard ships that he had left had been badly damaged. More important from the point of view of the safety of the islands, the stock of naval stores had been badly damaged as well, and he lacked the means of refitting his ships. However, in February 1781 news reached Rodney that Britain had declared war on Holland and he sailed to St Eustatius and took it without a fight. The harbour was filled with merchandize valued at £3 million. The booty made Rodney and his subordinates rich; it also checked the smuggling trade that had flourished through this hitherto neutral port – a commerce that many of the inhabitants of St Kitts had taken part in. More important strategically was the ending of the trade with French islands in naval stores, which was of considerable importance to the French – de Guichen's squadron had been refitted with Dutch stores after the action of 17 April.

The immediate result of the capture of St Eustatius was that Rodney stayed at the island and missed the chance of intercepting a large French convoy sailing to Martinique and subsequent bad health kept him inactive while the Comte de Grasse seized Tobago. Rodney returned to Britain to recover his health. The rest of 1781 saw no significant changes in the balance of power in the Caribbean though Rear-Admiral Sir Samuel Hood made a masterly defence of his squadron at St Kitts. He failed to save the island however, and it capitulated to the French, who also took Nevis and Montserrat. St Eustatius had already fallen, so too had Tobago, though St Lucia had withstood an attack by the Marquis de Bouillé early in May. Thus 1781 was an inauspicious year for Britain in the Caribbean, and news from North America was even worse, since Yorktown fell the same year. Rodney's victory of The Saints on 12 April recovered Britain's prestige to a large extent, for after some days of manoeuvring he managed to bring de Grasse to a battle which proved to be decisive. The deciding feature of the battle was the breaking of the French line in three places; this allowed Rodney to concentrate his forces in superior numbers against sections of the French line and bring his carronades into effective use. These mortar-like guns wrought considerable damage on the hulls and rigging of the French ships and were the means of disabling and destroying most of the French squadron. The outcome of the battle was that although Rodney, exhausted by the effort, was unable to conduct the general chase that Hood desired, the French Caribbean fleet was largely destroyed. De Grasse was unable to attack Jamaica as he had planned and the West Indies campaign was effectively at an end. Peace was signed the following year.

The War of American Independence had severely damaged the economy of the British islands. Many had been captured by the French during the course of the war, and even those which had escaped had suffered from a shortage of provisions and steeply rising costs which had brought many planters close to bankruptcy. The supply of North American provisions had been cut, American privateers, operating from French as well as American ports, had taken many prizes from the inter-island trade. St Kitts merchants were forced to trade at St Eustatius to obtain provisions to feed themselves and their slaves as well as the hoops and oak staves which traditionally came from North America and without which the sugar crop could not be exported. The cost of sending their sugar, molasses and rum to Britain rose: insurance and freight charges were high; insurance had increased 20 per cent in 1776 and the risk from American and, from 1778, French privateers kept rates higher thereafter. The general shortage of provisions – corn prices rose 400 per cent during the war – meant that many planters could not afford to buy adequate supplies to feed all their slaves and many died of starvation. The war impoverished the British islands and made it essential after 1783 to reopen the traditional commerce in provisions and lumber, as well as the market for molasses, with North America.

After considerable debate, commerce was reopened with the independent United States through the free port system, which was revised and enlarged in 1787 and 1792 to allow small American vessels to participate in British Caribbean trade.[46] This helped to aid the recovery of the British islands, and exports from Britain increased as the purchasing power of the planters rose.

Table 6.11 BRITISH TRADE WITH JAMAICA

| | (£000) | |
	Imports	Exports
1783	2,892	1,792
1784	3,405	1,370
1785	4,354	1,236
1786	3,443	1,336
1787	3,783	1,733
1788	4,088	1,766
1789	3,906	1,764
1790	3,891	1,986

Source: B. R. Mitchell and P. Deane, *Abstract of British historical statistics* (Cambridge 1971), p 311.

When war once again broke out with France in 1793, Britain was well prepared. Naval administration had been extensively overhauled by Admiral Sir Richard Middleton and large stocks of naval stores were held in the dockyards. The Spanish crisis of 1790 had demonstrated that the navy could be quickly brought into commission, and the numerically small forces in distant waters – the West Indies had only three 50s and five frigates – could be rapidly reinforced when war broke out. The wars with Revolutionary and Napoleonic France witnessed a further increase in the quantities of sugar and other commodities imported from the Caribbean and a rise in the value of exports to the islands *(see table p. 202)*.

There was no serious threat to the British islands during these wars, except in 1795 when Grenada, Dominica and St Vincent were held by rebels sympathetic to the French, and in 1805 when Missiessy raided the Leeward Islands. The Maroon War of 1795 in Jamaica between blacks and whites caused considerable alarm and serious dislocation of the island's economy until it finished in March 1796 with the total surrender of the remaining Maroons.

The naval campaign opened with a successful assault on Tobago, which was taken after a day's fighting on 15 April 1793. On the 16 June a force was landed on Martinique in response to royalist requests, but those who came forward to help the British force proved of little value and the force was re-embarked when it became clear that the defences were too strong to be stormed with the available forces. Another attempt was made on St Domingue, again in response to royalist requests. The landing, in September 1793, was unapposed and to begin with the troops made good progress. Eventually they were defeated by yellow fever and the excellent generalship of the mulatto general, André Rigaud, who commanded

Table 6.12 BRITISH TRADE WITH THE WEST INDIES

| | (£000) | |
	Imports	Exports
1793	4,392	2,695
1794	4,783	3,633
1795	4,099	2,461
1796	3,967	3,223
1797	4,309	3,144
1798	5,419	5,198
1799	6,162	5,947
1800	7,369	4,087
1801	8,436	4,386
1802	8,351	3,926
1803	6,132	2,380
1804	7,682	4,282
1805	6,720	3,832
1806	8,815	4,734
1807	7,980	4,579
1808	8,778	5,929
1809	7,703	5,975
1810	8,258	4,790
1811	8,452	4,123
1812	7,487	4,767
1813	N/A	N/A
1814	8,497	6,315
1815	8,527	6,916

Source: *ibid.*

French troops in the south of the island. The five years' occupation of the island cost the British at least 20,000 dead from disease; the 96th Regiment was totally destroyed.[47] In 1798 the island was evacuated and quickly overrun by the negro general Toussaint l'Ouverture. In the Lesser Antilles the British had more success. In February 1794 Martinique was captured after a brief campaign; in April St Lucia was taken, as were the Saintes and Guadeloupe, the latter capitulating on 21 April. However a French force under the command of Victor Hugues recaptured Guadeloupe in June and St Lucia was retaken, its small garrison weakened by fever, in June 1795 – a serious loss to Britain in view of its strategic importance. Fighting took place also in the other islands where discontent was fomented by revolutionary propaganda and French planters, but no others were lost.

The most serious problem was the defence of the returning trade. From the outbreak of the war all ships were again encouraged to sail in convoy – it became a legal requirement in the Compulsory Convoy Act of 1798 – and large numbers of ships sailed to and from the Caribbean each year. Hundreds of ships sailed from London alone –

many more than from Liverpool, Bristol and the other outports, though their trade was also considerable. The huge size of these convoys offered opportunities to French privateers to attack the inter-island trade and the returning convoys. Privateer brigs and schooners operated from French and, after 1796, Spanish ports in large numbers. French ships regularly patrolled the difficult passage of the Florida Straits, where convoys traditionally became separated while trying to adjust their speed to the fast flowing currents, navigational hazards and the ever-present risk of gales. The worst year for British trade, both in the Caribbean and European waters, was in 1797, and a correspondingly large naval force was assembled to meet this threat, consisting largely of frigates and sloops. By 1800 this force consisted of six warships, a 50-gun ship, forty-five frigates and forty-three sloops based at Port Royal and English Harbour, Antigua. These kept losses within acceptable limits, and there was no serious criticism of the Admiralty's organization of commerce defence in this war.

However, planters again had to face higher wartime costs and although their exports of sugar, cotton, wool and coffee increased during the war, many found that their incomes were declining. The soil was also becoming exhausted and required increasing quantities of fertilizer and a larger labour force to maintain profits at anywhere near their peacetime level. It was not clear until much later that this trend was irreversible and that the Caribbean plantations were declining. The fortunes of planters and merchants sank further in the Napoleonic wars. Outwardly there was considerable prosperity; there were bumper crops of sugar and the trade was not seriously disrupted. But from 1806 the market was seriously depressed. Napoleon's conquest of much of Europe closed many of the markets that had earlier remained open, and the price of sugar fell from 72 shillings per hundredweight in June 1798 to 38 shillings in December 1806.[48] To make matters worse, the French were able to bring home much of their sugar in neutral ships at lower cost and there was not even an incentive to smuggle the surplus across the Channel.

Nonetheless, the commerce of the West Indies islands had to be defended. French raiding squadrons occasionally sailed across the Atlantic; in February 1806 Admiral Sir John Duckworth destroyed Admiral Lesseigues' off St Domingue. Later the same year another French squadron commanded by Admiral Jean-Baptiste-Philibert Willaumez captured vessels at Montserrat and Nevis and chased others near St Kitts. A large convoy of 280 ships was anchored off Tortola but was protected by a squadron under the command of Sir

Alexander Cochrane. The British navy was supreme in the Caribbean, and naval activities from the time of Trafalgar were limited to seizing the islands used as privateer bases. Deseada and Marie Galante were taken in 1808, Cayenne was captured by a combined Anglo-Portuguese force in 1809; Martinique fell to British arms the same year. By 1810 all European colonies in the West Indies, except those belonging to Spain which was in alliance with Britain, were in British hands.

There were few other events of importance until 1812, when the American Congress declared war on Britain in June, the result of friction from commercial restrictions and the searching of American ships for deserters. The result was the renewed presence of American privateers in the Caribbean. In 1813 there were so many that they almost blockaded the Jamaican coast and some settlements were burnt in revenge for the burning of part of Washington by British troops. In the closing stages of this war with France and America the convoy system was developed to an unprecedented level of complexity and efficiency. In the case of the West Indies trade, there was provision for convoys to be sent monthly when required and every effort was made to restrict losses. It is small wonder that in the final years of the war, 1810–14, Britain's imports from the Caribbean and her exports thence were at an unprecedented level.

Nonetheless, the West Indian sugar plantations had begun a decline from which they never recovered, and one feature of the period 1688–1815 is that it includes the greater part of the golden age of sugar production. At the beginning of the period the planters were emerging from a period of dependence on British merchants. Labour was imported in the form of indentured servants and the islands' population was growing slowly. Tobacco was still an important cash crop. By the end of the period the leading planters were rich men, often compared to nabobs and able to influence government policy. Much government revenue came from the Caribbean trade and it was essential to protect it from naval and privateer attack. It is worth noting that the Admiralty succeeded, against considerable odds. The islands were scattered over a large area; the prevailing winds prevented those naval forces to windward from giving help to the Leeward and Windward chain, privateers were fitted out in large numbers and cruised off many of the islands. The conflict between the material interests of colonists who made money from smuggling and the need to keep trade within strictly controlled limits frequently embittered relations between colonial legislatures and commodores. Against all these odds, and the occasional risk of a larger French squadron overpowering British forces, it was possible for successive Boards of Admiralty to devise a system of commerce defence which largely checked privateering, held the naval forces at bay and occasionally inflicted serious damage to them, and controlled the movement of British merchant ships in order to give them protection. That the colonial economy declined after 1800 is no fault of the Admiralty; rather the reverse, since the crisis was partly caused by over-production of sugar and the success of the Admiralty in escorting it to a market in Britain. External competition in the production of sugar and cotton and decline in soil fertility ultimately caused the downfall of the Caribbean.

7

East Indies

BRITISH OVERSEAS TRADE in this period can be divided into two parts. The first consists of the geographical areas that have already been discussed: Europe, the Mediterranean, North America and the West Indies. The other contains India, China, the Persian Gulf, the Red Sea and Sumatra. In the eighteenth century the two sections presented sharp contrasts in the content and nature of their trade. The colonial markets of America and the Caribbean supplied tobacco, sugar and a variety of other raw materials to mass markets in Britain and the continent of Europe. These overseas colonies were also to a large extent captive markets for British manufactured goods. The East Indies trade differed from this in almost every respect. Britain possessed no colonies in the East Indies in this period and experienced many difficulties selling the traditional British exports, which were often unsuitable for eastern markets. On the other hand, only one of the commodities imported into Britain by the East India Company stimulated mass consumption – Bohea tea, a coarse and relatively inexpensive leaf. One other item was of strategic importance – saltpetre, an essential ingredient for the manufacture of gunpowder.

The bulk of the trade of the East India Company was in luxury goods for the British and continental wealthy and leisured classes. Indian cotton goods, finely woven and gaily coloured, had no rival in Britain before the mass production of the factory age. Porcelain, shipped from China in bulk and used as ballast, attracted buyers for its quality and design and together with Chinese lacquer work strongly influenced British design and craftsmanship. Coffee, another important import, never attracted a mass market in Britain, unlike tea, and pepper, cloves and cinnamon and a variety of spices were imported for a tiny market. Consumption was small on account of

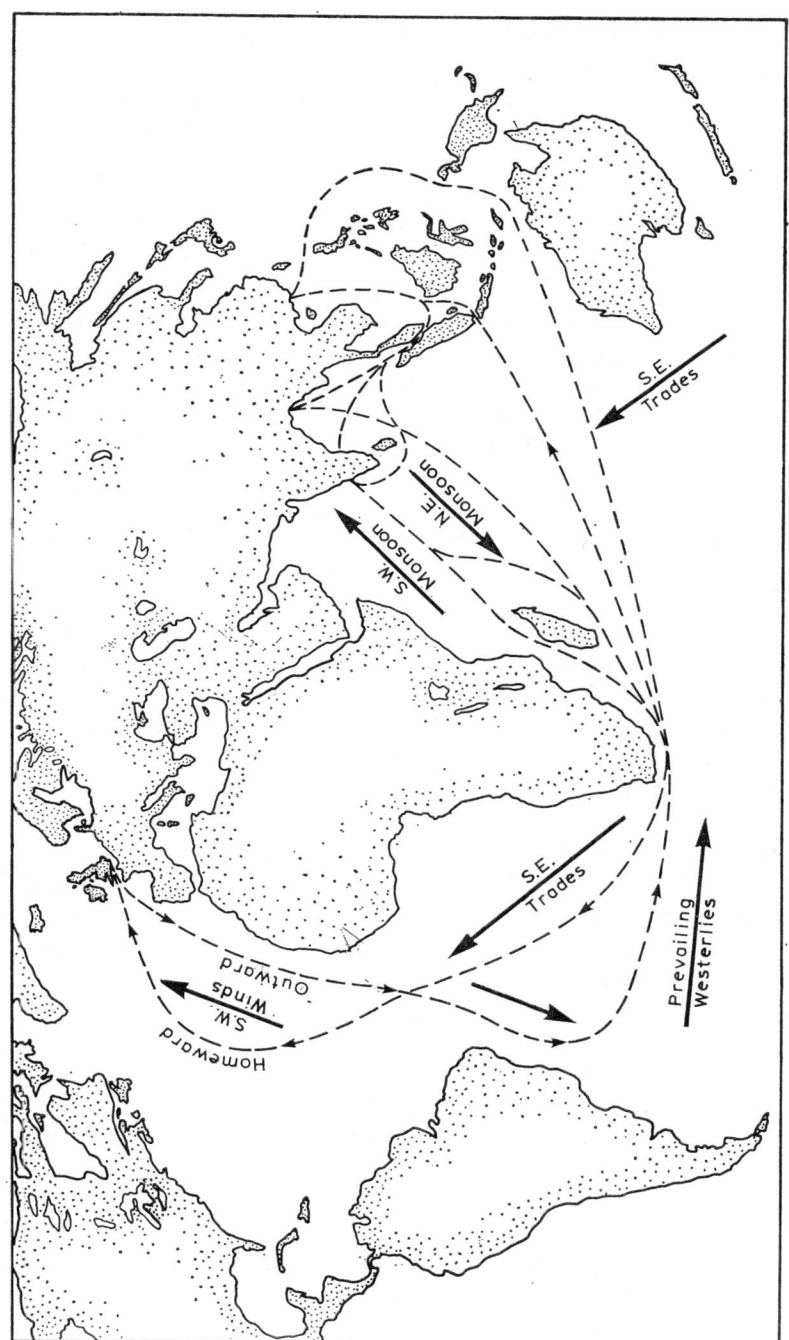

12 East India trade

the high cost, and also because their use was confined to a more sophisticated minority.

Controlling this important British trade was a small group of merchants, the elite of the commercial aristocracy, who possessed large fortunes and were highly respected in British society. The company which they controlled, the East India Company, reached its zenith by the mid-eighteenth century. Thereafter it gradually lost its function as a trading company as large numbers of young men entered the company's service to try and make their fortune and emulate Clive and other nabobs. Gradually the duty of administration of the company's lands was assumed by government. As will be seen however, the value of its trade remained high, and indeed steadily increased. This made it essential that the company's ships should be given the fullest protection of the navy in waters where privateers and warships were expected.

This brief outline however is no more than the historians' comment on the growth of the company and its ultimate decline. At the beginning of the period under review, the company faced serious difficulties. From its foundation in 1660 by royal charter, the company had co-operated closely with the Stuart kings and had won a privileged commercial position. In 1688 this almost proved the company's undoing. The Glorious Revolution discredited the company as well as the Stuarts and in 1698 parliament authorized the foundation of a rival company. The eastern trade demanded large capital resources and strong nerves. Merchants who contributed wealth to the costs of this trade could expect slower returns on their investment than in other sections of British commerce. The risks were high; each ship carried a large and expensive cargo. The sums needed for constructing and fitting out these large, specialized vessels were beyond the means of all but a small minority of merchants. By the end of the seventeenth century this had changed. There were other wealthy men eager to participate. They too possessed the resources and commercial acumen needed and at least some of these began to trade on their own account. The Revolution of 1688 gave them the opportunity to challenge the company's monopoly.

Thus by 1698 there were two companies, the older with a royal charter, the new with a parliamentary one. This was unsatisfactory for all concerned. It increased the competition in Britain for suitable trade goods and bullion, as well as risk capital, and in India there was greater rivalry for commodities to bring back to London. This specialized trade, with its small market, high costs and substantial risks could not stand too much competition. There was in any case

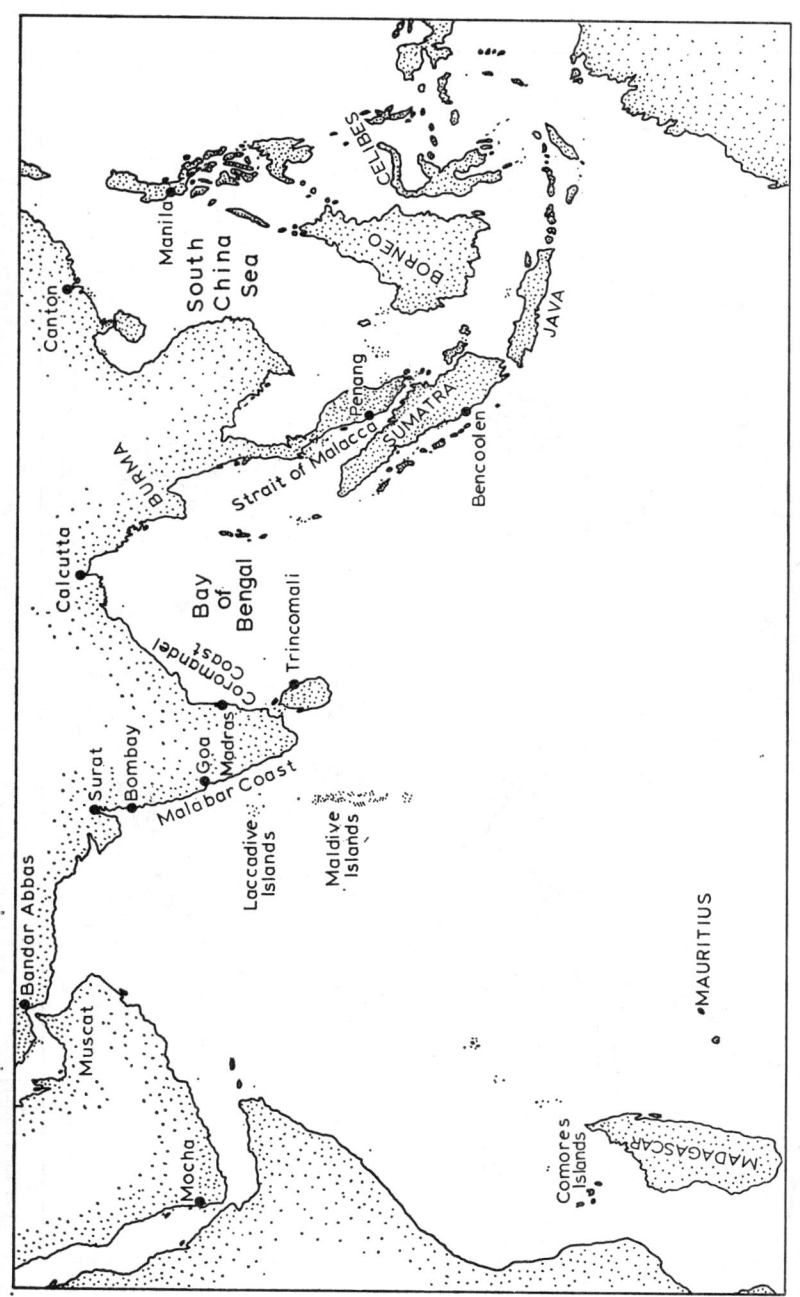

13 East India ports

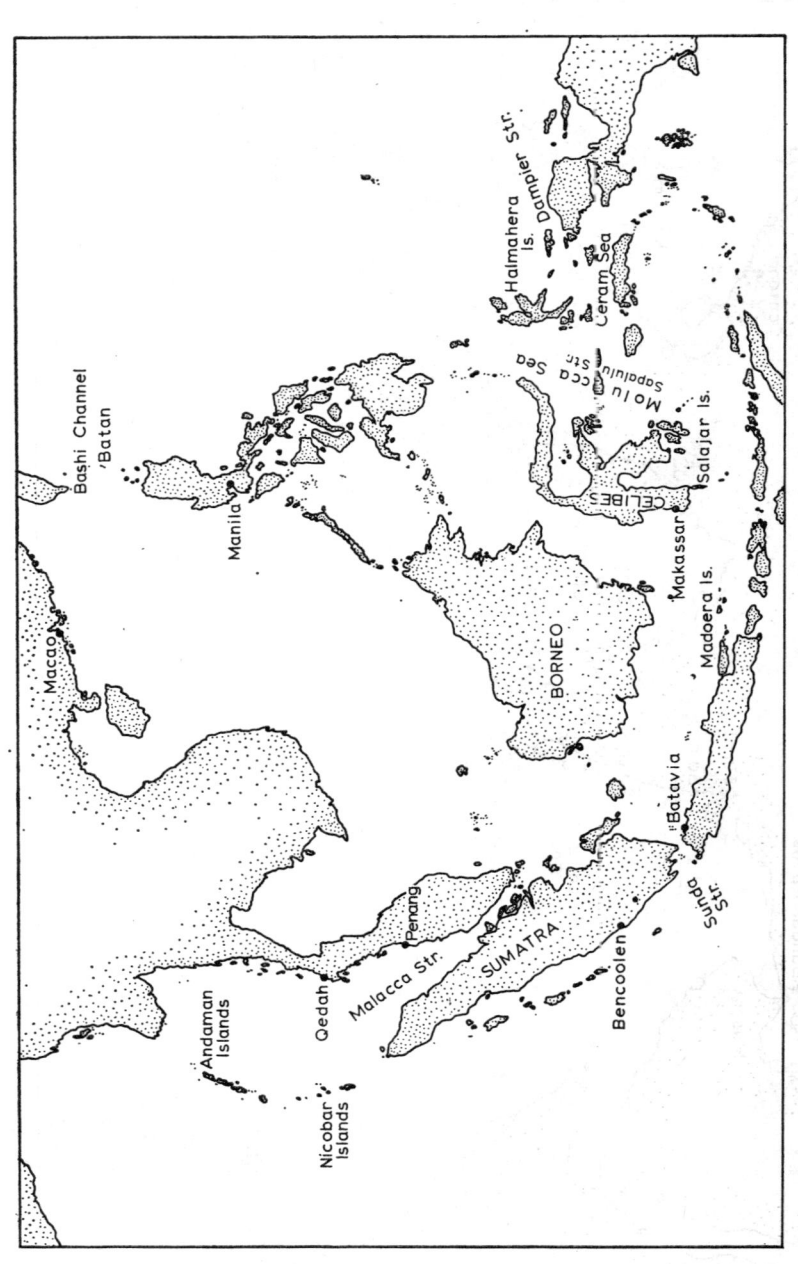

14   Far East India ports

rivalry between the English merchants and others: the Portuguese government sent ships to India, and so too did four or five European companies. The main rivals were the Dutch Vereenigde Oost Indische Compagnie established in 1616 and the French Compagnie française des Indes orientales, created by Colbert in 1664, although the Dutch concentrated their efforts in the spice islands. Against these rivals the English merchants had to form a united front. In 1709 they finally settled their differences and a new United Company of Merchants trading to the East Indies was formed, though they had to make considerable loans to parliament to regain the privileges of the older company. This left the new company with little trading capital.

From 1709 the new company slowly gained strength. It was organized on the same lines as the old. Power was in the hands of a group of twenty-four directors, elected annually by the shareholders. The day to day business was in the hands of a number of committees, each concerned with an aspect of the company's organization and to a certain extent overlapping in responsibility. These committees hired the ships and men to form their crews, they purchased the bullion and trade goods and warehoused and finally sold the goods imported on the company's account. Originally the company had owned the ships it used, but that practice had died out by the end of the seventeenth century. In place of this was the practice of hiring the ships that were required. This may originally have been intended to stimulate competition between owners and keep the company's costs down. In practice competition between owners steadily declined. Each ship was specially built for the trade and was unsuitable for any other. The owners of such ships had to preserve their patronage. The disadvantage was that it created a privileged group of owners who kept up rates by collusion and resisted any attempt by outsiders to share in the trade. The company came to accept that rates for charter should be high to compensate for years when the ship was out of service, and gradually this led owners to build more ships than the trade required. It was almost impossible for the company to check this practice, because many of the directors were also owners or part owners of ships, and as a compromise it was agreed that new ships should only be built 'on the bottoms' of old, that is as old vessels were scrapped. This at least checked the increase. In the same way the post of captain came to be regarded as personal property, to be bought, sold or passed on without consideration for the company's interests. These two aspects of commercial activity demonstrate how the interests of the company were being disregarded by the mid-eighteenth century. The widespread misuse of company authority after 1763 for private gain falls into a tradition that was already well established.

The acquisition of territorial rights after 1763 placed a heavy burden on the company whose servants were totally unfitted for the task of administration. Moreover, the opportunities for private enrichment drew a crowd of men who proceeded to fleece the native population and engage in large-scale private trade. The company saw no benefit from this, and although the level of imports steadily rose, so too did the flood of money remitted to London. This put a strain on the company's finances, for they were usually remitted in the form of bills that had to be met out of the proceeds of the annual sales. This also decreased the amount of money available to pay the large dividends that shareholders had become accustomed to. The crisis came in 1772 when the company found that it could not pay the dividend of 12½ per cent that it had promised. It tried to delay payment, but was forced to turn to the government. Help was given unwillingly, on the understanding that dividends should be limited in future and accounts submitted regularly to the Treasury. It was a stopgap measure and failed to halt the decline. In 1773 the Regulating Act showed that the government understood the real cause of the problem and was trying to check administrative malpractice by instituting government control. Pitt's India Act of 1784 marked the final stage of eighteenth century government activity by appointing a Board of Control – a committee of the Privy Council – with power to approve and if necessary amend the directors' despatches to India. From there it was a short step to the assumption of responsibility for administration of Indian territory through the appointment of a Governor General.

The maladministration was well hidden by the rise in the company's trade which in the eighteenth century was phenomenal. According to official Customs returns the value of imports rose from £787,731 in 1700 to £1,104,180 in 1750 and £1,933,096 in 1773, the year of the Regulating Act[1]. When the crisis struck, the company appeared to be enjoying an unprecedented boom, for which a dividend of 12½ per cent was justified. Appearances were, as noted already, deceptive. In addition to the payment of bills from India, the real value of commodities imported by the company had declined and the revenue from the company's annual sales was less than the Customs returns indicated. It was a poor guide on which the government might guide its strategy. The increasing flood of tea, coffee and other goods had lowered their value in European markets, and the opening of the trade after 1813 released a further flood on to the market. This trend may be seen from a comparison between figures used by Professor Davis in his study of English trade, which are calculated from the Customs returns, and those of Mrs Schumpeter which are based on market values.

Table 7.1 IMPORTS INTO ENGLAND FROM THE EAST INDIES. ANNUAL AVERAGE VALUES

| | (£000) | | |
	Customs returns	Professor Davis	Mrs Schumpeter
1699–1701		756	
1701–5	551		551
1721–5			936
1722–4		966	
1751–5			1,121
1752–4		1,086	
1771–5			1,753
1772–4		1,920	

Note: The Customs returns for 1701–5 have been added because Professor Davis' 1699–1701 figures are not directly comparable.
Source: Whitworth, *Trade of Great Britain*, p 9; Davis, 'English overseas trade 1701–1744', table facing p 118; Schumpeter, *English overseas trade*, p 18.

The reverse trend is to be seen in the company's exports, where the real value of commodities increased:

Table 7.2 EXPORTS FROM ENGLAND TO THE EAST INDIES. AVERAGE ANNUAL VALUES

| | (£000) | | |
	Customs returns	Professor Davis	Mrs Schumpeter
1699–1701		136	
1701–5	113		113
1721–5			113
1722–4	112		
1751–5			787
1752–4		748	
1771–5			912
1772–4		780	

Source: Whitworth, *Trade of Great Britain*, p 9; Davis, 'English overseas trade', table facing p 119; Schumpeter, *English overseas trade*, p 17.

In attempting to assess the impact of war on the company's trade, a choice must be made between the two sets of figures. Mrs Schumpeter's figures are useful for assessing the values of trade, but for year by year fluctuations it is necessary to turn to the Customs returns until 1773, where the figures are based on a set of book values. The disadvantage is that for only about the first fifty years do the two sets of figures correspond closely in real values. The tables shown below cover the years when Britain and France were at war:

Table 7.3 IMPORTS AND EXPORTS BETWEEN ENGLAND AND THE EAST INDIES

| | (£000) | |
	Imports	Exports
1697	263	67
1698	356	451
1702	247	87
1703	596	135
1704	758	564
1705	391	27
1706	647	27
1707	356	56
1708	493	61
1709	327	168
1710	248	126
1711	637	152
1712	457	142
1713	953	94
1714	1,046	77
1744	743	476
1745	973	293
1746	647	894
1747	822	346
1748	1,098	306
1756	796	489
1757	1,112	845
1758	222	922
1759	974	665
1760	1,786	1,162
1761	841	846
1762	973	1,067
1763	1,059	887

Source: Whitworth, *Trade of Great Britain*, pp 9, 10.

From 1773, as values shown in the Customs returns and the real values continue to diverge, it is better to use the figures for average annual values of imports and exports calculated by Mrs Schumpeter.

Table 7.4 IMPORTS AND EXPORTS BETWEEN ENGLAND AND WALES AND THE EAST INDIES. AVERAGE ANNUAL VALUES

| | (£000) | |
	Imports	Exports
1776–80	1,303	906
1781–5	2,030	930
1791–5	4,024	2,544
1795–1800	4,834	2,211

Source: Schumpeter, *English overseas trade*, pp 17, 18.

A comparison of the above tables shows that in general imports were lower in war than in peace. This is to be expected. It also shows that there were considerable fluctuations from year to year and not, as in other trades, a fall in the first years of the war followed by a gradual recovery. This may be explained in a number of ways. In the first place, the variation was caused by differences in the crops of tea, coffee, silk and other commodities. Imports were also slightly affected by privateer and pirate activity at the focal points of trade, which will be discussed later in this chapter. Nor was there any direct relationship between import and export figures as in other trades, where ships made a single voyage each year. In the East India commerce, vessels took varying times to reach and return from their markets in India, China and elsewhere. One year's exports were reflected in the imports of three or four years later. Nonetheless the value of these figures is that they reflect the current financial position of the company, and it was on these figures – real values and not those of the Customs returns – that the company fixed its annual dividend. War therefore played a small part in that.

More important as a means of assessing the impact of war on the company were the figures for the number of ships hired each year and the freight rates that were charged. The following table shows how these progressed in the period to the company's crisis. In the case of freight charges, rates for 'fine' goods – silks, calicoes, indigo, drugs and spices – were higher than for 'gross' or 'gruff' goods that were cheap in relation to the cost – saltpetre, sugar, pepper and tumeric *(see table p. 216.)*

The evidence of the table suggests that the company was affected less by the war of William III than other trades. In spite of privateering and the formidable *guerre de course* from 1695 the East India Company continued to send its richly laden ships to sea. Of the fifty-six chartered between 1689 and 1697, the company lost only eight – a creditable performance in view of the serious losses in other trades. In successive wars the numbers steadily rose as trade increased. By the end of the period the company was hiring over forty ships a year, of which over thirty were large vessels of 800 tons and more. Records of charter are to some extent misleading. At no time did the company hire complete vessels. For the first seventy years of the eighteenth century it hired 499 tons, made up of 404 tons of cargo at the rate agreed in the charter party, 80 tons of ballast or kintledge at a low rate, and 150 tons for the company officers. Before 1773 many ships may have been constructed at around this tonnage, but in that year the ships were measured and their tonnage published in Hardy's

Table 7.5 HIRE OF SHIPS AND FREIGHT RATES, 1689–1772

	Number of ships	China		Malabar Coast and Bay of Bengal		Bombay and Surat	
		g	f	g	f	g	f
1689	2						
1690	3						
1691	9						
1692	5						
1693	8						
1694	7						
1695	9						
1696	4						
1697	9						
1698	14						
1702	12			30	30	30	30
1703	13			33	36	33	36
1704	17			33½	36	33½	36
1705	9			31	35	32	34
1706	9			30	33		
1707	15			31	36	33	34
1708	10			30½	37	34	33½
1709	12			30½	37	34	33½
1710	15			30½	37	34	33½
1711	12			30½	37	34	33½
1712	8			24	29½	26	27
1713	11			22	27¼	24¼	25
1714	9			21	26	23	24
1744	16			32	37	34	35
1745	22			32	37	34	35
1746	24			32	37	34	35
1747	24			32	37	34	35
1748	14			26	31	28	29
1756	20			31½	34	34½	37
1757	21			33	36	36	39
1758	24			34	37	37	40
1759	22			35	38	38	41
1760	21			37	40	40	43
1761	22			37	40	40	43
1762	23			37	40	40	43
1763	28	31	34	31	34	34	37

Source: India Office Library, Marine Misc., 504A, pp 24–129; Davis, *Rise of English shipping industry*, pp 262–3.

Register. At that point many of the ships weighed between 850 and 1000 tons. Thereafter the tonnage of East Indiamen was increased; after the War of American Independence it was appreciated that a larger ship could defend itself better than a smaller. In 1786 the

Nottingham of 1,152 tons, was launched, and this marked a new stage in the construction of big ships. Yet it carried a crew of only 104 men, hardly more than an 800-ton ship, and a cargo of 1,570 tons of tea.[2] This proved the potential improvement in reducing shipping costs; by 1810 thirty-four ships of 1,200 tons had been constructed and were in regular use. This was important in wartime, for not only were the larger ships capable of a determined defence against privateers and even warships, but they could also fight in a line with naval frigates. On occasion they were even mistaken for naval frigates.[3] The added security which the construction of large vessels gave to this trade meant that freight rates fluctuated less than in other trades. Between 1702 and 1777 rates did not fluctuate more than £19 per ton between peace and war on any route – lower than in many other trades.

The first stage in the annual cycle was the hiring of ships by the Committee of Shipping. This took place in August, and the Committee maintained the pretence that freight rates were kept down by competition between owners who wanted to have their ships hired. Each submitted a sealed bid, but as there was seldom any difference between bids, it was clear that the owners consulted each other to decide the annual rate. However, owners made good profits from their ships and occasionally an outsider tried to break into the charmed circle. In 1756 all except the owners of the *Fox* submitted bids for £32 and £35 per ton for a voyage to 'Coast and Bay' – India and the settlements in Sumatra. The *Fox* was tendered at £31 and £34.[4] This started a battle between the owners, who were caught by surprise. The other owners petitioned the Court of Directors to have the bid rejected, and were successful. A week later discussions were reopened; the matter was clearly not finished. The owners of another vessel, the *Prince Edward*, took fright and tendered her at £31.10s and £34.10s, and the bid was accepted on 25 August. The *Fox* was finally chartered on 1 September on the condition that her master satisfied the Committee of Shipping of his ability as a seaman. It was a face saving compromise.

After the elaborate charter party had been signed the company assumed full responsibility for the vessel. The first task was to procure the cargo that might be sold at the ports for which the ship was destined. Throughout the period the company experienced great difficulty selling British manufactured goods in Indian and Asian markets. British woollen goods and the variety of commodities known collectively as 'dry goods' – furniture, kitchen ware, clothing, iron nails and the like – could not easily be sold outside European and colonial markets. Much was unsuitable on account of the climate, and British manufacturers paid no attention to the possible requirements of these markets. Canton merchants were scornful of most British goods and the Parsees, Persians and others either could not afford them or had no need of them. The company was forced to export British manufactures and metals however – by its charter it was bound to export British manufactures worth at least one-tenth of its trading capital in any one year – and supplemented these with large quantities of silver which was readily accepted in every market. Not all the silver required was taken from Britain; much of it was acquired from Manila.[5] The company bought its silver for export from Portuguese and Spanish merchants; at times Dutch merchants offered silver but were politely and firmly rejected. In any case, the company did not export more silver than it had to; mercantilist theories firmly rejected the notion of exporting bullion – the nation's wealth – and in most cases the bullion requirement could be met from eastern sources. In any case, most of it originated from one area, the Peruvian silver mines, and the company did not need to buy it when it could be obtained easily in the east.

While the company was obtaining cargo for the outward bound ships, agents were hiring seamen. East Indiamen were throughout the period the largest merchant ships afloat and their requirements for experienced seamen were prodigious. Under normal circumstances the company had little difficulty recruiting suitable men. Many were attracted by the opportunity for a little private trade, some were obtained by crimps and entered the service unwillingly, but the voyages though long held no more hazards than the Caribbean trade and was far healthier than the African. In wartime recruitment became more difficult. There was more recourse to crimps, and the company sent agents to the outports – especially Scotland – and even to the continent. During the Seven Years War the company's agents actively recruited men in Bremen, Lübeck and Hamburg, a most suitable choice because ships sailed from there to Canton and there were seamen in the ports with experience of the trade. Language does not seem to have presented any difficulty and the practice was probably repeated in other wars. During these wars, especially when the fleet was being fitted out in the early stages, press gangs roamed the streets of dockside London seizing every able-bodied man. Under such conditions the protection from impressment issued by the Admiralty was ignored. Only apprentices could be released, since their impressment was illegal. It was of course only during war that the company was able to employ large numbers of foreign seamen. During peace the Navigation Act strictly limited the number of foreign seamen employed in British ships, but in war the regulations were relaxed.

Loading the ships for their long voyages presented many difficulties that were not easily overcome. Many Indiamen were loaded in the Thames at Deptford from lighters, barges, billyboys and other small craft, but this had many disadvantages; vessels were damaged in the general press of shipping in the Thames and stores and cargo pilfered. Some used the Howland Wet Dock at Rotherhithe which offered more security, but it was small. It was important mainly as a pioneering work in dock construction, completed in 1709, and served as a model for docks in Liverpool and elsewhere. The problem of overcrowding in the Thames became steadily worse as the century progressed. Although at the beginning of the period the company only sent about a dozen ships a year, by the middle of the century this had increased to between twenty and thirty and by the end of the century there were perhaps fifty, including extra vessels hired by the company in addition to the usual chartered ships. This was reflected in the rise of other trades as well and the Thames became crowded with vessels in the spring and summer. The practice of organizing trades into convoys only made the situation worse, for it concentrated shipping activity into a comparatively short period. So serious had this congestion become by the end of the century that the East India Dock Company was formed to construct new docks. These were opened in 1806 and did much to ease the congestion and provide security. They also reduced the cost of loading and unloading the Indiamen, though not as much as the directors had intended.

When the ships were almost ready to sail, the East India Company's Secretary wrote to the Admiralty requesting a convoy for their passage through the English Channel and Soundings. This was for security – the ships were never obliged by law to sail in convoy. The ships did not all sail together, but left the Thames between mid-October and the following May. The first ships were those destined for Canton and the company's settlements in Sumatra. In mid-November they were followed by the vessels for Madras and Calcutta, some of which subsequently went on to China, and they were followed in December by ships for Bombay and China and for Bombay and Calcutta. The majority left the Thames before the end of the year, though there remained a few which sailed in the late winter. All had to be away by May or the company would be faced with additional demurrage charges. This order of sailing was related to the pattern of winds in the seas they were sailing to. In the Indian Ocean and South China Sea the South-West Monsoon blew steadily from May to September. Ships destined for Canton had to reach the latter sea by early to mid-summer to make their passage, until an alternative route was discovered in 1759 through the Celebes. Ships for the Coromandel Coast had to sail next to make their passage and leave the coast again before the monsoon changed in September, a period of storms and heavy weather. Finally, Indiamen destined for Bombay could sail later. They gained the South-West Monsoon in the Indian Ocean, but because the harbour of Bombay was sheltered from the monsoon, they could continue there later in the year.

These were the factors which governed the time when the Indiamen set sail. After completing their lading they slipped down river to Gravesend to take the first passengers and recruits on board for the company's service in India. At the beginning of the period there were comparatively few, some writers for Fort St George, Bombay or Calcutta, a number of factors for Canton or Bencoolen and perhaps a few soldiers for the small military force kept at the company's Indian factories. By the mid-century the number had increased slightly, but after Clive's success there were many more. Most of these joined the ship at Gravesend; the most important came on board in the Downs; so too did the regular soldiers, for in war the government used Indiamen as troop transports. The navy also searched the ship for deserters. In the month that the ship stayed at Gravesend there was considerable activity as the passengers and their luggage were taken on board, stowed, and arrangements made for providing cabin accommodation. The captain was seldom seen during this period. He was too important to participate in the arguments over precedent among the more distinguished passengers or to get involved in the squabbles of the rest. These were the responsibility of the chief mate and the captain only came on board permanently when the ship was almost ready to sail.

The month was also used for checking provisions and stocks of water and beer. Substantial quantities were carried of both: at least 40 tons of water – a hundred if soldiers were carried – 28 tons of beer, barrels of salt beef and pork and biscuit, additional stores for the petty officers and finally a quantity of livestock. The company allowed a generous provision of food for the officers and petty officers: the chief mate had 24 dozen bottles of wine, beer or other form of liquor, two firkins of butter, a hundredweight of cheese, another of groceries, four quarter cases of pickles and usually a puncheon of rum. [6] In the last few days before the ship left Gravesend the livestock were brought on board: poultry, cows and sheep were penned on the poop and in the waist of the ship, and by the end of the eighteenth century it was customary to carry at least one milch cow as well. These were not for general consumption. Only the captain and his chief passengers enjoyed them as a change from the dull standard fare. Nor were they regarded as a means of warding off scurvy – a major problem on the long voyages. It was not until 1795 that the company experimented with the use of lime juice as an anti-scorbutic on the *Suffolk*, and the results were so impressive that thereafter lime juice was regularly carried on board Indiamen and formed part of the stores loaded on board in the Thames or at Gravesend.[7]

When the final cask, bag and passenger had been taken on board, the Indiamen sailed down to the Hope, at the mouth of the Thames. Here the captain ensured that the cargo was properly stored and put the crew and passengers through gunnery drill. This was particularly important in wartime, but the fear of piracy made this essential even when there was peace in Europe. The company's instructions were specific on the action the captain should take: 'You are there [at the Hope] to stow away your goods and put your ship in the best posture of defence by quartering your men, getting your guns all in order and shotted, and your small arms in readiness, that you may be ready to defend your ship against an open attack or a surprize'.[8] It is hard to tell whether these instructions were fully carried out. At times the cargo and baggage interfered with gunnery practice, although it was usually only on the return voyage, when the ship was heavily laden, that the guns could not be worked satisfactorily.

It was a heavy responsibility for the captains of escorts to defend those ships against privateers in the English Channel and Soundings. The Indiamen were all specially built for the trade, mostly at a few yards on the Thames. They were the largest merchantmen afloat and their cost was prodigious. The *Grantham*, 567 tons, was built and fitted out for £12,000 in the early 1740s; by 1793 the cost of construction alone amounted to £11,200 for an 800-ton vessel, and continued to rise thereafter. Besides the initial cost of building and fitting out, the cargo carried by the larger vessels was valued at anything from £20,000 to £60,000, In exceptional cases the value might be even higher: the *Duke of Richmond* carried goods valued at £80,967 in 1760. To defend these ships the company usually insisted on an escort of at least a 40-gun ship, which would join the Indiaman at the Nore or in the Downs, see them down the English Channel and for the first 100 or 150 leagues of their voyage. The best defence was when the Indiamen joined a convoy for the West Indies or North America and sailed with that until past the island of Madeira. Occasionally, Indiamen were able to sail to India with a naval squadron, as in 1754 when Rear-Admiral Watson was appointed to the Indian station, or in 1760 when Captain Kempenfelt was sent with two frigates and half a dozen transports to Madras. The disadvantage was that the naval squadrons often had to go to Kinsale to take provisions on board. This took time, and the roadstead gave little protection to the assembled fleet. Indiamen caught and damaged by a rising storm had to go to the nearest naval yard for repair, for no merchant yard had masts or spars to fit such large vessels. Fortunately for the company this seldom happened, for in extreme cases it could mean that a ship could miss her passage or not have enough time to load a full cargo before returning to Britain.

There were advantages for the Indiaman who sailed under naval escort. Naval vessels, especially those destined for India and other distant waters, carried some naval stores and could offer assistance in any emergency. Captain James Dale of the Indiaman *Falmouth* had reason to be grateful for the presence of the *Colchester* in 1757. The latter formed part of the squadron of Admiral Stevens; when the *Falmouth* damaged her bowsprit and part of her rigging in an Atlantic storm she received replacements and a carpenters crew of eight men to help carry out the repairs.[9] This ensured that the vessel was seaworthy and could be properly manoeuvred – a great asset if the Indiamen met hostile forces.

The company ships which were only escorted through the English Channel and Soundings followed a southerly course which took them within sight of the coast of Galicia. Their first port of call was Funchal on Madeira, which they generally reached in seven or eight days sailing when they had favourable winds. There was no harbour at Funchal and the ships had to lie in an unprotected roadstead, which they had to leave if the wind rose. Nonetheless, the island had many attractions. It gave the passengers the chance to stretch their legs and drink the island's wine. Captains sent their water casks on shore to be replenished and arranged for fresh vegetables to be bought. They also bought, through the company's agent, casks of Madeira wine for shipment to India, where it became popular with company officials towards the mid-eighteenth century. Many captains, especially after 1750, shipped extra casks to take back to Britain, for it became a fashionable drink and benefited from the extra time in cask. This indirect method of importing wine into Britain reflected the way in which the taste was acquired there, as officials returning from India at the end of their service with the company brought it back with them.

A further benefit from the stay at Madeira was the opportunity it gave to captains to check their progress. Eighteenth century methods of navigation were notoriously inaccurate, for before 1755 there were no means of measuring longitude at sea with any precision. The East India Company put considerable stress on accurate navigation, and in the first half of the eighteenth century company officers used the log line for estimating elapsed distance and the octant for calculating latitude. After this two methods became available for calculating longitude. In 1755 Tobias Mayer completed his tables for forecasting the motions of the moon and demonstrated that it was possible by estimating lunar distance methods to calculate Greenwich time. Significantly, it was tested in 1761 by Nevil Maskelyne on a voyage to St Helena.[10] The other method of calculating longitude was through the use of an accurate timekeeper, and Harrison's first chronometer demonstrated the possibilities of its use on a voyage to Lisbon and back in 1736. Both methods were improved and used by the East India Company as they became available. By about 1790 the company issued its ships with new log books and included spaces for the daily noon recording of three longitudes, by estimate, by lunar and by chronometer. The arrival of Indiamen at Madeira provided the captain with the opportunity of checking the methods he was using.

As the ship left Madeira, they sometimes sighted French and Spanish privateers cruising south of the island. These were waiting for stragglers from the West India and North American convoys and were not prepared to attack the Indiamen, which carried a crew of around a hundred and were pierced for over thirty guns. The captain shaped a course for the Canary Islands, where ships met the full force of the prevailing trade winds blowing almost directly from the east.[11] From there vessels steered for the Cape Verde Islands, which provided wood and water for any that had been prevented by stress of weather from calling at Madeira. Many Indiamen kept clear of these islands, especially in wartime, for they were used by ships of all nationalities. Commodore Johnstone was caught there by the Bailli de Suffren in 1781, and only saved because Suffren was not supported by his captains. Most Indiamen accordingly passed to the east of the group and made a sighting of St Anthony.

Once past the Cape Verde Islands the captain of an Indiaman had the choice of following the trade wind or steering directly for the coast of Brazil. The first guaranteed good progress, but might take him too far to the west, and most captains compromised. They passed more slowly through the variable winds and crossed the Equator between 18° and 23° W. Sometimes the 'Neptune's rites' were performed but not invariably, for at times they could result in much brutality when relations between the crew and passengers and soldiers had become strained by the monotony of the voyage. In one extreme case the Bombay court fined a captain of the *Scaleby Castle* 400 rupees for the rough treatment of a passenger.[12] More sensible was the decision not to hold the ceremony which in any case had not become traditional by the beginning of the nineteenth century.

It was vital that outward-bound Indiamen should be warned if French vessels were cruising in the same area. Ships passing at sea always exchanged information, but in the South Atlantic most vessels followed the same course along the east coast of South America and few ships met. Fortunately for the company, the small island of Fernando Noronha lay in the track of outward bound and returning vessels. Captains made a point of calling there with information on enemy shipping, to replenish water and check their position. Its value was incalculable, for it was the one point at which the outward and return passages crossed, and where accurate, up-to-date information could be exchanged. From there vessels continued down the coast, occasionally calling at one of the rich tobacco or sugar ports – Bahia, Santiago or Rio de Janeiro – for provisions. This was the point at which most captains began to be concerned about the health of their crews. Many began to show symptoms of scurvy because of the diet of salt pork and beef, and before the introduction of lime juice at the end of the eighteenth century captains were tempted to call at Rio de Janeiro for fresh vegetables. In wartime this was risky, for French vessels put in to these ports as well. The popularity of Rio prompted the Comte d'Estaing to plan its seizure in 1763 and in May 1800 the *Exeter* Indiaman sent the French frigate *Medée* there as prize.[13]

The captain was obliged to press on for the Cape of Good Hope or Madagascar with all speed to avoid losing too many men from scurvy. However he needed considerable experience to do so. There was no lack of nautical guides for sailing in these seas, but they seldom told the whole story and were occasionally inaccurate. Experience counted for a great deal. The captain's object was to get his ship into the South-East Trade Wind as quickly as possible, and he did this in latitude 30° or 40° S. But, as Captain Hall pointed out:

> An experienced sailor, on first entering the south-east Trade, is very apt to be too solicitous about making southing; whereas rather he ought to keep his ship off a little, give her a fathom or two of the fore and main sheets, and take a smart pull of the weather topsail and top-gallant braces, to ensure making good way through the water. Indeed, many officers go so far as to recommend flanking across the south-east Trade

with a fore-top-mast studding-sail set. . . . In this respect, it may be remarked, that the scale of navigation on every Indian voyage is so great, and the importance of getting into those parallels where favourable breezes are certain to be met with, of much more consequence than the gain of mere distance, that two or three hundred miles to the right or left, or even twice that space, is often not to be regarded. Accordingly, in cutting or flanking across the south-east Trade wind, the object, it should be remembered, is not to shorten the distance, but to reach those latitudes where strong westerly gales are to be met with, by help of which five hundred or a thousand miles of lost distance are speedily made up, and the rest of the voyage secured.[14]

This was sound advice, but not all the ships sailed from the South American coast together. Occasionally Indiamen would be escorted into the South Atlantic by a warship bound for St Helena to escort the trade home. These steered a different course, closer to the African coast. At times they reached the trade winds in 10° S. The majority of Indiamen were bound for the Cape of Good Hope to take on provisions or fix their position from the Aghulas Bank. Little was known for most of the period about this current which set westward on the bank, but by the end of the eighteenth century Indiamen either approached the Cape on the latitude on which it lay or from the south-east after making faster progress in the stronger and sometimes stormy winds in latitude 40° S, the Roaring Forties. The Cape was an excellent port of call, except during the Anglo-Dutch war of 1781–3 or when French ships were known to be cruising off it. The climate was mild, fresh vegetables, meat, fruit and excellent wine were all readily available and sailors sick from scurvy recovered quickly. It was the best point at which to refresh crews and passengers, many of whom enjoyed the neat appearance of the colony and the beautiful gardens established by Ryk Tulbagh in the 1750s and 1760s. Those who rode or took a carriage to Table Mountain were less impressed by the primitive Hottentots, the slaves and the household drudges, who, according to William Dampier, stank abominably. A visit to the Cape was a normal part of the leisurely voyage to the east. It was the half-way house of those great sweeps across the Atlantic and Indian Oceans and was not always pacific. Sometimes vessels were struck by storms at the Cape and reminded of its earlier name 'Cape of Storms'. Many preferred to anchor in False Bay to the east, which was protected and had better holding ground.

From the Cape the Indiamen sailed on eastwards and their captains faced one of the most serious hazards of the voyage. The full effect of the westwards Aghulas Current was not always fully appreciated and captains who underestimated or ignored its strength misjudged their easting and were wrecked. Fortunately for the company this did not happen often, but the *Dodington*'s loss in 1755 emphasized the need for caution. The plight of the shipwrecked was heartrending. The *Dodington* was wrecked in heavy surf and few managed to get ashore alive. The vessel rapidly broke up and all that could be saved were the company's packets, a box of treasure and another of plate.[15] Many of those who survived the wreck died later of exposure on this inhospitable shore, and only a handful eventually reached Madagascar in the summer of 1756 in a boat constructed from the wreckage. Other, more fortunate, ships rounded the southern tip of Africa safely and their captains had a choice between passing to the east of Madagascar or to the west. Any that had not been able to call at the Cape of Good Hope steered for St Augustine's Bay in Madagascar with many sick from scurvy – as many as twenty died on these long ocean voyages. St Augustine's Bay was not a thriving colony like the Cape, but the islanders became accustomed to trading cattle, limes and oranges with European ships and the bay offered a good anchorage. The sick were put ashore, water casks refilled and the crew refreshed. Some captains believed that the smell of earth was beneficial to sufferers from scurvy and put them ashore at the earliest opportunity. Before 1730 few captains wished to stay long at the island, or even to visit it. Pirates, mostly renegades from the American colonies, used Madagascar as a base from which to attack shipping in the Mozambique Channel and engage in the East African slave trade. Usually they preyed on Arab and Indian craft, but occasionally they attacked Indiamen. The *Cassandra* bound for Bombay in 1720 was captured after a fight lasting over two hours, and in which the *Greenwich* Indiaman and an Ostend ship deserted her. So well known were these pirates – many of whom had been driven out of the Caribbean by Kidd and others – that Defoe based a novel, *Captain Singleton* on the exploits of one, the infamous Captain Avery.

These men were usually a nuisance rather than a menace to Indiamen and when escorted by naval vessels, the Indiamen were never attacked. Even after 1730 the strait was still dangerous for shipping to pass through; it was a focal point of the passage to India and French naval vessels and privateers occasionally lay in wait for ships. They usually chose the Comoro Islands at the northern end of the strait, for Indiamen occasionally made for the island of Johanna to do a little trading. The passengers and crew amused themselves there by giving the natives who came on board the names of European statesmen whom they least resembled, and the names stuck.[16]

It made a little light relief after about four months afloat. Most ships were on the last leg of their voyage, and passengers and crew were anxiously looking forward to reaching their destination. In the early part of the eighteenth century and the last decades of the seventeenth, most of the few ships that sailed for India were destined for Surat. It was then the chief mart of the Indian continent open to Europeans, and had important links with the Red Sea and Persian Gulf as well as the cotton-producing areas of India. To begin with, Bombay to the south was no more than a convenient port of refuge during the period of the North-East Monsoon. On the eastern coast, Fort St George grew slowly from a small collection of huts of baked brick to a sizeable fort and Calcutta from a squalid group of buildings on the banks of the Hughli to a thriving emporium. As the eighteenth century progressed, so too did the volume of trade at each of the company's factories and the commerce with Surat declined. It changed the organization of the company's trade within the Indian subcontinent and the destination of the growing fleet that serviced it.

Thus one can say that at the end of the seventeenth century the Indiamen sailed from Madagascar to Surat, and a few took course to the other factories. As the trade developed, so too did the routes that ships took to reach them across the Indian Ocean. The route to Surat and Bombay was straight forward provided it was made with the South-West Monsoon, and the captain took care to avoid the Indian pirates who were to be found off the Malabar coast. Ships destined for Madras – Fort St George – or Calcutta, usually steered further to the east from the Comores and towards the Inward Passage between the Maldive and Laccadive Islands. East India captains generally regarded this as the quickest passage to the Coromandel coast. They had to make considerable easting in order to run down to Madras and sometimes vessels sailed almost to Sumatra. Ships sailing to Calcutta followed a similar course, except that they had to brave the treacherous navigation of the mouths of the Hughli, where the sandbanks continually changed shape and experienced pilots were needed to guide the large, unwieldy ships up the river at high tide. At times it was necessary to put boats out and tow them up river when the wind was unfavourable, and a short voyage from the Sandheads to the company's factory was often a trying experience. The alternative route was for ships that made the Malabar coast successfully to touch at Goa for news and then follow the coast round to their destination. They had to round the southern tip of Ceylon, for the passage that separated it from India, Palk Strait, was dotted with small islands and shallows and was only navigable by native boatmen in small, shallow draught vessels. When the ships all reached their destinations, they unloaded their cargoes, put the passengers ashore and prepared for a long wait as the company's factors collected a suitable cargo, and the captain and crew engaged in a little private trade on their own account. Bombay offered the best facilities for docking ships, for it possessed an impressive natural harbour that was greatly improved during the course of the eighteenth century. Madras was the worst. There was no harbour off the gently shelving beach, on which heavy surf continually roared. Goods and passengers were carried through it on primitive outriggers which occasionally capsized.

Not all the company's ships sailed to India; some went direct to Canton, but Bengal played an important part in the trade between India and China. During the second part of the eighteenth century the company found that the Chinese at Canton were prepared to buy opium, and a flourishing commerce developed within this commodity, though officially it remained in the hands of independent merchants. Two other commodities which the Chinese were prepared to purchase were tin, from the Malay peninsula, and silver, which was obtained from Manila by British and Indian merchants who used ships that were to all appearances Indian-owned. Calcutta and Madras were partners in this China trade, for both received Spanish silver in this way and sent company ships to Canton. They faced formidable difficulties in wartime. The usual route from Madras and Calcutta to Canton was to pass through the Straits of Malacca, round Singapore Island and sail northward for the Chinese coast across the South China Sea. In order to reach their destination by the autumn, when the tea sales were in progress, ships had to leave the Coromandel coast and Calcutta by mid-summer. Their sailing times were well known to all who visited China, so too was their course. Ships that sailed directly to China from Britain differed only in their route across the Indian Ocean. Their progress was predictable and their ships easy to intercept. This could have made French privateering on the China route successful. In practice this was not so. The number of ships sailing to China was never large; the first had sailed to Amoy in 1685. Between 1690 and 1696 only eight sailed to China, between 1697 and 1703 – a period of bitter rivalry between the old and new companies – twenty. Thereafter there was a steady trickle of ships, rising to around half a dozen by the mid-century and a dozen by the end. The company's ships were convoyed from the Seven Years War, when there was a naval squadron in Indian waters. Before that date French privateers were occasionally active; the *Canterbury* was taken in the Straits of Malacca in 1703 and the *Halifax* had a lucky escape in the same year when the two French ships it met were not aware that war existed.[17] In 1815 the American sloop *Peacock* took the Indiaman *Nautilus* off the Sunda Strait. The strangest episode was a meeting between Commodore Nathaniel Dance and Admiral Linois in 1804.[18] Dance was leading a fleet of sixteen Indiamen and eleven country ships back from Canton when off Pulo Aor in the Straits of Malacca he sighted a French squadron of four. Dance's ships were all large and most had the appearance of warships though they did not carry as many guns as they were pierced for. Linois had the *Marengo* 74 guns, two frigates *Belle Poule* 40, and *Semillante* 36, and a brig the *Berceau* 24. Linois was puzzled to find so many ships and suspected that the convoy contained warships. Dance encouraged him to believe this by hoisting a blue naval ensign instead of the company's blue swallowtail pennant and made no attempt to escape. He lay to under easy sail that night and made slow progress the following day. When Linois tried to cut off some of the rearmost ships, Dance ordered his convoy to tack in succession and engage the enemy. Dance reported that this manoeuvre was correctly performed and the leading Indiaman, the *Royal George*, fired at the enemy. Linois decided that he was being attacked by superior naval forces and broke off the engagement. Dance gave the signal for a general chase and for two hours the Indiamen chased French warships. This however was exceptional.

Dance was lucky; his bluff succeeded, and it should be emphasized that from the mid-eighteenth century many East Indiamen were convoyed from India to China and back into the Indian Ocean. Linois to some degree was unfortunate. Before the Seven Years War the Indiamen sailed independently or in small groups and presented an attractive target to French ships. In 1755, when there was a prospect of war being renewed between Britain and France the East India Company took steps to provide its own defence in eastern waters. The Court of Directors agreed that prospective owners should be allowed to build ships with a third deck fitted to carry nine-pounder guns. One result of this decision was probably the building of the *Pitt* as a larger and more heavily armed ship. In place of the usual complement of 100 men for the 500-ton vessels, the *Pitt* had 250 men and carried 50 guns.[19] She was hired by the company at 600 tons on 2 November 1758, and sailed for Madras on 6 March 1758 under the escort of the warships *Grafton* and *Sunderland*. She carried men from Lieutanant-Colonel Draper's regiment and a cargo valued at £31,832. On 14 September 1758 the *Pitt* reached

Madras and the cargo and soldiers were unloaded. It is hard to tell how the company planned to use her; it was too late to act as escort to the China trade, for that had sailed already. It was also too late to load the *Pitt* for Canton if she were to use the usual route, for she had missed the favourable monsoon in the China Sea. Admiral Pocock was anxious to incorporate her into his own squadron, and as a new, well-armed vessel she could have acted as a naval frigate.

The *Pitt* remained at Madras only nine days, long enough to unload the soldiers and cargo for Madras. Even that took her close to the stormy period of the changing of the monsoon. It was long enough for Captain Wilson of the *Pitt* to arrange to discover a new route to China; a venture in which he had the support of Alexander Dalrymple, an official in the company's service at Madras and later hydrographer to the company. For some years Dalrymple had been interested in exploring the coast of Borneo and the Sulu Sea as a means of opening a new trade in spices. The power of the Dutch East India Company was no longer adequate to control the whole area where it claimed a commercial monopoly and was on the defensive. Dalrymple had been hoping to begin exploration of this Dutch preserve in that year but had been prevented by Lally's siege. Captain Wilson provided the ideal opportunity to combine exploration for commercial exploitation with the possible discovery of a new route to China.

Six days after the *Pitt* had left Madras a strange sail was sighted. It proved to be the *St Louis*, a large French frigate, cruising to intercept British trade off the Coromandel coast. The two vessels exchanged broadsides but then Captain Wilson broke away; he found that he could not open the lower tier of gun ports without flooding his ship and with these out of action the *St Louis* had a superiority of thirteen guns. Neither captain appeared anxious to continue the action and the *Pitt* sailed on, first to Quedah to rejoin the snow *Surprize* which was to accompany him, and then to Malacca. Here he exchanged his sand ballast for shingle – sand tended to clog the pumps – and sailed on to Batavia. Ostensibly he called to purchase provisions, claiming that he was planning to attmpt to sail to Canton through the China Sea. In reality he wanted to obtain Dutch charts. His own were totally inadequate, unless Dalrymple had already been able to get some and give him copies, which is unlikely. The Dutch guarded their charts jealously, and when the governor of Batavia became suspicious of Wilson he sent boats to try and discover the real purpose of his visit. He failed to do so; Wilson complained at this interference, there was a dispute over saluting and Wilson anchored outside the port. When he had taken provisions on board he sailed east along the north coast of Batavia. He was now in waters where no British ship had sailed for over a century, apart from Woodes Rogers in 1710 and Dampier in 1700. The *Surprize* was used to sound a passage and the two vessels slowly progressed to the island of Madoera at the eastern end of Java and thence to the southwest corner of the island of Celebes. Here Wilson had a stroke of luck. He met a sloop sailing from Java to Makassar, and gave the master a barrel of beer. In the ensuing conviviality the master warned him that he was near a dangerous shoal and described the course that Dutch ships usually took when sailing to Makassar and the more northerly settlement of Bandar. He also gave Wilson a chart of the area.

Further progress was necessarily slow. On 6 January the *Pitt* passed through the straits between Celebes and the island of Salajar and four days later anchored in the Straits of Boetang. When he went on shore to obtain fresh provisions, Wilson was treated with great suspicion. There was a delay while the local ruler considered whether it was safe to treat with this stranger, but ultimately Wilson was given provisions and a pilot for the straits. Wilson, no doubt prepared for such an eventuality, presented the king with a silver-mounted broad sword, a small British flag and another, smaller sword and received two native boys in exchange. Thereafter the *Pitt* and *Surprize* moved slowly eastwards through the Ceram Sea. Wilson's original intention was to pass through the Sapalulu Straits, through the Molucca Sea to the west of Halmahera Island and thence into the Pacific. When surveying the Sapalulu Straits the boats crews were nearly drowned by tidal waves that probably originated in earthquakes to the north. Wilson was forced to sail instead to the straits that Dampier had discovered in 1700, and on his way was careful to claim to all native craft that he met that he was Dutch. On 15 February he came in sight of the Dampier Straits and took the opportunity of exploring a small strait that Dampier had seen but had not been able to explore. Wilson named this Pitt Strait after the ship, and several headlands and islands in the strait after members of the royal family. Once safely into the Pacific the remaining part of the voyage to Canton was straightforward. The *Pitt* sailed north to the Bashi Channel and thence west to the China coast. He reached Macao on 4 April.

The voyage had dramatic implications for the East India Company. It was the first time that an Indiaman had sailed eastwards through waters where the Dutch had a monopoly. Captain Wilson had performed his task with quiet efficiency and great diplomatic skill. It was a considerable feat to take a vessel of the *Pitt*'s size through such uncharted waters and to show that it was feasible from both directions he returned by the same route, leaving Canton on 12 June and reaching the Thames on 27 April 1760, six months earlier than expected. The voyage was a personal triumph for Wilson; the directors of the East India Company awarded him a medal to the value of 100 guineas. The practical results of the voyage were that the company possessed a set of charts for the new route that had been made with considerable care and could be used by other captains. Wilson had taken the French *Neptune* sea atlas, the British *Sea Atlas* based on it, Dampier's account of his circumnavigation, Richard Walter's, *A voyage round the world by George Anson*, and the *New Directory*. He had made careful soundings along the route, had checked the position of islands shown in plane and mercator charts by the use of a Morgan azimouth compass and Hadley quadrant and had obtained a number of Dutch charts. Wilson had spent part of his time at Canton having two copies made of each of these charts; one was left with the supercargoes in Canton and the other was sent to Madras where further copies were made.

The company quickly made use of these, stimulated no doubt by an interest in Dalrymple's voyages. In 1760 when news of d'Estaing's ships in the Straits of Sunda reached Madras the Council ordered the *Caernarvon*, *Princess Augusta* and *Warwick* to use Wilson's route to avoid them. Others followed, including the *Osterley*, *Worcester* and *Prince George* and by the end of the Seven Years War copies of the charts had been sent to the company's trading posts on the route to China. It was not the company's intention to publicize this new route, but inevitably news reached the Dutch in Batavia. The Vereenigde Oost Indische Compagnie regarded this as an incursion into their commercial territory, a direct challenge that they could not afford to ignore. Towards the end of 1761 the Indiaman *Warwick* returning from China along *Pitt*'s course was boarded near the Moluccas by the Secretary of the Dutch settlement on Tidore, an island in the Ceram Sea. He claimed that the *Warwick* had no business to be there because all the islands belonged to the Dutch. It needed more than verbal complaints to deter the East India Company. By the beginning of 1762 some form of trading or supply settlement had been established on Salawati and Batanta islands, near the western entrance to Pitt's Straits. When the Dutch heard of the Salawati settlement they sent an expedition to destroy it. The significance of the new route remained however, for it provided the means by which ships could be sent to Canton at any time of the year.

Moreover, when there was a French threat in one strait, ships could be sent by another, and the regularity of these voyages contributed a great deal towards the growth of British trade among the Dutch islands as well.

These new arrangements were especially important in the second half of the eighteenth century. French privateers had already begun to use the Burmese ports of Mergui and Tenasserim as repair bases for their ships and threatened to interrupt the passage of Indiamen through the Straits of Malacca. The French and British companies had factories at Syriam, though the British were turned out in 1742 and later established a base at Negrais. The troubled state of Burmese affairs during the rise of the Konbaung dynasty was a comparatively minor threat to the company's trade with Canton, though it offered France the opportunity of using Burma as a base for commerce raiding after the French factories in India had been captured. It was at this point that it became necessary to establish a forward base for commerce protection. The choice fell on Penang, the half-way house on the route to China. Penang, or Prince of Wales Island as it was called under British rule, was a thickly wooded island about fifteen miles long that provided shelter and a safe anchorage in the Malacca Straits. It was rented from the Rajah of Quedah by the East India Company in 1786 and became for a time, in 1805–7, a naval base for the eastern half of the Indian naval command.[20] It was given an imposing fortress, Fort Cornwallis, and when the ancient Malay capital Malacca fell into British hands in 1795, it gained much of the latter's trade. The native population grew apace and in 1805 Mr Philip Dundas was sent by the First Lord of the Admiralty, Henry Dundas, Viscount Melville, to be the first governor. He was also the last. Penang was also extremely unhealthy and Philip Dundas was dead within two years. It was also realized that the fort, though imposing – it had apparently impressed the native population who had flocked to enjoy its protection – would not withstand any attack. Its value as a forward base for commerce protection was therefore extremely limited and the settlement was reduced to its former status, though not before Philip Dundas and all the members of the Council had died.

The problem of a forward base remained. Ultimately it was solved after Stamford Raffles had bought Singapore Island from the Sultan of Jahore in 1819 on behalf of the East India Company. Some considered Bencoolen a suitable site, but that too was unhealthy. Another alternative was the proposal in 1779 to occupy the Bay of Tourane on the Annam coast.[21] This would have provided a secure retreat for Indiamen which were in danger of losing their passage to China and a base from which to intercept Canton trade. The company rejected this proposal because of the low state of its finances. There were no other alternatives. Manila, seized in 1762 after Spain had entered the Seven Years War, was never intended as a permanent accession to British power and was returned at the peace. Java was likewise returned to Holland in 1815. These naval and commercial posts were not intended to protect Indiamen solely against French privateers and warships, though they are usually prominent in discussions of commerce raiding. There were also pirates. Vessels engaged in the country trade with the Dutch spice islands had to keep a weather eye open at all times. Many of the country traders were in any case liable to have their ships seized if caught by the Dutch and the natives with whom they traded suffered harsher penalties. The seas were not safe for European and Indian ships. The Spaniards tried to capture the piratical Sulu Islands in 1751, but were beaten off and the Philippines were ravaged for three years in retaliation.[22] The Dutch built a Venetian type of galley to fight the swift Malay 'prahus' and in 1756 Bugis from Riouw and Selangor under Daing Jamoja attacked Malacca. An Indiaman, the *Fame*, was surprised at the north end of the Lombok Straits in 1756 by Malay pirates and lost thirty-nine men beating them off.

These were the everyday risks of the China trade. Ships were generally safe from attack when they travelled in groups or under the escort of a naval frigate. Only when sailing singly, as they were forced to do in the early wars, were they likely to be taken, and then only by the French. This is not to say that the outward voyages were always uneventful. Apart from the risk from pirates already referred to, there were at times storms in the China Sea and ships occasionally called at the island of Pulo Condore, off the coast of Cochin China, for a little private trade.[23] Later in the voyage the Indiamen passed over the Macclesfield Bank and reached the Portuguese settlement at Macao. Their first task was to obtain a pilot to take the boats up river to Canton. There was throughout the period a complicated procedure for entering the river. It was unsafe as well as illegal to proceed up river without a pilot, for there were many islands off the coast that looked similar, and strong currents further hindered navigation. One characteristic of this trade was the shrewdness with which the Chinese exploited this European trade. The pilots charged exorbitant fees and the Canton merchants who traded with the Europeans established a monopoly, the Co-Hong, that lasted until 1771. At the mouth of the river there was an anchorage known as the

Bocca Tigris or Bogue, where all ships were inspected and measured for port duty, given permits and paid taxes before proceeding to the principal anchorage at Whampoa. The custom of the Chinese officials was to measure the distance between the fore and mizon masts and base the port duty on that, a factor that may have influenced the design of the country vessels that later in the century carried the opium to Canton.

There was always considerable delay on the part of the Chinese officials, and this may occasionally have been deliberate to emphasize the inferior status of Europeans in Chinese eyes. At the beginning of the period in particular there was a tendency for each commercial transaction to be the subject of prolonged and tortuous negotiation. Occasionally this was too much for British captains. In 1689 the captain of the *Defence* found he could not take his cargo from the customs officials, perhaps because he had not paid the 'presents' which were frequently expected. When he tried to seize it by force the Chinese authorities swiftly moved against him and he hurriedly sailed, leaving six of his crew and the supercargo on shore.[24] Behaviour such as this tended to confirm the Chinese in their prejudices: Europeans were no more than untrustworthy barbarians who were violent, boorish and difficult to comprehend.

At the beginning of the period the East India Company was trading to Amoy, and sent its first ship, the *China Merchant* in 1685. This was the first direct venture to China – earlier imports of tea had been bought from Portuguese traders and country ships at Surat and Madras and from Chinese merchants in Bantam. Tea was also purchased from Holland, and it was to lower the cost that the East India Company began direct trade. When Parliament sanctioned the new company, that too sent ships to China, though they went to Canton. The first set sail in 1699. From that point the company ships monopolized the import of tea into England. In the first half of the eighteenth century the Chinese authorities allowed Europeans to trade at Canton, Chusan, Limpo and Amoy. The companies maintained modest factories at each, but relied on supercargoes to purchase tea when they reached their destination. The voyages became a race, as each company tried to get its ships to China first. There was considerable competition between the Europeans, but on the Chinese side the annual trade came to be controlled by a small group of merchants. These found that they could to some extent play the Europeans off against each other. The Europeans played into their hands. They came to concentrate their attention on Canton; it had a good anchorage at Whampoa, ten miles from the town, and even the largest ships could sail there. There were plentiful supplies of tea available from the province of Fukien, and much porcelain of neat and ornate design together with woven and raw silk. The concentration of European interest at Canton enabled a group of twenty Chinese merchants to form an executive council to superintend the trade. This council, the Co-Hong, was responsible to the chief customs officer, the Hoppo, through him to the governor and thence to the viceroy. It formed a neat and orderly chain of responsibility. Attempts to gain permission to extend trading rights to Limpo and Chusan failed, as did Macartney's mission in 1792.

Tea was the company's principal import from China; it was all black tea, ranging from the expensive Pekoe from the first picking each year, to Bohea, a coarse mixture that could contain sloe or liquorice leaves, old tea, ash or elder leaves and was at times coloured with Terra Japonica, copperas, sugar, molasses, clay or logwood.[25] Tea was packed in lead-lined chests to preserve its flavour and other commodities – silk and porcelain – were shipped in comparatively small quantities to fill the remaining space. Demand for tea increased steadily, stimulated by tariff reforms in 1745 and 1784 which helped to reduce the price. Demand in the first half of the eighteenth century seems to have been met partly by imported teas from Holland, from the illegal re-import of teas nominally shipped abroad, on which the drawback had been paid and from a limited amount of illegal importing of tea by captains and crews of returning Indiamen. At all events, from the company's point of view, the volume of tea imports steadily rose, from 91,260 lbs in 1700 to 1,901,389 lbs in 1780.[26] By the end of the period the average yearly import was around 4 million lbs.[27] It was matched in Britain by a corresponding increase in consumption and a decline in the average real price *(see table p. 237)*.

The table demonstrates the importance of the tea imports for the East India Company. The company's ships left Canton early in the year and sailed back across the China Sea or occasionally through the route pioneered by Captain Wilson in the *Pitt*. The first part of the voyage was uneventful, though there were occasional scares that French warships might be cruising off the mouth of the Canton River. These always proved false. Nor was there any danger from French Indiamen, for these had been scrupulously avoided at Canton, partly to prevent violence between the crews which would disrupt trade, and partly because the merchants and crews were not allowed to move beyond their ships and factories. The first sign of danger on the voyage home was in the straits that connected the Bay of Bengal with the China Sea: the straits of Malacca, Banda and Sunda. Ships

Table 7.6 ESTIMATES OF THE REAL PRICE AND CONSUMPTION PER HEAD

Excise years ending at midsummer	Average real price of tea (1725=100)	Average annual consumption per head (lbs)
1726–30	93	.10
1731–35	89	.11
1736–40	80	.17
1741–45	78	.13
1746–50	67	.41
1751–55	60	.51
1756–60	58	.62
1761–65	60	.68
1765–67	53	.64
1768–72	38	1.00
1773–75	41	.76
1776–80	43	.68
1780–84	45	.66
1787–91	25	2.09
1791–95	23	2.24
1796–1800	22	2.54
1801–05	24	2.33
1806–10	29	2.07
1810–14	27	2.02

Source: W. A. Cole, 'Trends in eighteenth-century smuggling', in *The growth of English overseas trade in the seventeenth and eighteenth centuries*, Minchinton (ed), p 128.

were sometimes lost there to French warships and privateers, though Linois had suffered the supreme indignity of being chased by merchantmen. There were also navigational hazards, for instance shallows in the Straits of Banda. Indiamen usually called at Bencoolen on the Island of Sumatra for pepper and were sometimes caught at anchor. Bencoolen, one of the company's factories and a focal point for trade, attracted the attentions of French vessels from time to time.

The first important attack on Fort Malborough was made by the Comte d'Estaing as part of a cruise that was notable for its intelligent use of mobility and surprise. D'Estaing had gone to India to serve in the forces of the French East India Company. A young man of considerable resource and bravery, he had risen to the rank of brigadier before being captured at the siege of Madras in December 1758.[28] The following May he was sent to Île de France, the modern Mauritius, to be returned to France on parole and exchanged. He decided instead to break his parole and make a privateering raid in the Bay of Bengal. Because of rivalry between the French governor René Magon de la Gervaisis and a military adviser Guérin de

Frémincourt, d'Estaing was given the use of an old 64 the *Condé* and a frigate the *Expédition*. The governor was anxious to gain prestige, spite his rival and gain a share of prize money. The nominal command was given to a naval lieutenant, des Essarts. D'Estaing's first task was to capture British prisoners for whom he could be exchanged, freeing him to assume an active role in the expedition. This was casuistry; he had no right to take part in a warlike venture while still under parole – the penalty was death if caught – nor had he the right to exchange except under normal procedure in Britain.

At the end of August the two ships set sail north for the port of Mocha. On the way he took a small number of Arab boats flying the British flag and learnt that there was a large British vessel lying at the port of Muscat. He sailed there and took it, violating the neutrality of the port. He next sailed for Bandar 'Abbās, where there was a small East India Company fort guarded by a few European and Indian troops. This fell to a swift *coup de main* and d'Estaing went on shore and was ostentatiously exchanged for the British prisoners. He now felt free to lead the expedition in person, though he was still a brigadier in the army and held no naval commission. It is clear from his subsequent actions that he possessed a clear grasp of strategy and the energy and determination of a young man; he was thirty. He had only two ships; one was an old and probably not fully seaworthy craft – the French naval base at Mauritius was never adequately stocked with naval stores – and the other a smaller frigate. He kept well clear of the Coromandel coast where the British squadron might be found and made a slow crossing of the Bay of Bengal to Sumatra in the teeth of the North-East Monsoon. He had two aims: to intercept an Indiaman returning from Canton and to seize British trading posts in Sumatra. Success in either should have made him a rich man and would have erased the stain on his character, at least in France.

His Sumatra venture was a model of swift action. He attacked Natal, a settlement approximately 400 miles north-west of Fort Malborough, the day after he reached Sumatra. It fell the next day. About 80 miles north-west of Natal was the settlement of Tapanuli, famed for its exports of camphor, gold dust and benjamin, a resinous juice used for making incense. The *Expédition* attacked Tapanuli on 8 February, but the British resident, Nairn, beat off the attack. A week later the *Expédition* returned with the *Condé* and the settlement surrendered after a brief cannonade. D'Estaing had now taken two settlements, but had little to show for his efforts, for he had arrived a month too early. The pepper crop was not harvested until April, and the Indonesian rajahs would not send pepper to the settlements while he was there. D'Estaing spent the next month trying to persuade the Dutch to accept the settlements – he was trying to foment discord between the companies – and prepared for an attack on Fort Malborough. As a military officer d'Estaing was well aware of the weaknesses of East India Company forts in such outlying areas. They were built to overawe the local population rather than withstand attack by Europeans, and Fort Malborough, faced with brick and built in 1714, was not as formidable as its imposing appearance suggested. On 1 April d'Estaing appeared off the fort, in hot pursuit of the Indiaman *Denham* and boldly sailed up river to the fort with the help of Dutch pilots. The *Denham* was burnt by the British to prevent it falling into French hands.

Within a few days Fort Malborough was forced to surrender, but d'Estaing was disappointed to find that the governor had sent all his silver to Batavia as soon as he had received notice of the French force on the coast, and there remained only the stocks of pepper and trade goods to a value of about £10,000. This was not enough to defray the costs of his expedition and it may have been difficult to realize the full value of what he had captured. The expedition was proving to be a failure, at least in financial terms, and he now had the gambler's choice: to cut his losses and return in comparative ignominy, or stay in eastern waters and hope to make a rich prize by taking an Indiaman. He chose the latter. It proved to be a disastrous mistake. Throughout the summer he remained at Fort Malborough, an unhealthy spot where his officers and men sickened and died of dysentery and fever. Then he replenished his stores at Batavia and cruised in the Straits of Malacca in late summer to try and intercept ships sailing to Canton. He was unsuccessful. He then cruised in the Straits of Sunda and had no more luck there. He failed to realize that the British had discovered a new route through the spice islands by which they could avoid the latter straits. The outward bound ships were also diverted from the Straits of Malacca when news reached Madras through the country trade of his presence in the area.

D'Estaing continued to cruise until early in the summer of 1761, taking no prizes and holding his small force together in the face of mounting losses through disease. Sanitation and cleanliness were traditionally ill-organized on French ships and d'Estaing may have accepted his losses as normal – d'Anville's expedition to Quebec in 1745 had been crippled by sickness. Nonetheless, this may have been a contributory factor to his almost total failure. He finally arrived back at Mauritius in June 1761. His cruise lasted twenty-two months and the sale of prize goods only defrayed the cost of the expedition. Of the officers and men who had sailed with him in search of wealth, twenty-three of the twenty-eight officers died on the voyage and three more were dead within weeks of his return. At Fort Malborough 126 men died and so did many more during the cruise in the Straits. On the other hand, the East India Company had suffered severe loss. In Sumatra the pepper crop for 1761 was completely lost and much damage was done to the plantations near the coast when it was feared that d'Estaing might try and seize the crop. The company had also lost prestige; its factories had been taken very easily and even Fort Malborough was not impregnable. Above all, d'Estaing had been able to cruise unmolested in the waters of Sumatra and Java for approximately seventeen months and had threatened company trade, though without taking any prizes. It demonstrated d'Estaing's qualities of leadership, imagination and determination and he was unlucky to fail in his main object.

He had been wise to keep away from the Coromandel coast. Other Frenchmen cruised there later with some success, notably Robert Surcouf in the years 1796–9 and 1807–9, but d'Estaing had at that time neither the naval skill nor the resources for such a venture. Madras, or Fort St George as it was often called, had been established by Francis Day in 1639 and fortified later against the general wishes of the company. It was a trading factory, and the fort was built to offer some protection to the company's goods and factors. It also had to secure the proceeds of taxation for which it was responsible to the Nawab of the Carnatic – part of the feudal obligations under which the company held the pocket of land on which the fort was built. The trade of Madras was never impressive. It exported some cotton piece goods and there were links through the country trade with the islands and their spice trade. Otherwise the East India ships brought out a variety of European goods for the large population, and took back these products of Indian commerce. Trade was hindered by the total absence of any dock. The sea shelved gradually from the shore, Indiamen had to moor up to two miles out and the goods and passengers were carried through heavy surf on catamarans and masullah boats. Strong currents and heavy winds completed the difficulties. Normally the Indiamen were able to ride at anchor in the roadstead in safety from May to October, but occasionally there were sharp, unexpected gales. In 1716 much damage was caused by one in early summer. The changing of the monsoon at the beginning of October heralded a season that was also wild and stormy and no merchantman was safe on the coast. So serious was the danger that it became normal commercial practice to refuse to insure ships on the coast at that time and the custom was emphasized by striking the flagstaff that was mounted as a guide to shipping on the roof of the Exchange. The main function of the Madras presidency was to keep the French out, and the Anglo-French rivalry on the coast was a symbol of this from the 1740s. Until 1745 the two companies had traded on the Coromandel coast in comparative harmony and in 1742 there had been an unofficial truce. This was changed by the actions of Dupleix and the decision by the British administration to fight in India. A naval squadron was sent out under the command of Commodore Peyton. Thereafter, in every war for the rest of the period there was a British naval squadron in the Indian Ocean, and a succession of actions were fought off the Coromandel coast. The East India Company played a comparatively minor part in these naval activities. It was anxious to preserve its commerce and pressed the naval commander for convoys for the China trade. East Indiamen were occasionally taken into naval service and at times fought in battle as frigates. The company was anxious that the trade should be able to arrive and depart in safety and accepted that this aim was best served by the maintenance of the British squadron as a fighting unit off the Coromandel coast. To this end the company provided repair facilities at Bombay. At times, notably in 1760 and 1795, British naval squadrons occupied the Dutch harbour at Trincomali. The advantage of this was that it was closer to the Coromandel coast than Bombay and when it was denied to the French, it forced the latter to withdraw to Mauritius to refit. Trincomali was also a useful base from which to intercept French privateers making a landfall at Friars Hood and ensure the safe departure of Indiamen for St Helena.

Although naval activity was concentrated off the Coromandel coast from the 1740s, the area of greatest commercial importance was Bengal. It would be wrong to assume that Calcutta suddenly acquired significance after Clive's successes and the financial mismanagement of the 1760s. Bengal's share of the company's Indian trade had been rising throughout the eighteenth century, except for the five years before Plassey *(see table p. 242)*.

The East India Company's factory had been founded in 1686, and at the start of the period was no more than a collection of huts of sun-dried mud on the banks of the Hughli River, a tributary of the Ganges. It was also almost a hundred miles upstream, and some of the company's larger vessels could not reach it. The anchorage was bad and after the melting of the winter snows the current became so

Table 7.7 BENGAL'S SHARE OF INDIAN TRADE

	Bullion	Goods	(£000) Total for Bengal	Total for India	Bengal's share (%)
1707–17	773	160	932	3,858	24.2
1718–27	1,332	227	1,559	4,614	33.7
1728–37	1,063	511	1,575	4,600	34.2
1738–47	1,703	643	2,346	5,855	40.0
1748–57	1,836	827	2,662	7,761	34.3
1707–57	6,706	2,368	9,074	26,687	
AVERAGE	134	47	181	534	34.0

Source: B. K. Gupta, *Sirajuddaullah and the East India Company, 1756–1757.
The background to the foundation of British power in India* (Leiden 1966), p 15.

swollen that it was well nigh impossible for ships to avoid straining
and at times breaking their cables. Nonetheless, because of its links
with the broad and fertile Ganges Valley, and its products of cotton
cloth and saltpetre, rice, silk and sugar it was the richest of the
company's factories, and it was to this region that the company
officials tried to go. After Clive's victories, Calcutta enjoyed a
prosperity that grew each decade, and an important trade in opium
was developed with Canton. The wealth of this area attracted the
attentions of French privateers.

The Coromandel coast and Ceylon, which formed the departure
area for Indiamen returning to Britain, was periodically ravaged by
French privateers. In the early wars of the period a small number of
vessels were fitted out at St Malo to cruise in the Indian Ocean.
These however were intended to combine privateering with trade;
two French ships that took an Indiaman the *Duchess* on the Malabar
coast in 1711 went on to Mocha, presumably to load coffee.[29] They
were followed by others, but in the main the activity off the Coromandel coast in the wars between 1744 and 1783 were naval battles of
varying intensity. Commerce raiding was practised on a comparatively
small scale by comparison with the determined squadronal raiding
in the English Channel in the early wars. This changed in the wars
with Revolutionary France and Napoleon. In 1793 and 1794 there
were heavy losses of Indiamen in the Indian Ocean and the focal
points of trade. The Admiralty did not have sufficient forces to
defend the convoys which had now grown considerably and there
was alarm at the company's factories as losses mounted.

The British naval commander in India was Commodore Peter Rainier, who reached Madras in 1794. He was immediately petitioned by the merchants to provide strong naval protection in the Straits of Malacca, through which so much British trade – both company and country – passed. His problem was the presence in Indian waters of four remarkable privateer commanders and a number of naval frigates which were harrassing British trade. He had not only to protect trade against these, if he could, but also to defend factories in India against naval attack. The four men who were most successful in this *guerre de commerce* were François Lemême, Robert Surcouf, Jean Dutertre and Mallerousse. They used Mauritius as a base for their operations. The most dangerous in British eyes was Surcouf, who arrived in the *Emilie* off the mouth of the Hughli in 1796. He was a remarkable man; his exploits were marked by daring and guile, unfailing consideration and courtesy to those unfortunate enough to fall into his hands as prisoners and unfailing good humour. He was still a young man in his early twenties.[30] His best known cruise was in a small pilot brig, the *Cartier*, which he had taken off the Sandheads. Although it was only a small vessel, it was able to cruise unobtrusively in the area and was bound to attract the Indiamen to it, for they would not expect it to be a French privateer. Another factor in his favour was the season; he had arrived during the North-East Monsoon, when privateers were not usually seen on that coast. On 29 January he took the Indiaman *Triton*, and it is worth remembering that the *Cartier* carried seventeen men and mounted four guns, whereas the *Triton* had a crew of one hundred and fifty and mounted twenty-six guns. Later, in 1799, Surcouf cruised in the Bay of Bengal in the *Clarisse* and the following year was given the command of a large vessel the *Confiance* which had 160 Europeans in her crew. In these two vessels Surcouf took a number of vessels in the Bay of Bengal and off the coast of Ceylon and though occasionally sighted by British warships was always able to escape by superior speed.

The Napoleonic War opened with another period of heavy losses of Indiamen to privateers and a warship, the *Marengo*, 84. This was a large vessel for commerce raiding – it was Linois' flagship – but it successfully evaded British warships. In any case, Rainier was unwilling to divert many ships to search for him in case he was faced with a major attack in India; the problem that had faced him in 1794. Linois' success was brought to an ignominious halt by his brush with Commodore Dance described already, though he was more successful later in June 1805 when he captured the Indiaman *Brunswick* off the coast of Ceylon. There were other French threats too. Lemême returned to the Indian Ocean in 1803 in the *Fortune*, 12, and a crew of one hundred and sixty. He soon took fifteen prizes and was only caught by a faster and heavier gunned ship, the *Concorde*, 48. This marked the end of his career, for he died on the voyage back to Britain. In 1804–5 Dutertre was active in the Indian Ocean with another well known privateer captain, Courson. *Guerre de commerce* was actively pursued in 1806 by two excellent frigates, *Piémontaise* and *Cannonière*, both 40s.

As the war continued the British shipping losses in the Indian Ocean continued to rise. Robert Surcouf returned in 1807 in the 18-gun *Revenant*, which had been designed as a privateer. It was the fastest vessel afloat in the Indian Ocean, and Surcouf was able to cruise successfully off the Sandheads and in the Bay of Bengal in perfect safety. No one could catch him, but it was his last cruise, for when he returned to France in 1809 he turned instead to owning privateers. His place was taken by a small squadron of four frigates: *Manche*, *Caroline*, *Bellone* and *Vénus*, commanded by Commodore Jacques Hamelin. Their actions in 1809 marked a new stage in the *guerre de course*; Indiamen in the main had not been taken in large numbers, but Hamelin and his ships took five, all homeward bound and several with valuable cargoes.

The East India Company's misfortunes were increased by the further loss of five more ships which foundered at sea and three more that were wrecked. In all this amounted to almost as much as the total loss during the previous war.

The best way to counter this commerce raiding was to try and prevent the privateers and warships having an effective base. The ideal solution was to seize Mauritius, but the fear of the British naval commanders was that it was difficult if not impossible without additional help from Britain, for to send the Indian naval squadron to attack Mauritius was to leave the Indian coast bare. That was to risk too much. The first attempt was planned in 1761, but failed because Keppel's reinforcements did not rendezvous with Cornish.[31] A second expedition was planned in 1794 but once again there were not enough ships available. In 1806 the prospects improved for Vice-Admiral Sir Edward Pellew, commander of the India squadron. A British force recaptured the Cape of Good Hope, cutting off the supply of provisions for Mauritius and Réunion. It also gave Pellew the chance to blockade the French islands. This was only moderately successful; for the winds were uncertain and the currents largely unknown, but Pellew did succeed in cutting supply links with France. Surcouf managed to capture enough rice ships in 1807 to enable the islands to hold out and Decaen fortified the islands in 1806 when he withdrew from Pondicherry. As the position of the garrison became desperate Decaen appealed to Napoleon for help, and the result was the arrival of Hamelin. The latter's success finally forced the British to attack Mauritius in 1810. The first attempt was unsuccessful. In August the attacking force under Captain Samuel Pym lost five ships, but then his luck began to change. He took the French flagship *Vénus* and severely damaged the other ships in the bombardment. Thereafter he was able to institute a close blockade, build up his attacking force out of sight of the defending garrison and finally launch a swift, well-conducted landing on 29 October. Decaen capitulated on 3 December. The only other base in French control, Java, fell to another well-executed attack in August 1811.

This ended the activities of French naval vessels and privateers in the Bay of Bengal and the straits, but there were other areas where they threatened. One was the approaches to the Cape of Good Hope and the Cape itself. It was the halfway house of the return voyages, valuable as a provisioning station for the British ships returning to the Thames and for the islands of Mauritius and Réunion which were not self-supporting. While Holland remained neutral, British ships called at the Cape, though they kept a close watch for French shipping. In the early wars of the period British ships joined Dutch convoys there, freeing the Admiralty from the responsibility of providing protection on this stage of the homeward voyage, though the problem remained of escorting Indiamen to the Thames from the Texel. At times even this was not enough defence, and convoys sailed to Cadiz to await additional support before attempting to enter the English Channel. In later years the Cape continued to occupy an influential position in British commerce defence, for though the ships no longer sailed with Dutch convoys, there was danger from French vessels which might use it as a base for commerce raiding. In 1781 the Admiralty sent an expedition to take it, but Commodore Johnstone was surprised *en route* by Suffren at Porto Praya in April and after a brief encounter Suffren reached the Cape first. The Admiralty had more success in later wars. The Cape was seized after a brief fight and considerable bargaining by Sir George Elphinstone and Major-General James Craig in June 1795. It was returned at the peace and again taken in 1806; this time it remained in British hands.

During the wars with Revolutionary and Napoleonic France the Admiralty agreed to extend its convoy protection from St Helena to the Cape. In all the other wars British defence did not extend beyond St Helena, and indeed was not instituted at that island until the war of Austrian Succession. It was of limited value to the East India Company ships. It could only act as a port of call to ships returning to the Thames, and offered a limited range of provisions to the Indiamen. Vegetable gardens had been established there early in the century and these produced a small surplus. The island also possessed a safe anchorage for the Indiamen and the returning naval escort but in all other respects was virtually defenceless, though there was a small body of company troops maintained on the island. The French made a number of plans to capture it but none succeeded. During the Seven Years War d'Estaing and Frogier de l'Eguille had both proposed the capture of the island, and in the War of American Independence Kerguelin planned another attempt – it was captured on board the *Libre Navigateur*. The only significant attempt to put such a proposal into practice was in 1758 when a warship and two frigates were sent to Mauritius for this purpose. The vessels sailed to St Helena but while they were off the island a violent quarrel developed between Marnière, a *capitaine de vaisseau* in the French navy and Marchais, a former captain in the Dutch East India Company. The cruise was a disaster from the French point of view; it failed to take the Indiaman *Tavistock* which arrived at St Helena while the squadron was cruising there and Marnière abandoned the attempt. It was in any case too easy for the Indiamen to sail to a port in South America for refreshments or to Barbados to join a West India convoy. St Helena was not indispensible to British East India commerce and there were no further attempts to attack it. Curiously, it was off this island that a death blow was dealt to the Dutch East India Company in 1794 when seven Dutch ships were captured by HMS *Sceptre* from a convoy returning to Holland.

The British ships left St Helena in July, usually under the escort of a naval vessel. To convoy valuable ships was by no means a sinecure, and escort commanders were frequently commended by the East India Company for the care and attention which they showed for the security of their charges. One example may suffice: the voyage of Captain O'Brian in July 1757. He had a reputation for fair dealing and humanity and the prospect of a harmonious voyage was assured when eight seamen who had previously deserted from the navy took advantage of an amnesty to ask if they could serve on board his ship: 'It being the first of His Majesty's ships as we are willing to serve His Majesty again.'[32] He had some difficulty keeping the convoy of eleven ships together and appointed the oldest captain to repeat his signals and carry lights at night. The task was made more difficult by the poor state of some of the ships, which had difficulty in keeping up with the convoy. When scurvy inevitably broke out, Captain O'Brian tried to alleviate the sufferings of the men with tea and sugar that he had bought. He shared his provisions when bad weather delayed the progress of the convoy and left to the captains of the Indiamen the choice of the twenty-five men that each should send into naval service. When several of the ships reported that they would have difficulty reaching a British port he made for Ireland; he was able to reach Cork where the East India Company had facilities for refitting ships and houses where men could recover. In this respect the company's men were more fortunate than naval seamen; there was no provision at Cork for them to be treated.

Captain O'Brian reached Cork in October and remained there until February 1758. This was by no means uncommon. In the early years of the period ships frequently put into Galway Bay or the Shannon and remained there until the Admiralty sent a frigate or warship to see them in safety to the Thames. The Admiralty may on occasion have suspected that there were ulterior motives behind the decision to put into an Irish port. Many of the crew deserted and formed gangs strong enough to fight off the naval press gangs, and left the lascars – Indian sailors – to bring the ship in safety to the Thames. It also gave the captain and crew an opportunity to dispose of their private ventures outside the company's monopoly, either by sale or smuggling. On occasions there were Indiamen which sailed northabout round the coast of Scotland. These made for Leith and were escorted to the Thames by an escort provided for the purpose. Such voyages were comparatively rare; the convoys from St Helena were usually strong enough to provide full defence to the Thames and additional support was in any case normally provided by cruisers in the Soundings, a practice that was observed in each of the wars from the mid-eighteenth century.

When the Indiamen finally reached the Thames the voyage was over. Vessels were moored off Deptford, Blackwall or Northfleet or in the company's wet dock at Rotherhythe, or, as at the end of the period, in the new East India Docks. These enclosed dock areas provided a measure of protection from smuggling and pilfering, though the institution of river police on the Thames in 1798 provided some protection. Before 1735 the company's trade could be stored in a few small warehouses in the city, such as the pepper cellars under the Royal Exchange. After Clive's success, trade grew and warehouses were constructed on twelve sites and riverside depots at Billingsgate and Ratcliffe; another at Blackwall was added later. Each specialized in one commodity: pepper continued to be stored at the Royal

Exchange for a time and was then transferred to the new warehouse at Blackwall, private goods were held at Billiter Lane, textiles were stored in the largest warehouses in Cutler Street, New Street and Devonshire Square, tea was kept at Fenchurch Street, Haydon Square, Cooper's Row, Jewry Street and Crutched Friars, spices were stored at Leadenhall Street and saltpetre at Cock Hill. Each was a bonded warehouse and each was considered 'splendid and commodious in the highest degree'.[33] From there the commodities were finally sold at auctions and the proceeds went into the coffers of the East India Company.

That the company had almost ceased to be a commercial body by the end of the period under review need not concern us here. The quantity of Indian and Chinese goods imported into London continued to rise and the revenue from duty formed a valuable part of the government's revenue, especially during wartime. It was this, and the political power of the directors of the East India Company, that ensured that the company's ships were given the protection of naval vessels in the approaches to the English Channel, the South Atlantic and, from the mid-eighteenth century, the Indian Ocean. Although there were a number of focal points for the trade, in practice the French found it hard to capture many Indiamen, for there were several courses that the Indiamen could follow, and the French never had the means of blocking them all. It was not until the end of the eighteenth century that French captures of Indiamen reached significant proportions, and these were the result of luck as much as daring, seamanship and courage. In any case, the company survived these attacks; more important was the decay within the company which ultimately caused its downfall.

Notes

Chapter 1 *French Privateering and British Trade 1689–1815*

1   R. P. Crowhurst, 'Bayonne privateering 1744–63', (Paper presented at the XV International Seminar on Maritime History held at the XIV International Congress of Historical Science, San Francisco, 1975), p 453.

2   Three or four hundred men sailed each year from St Malo and Granville to Newfoundland at the end of the seventeenth century; J. Delumeau, 'Le Commerce malouin sous l'Ancien Régime d'après les registres de l'Amirauté', in M. Mollat (ed), *Les sources de l'histoire maritime en Europe du Moyen Age au XVIIIe siècle*, (Paris 1962), pp 306–7.

3   Other ports were Havre 114, Dieppe 96, La Rochelle 93, Nantes 84, Dunkirk 69, Bayonne 61, Marseille 47; *ibid*, p 300.

4   A. Morel, 'Les armateurs malouins et le commerce interlope', in Mollat, *Sources de l'histoire maritime*, pp 311–14.

5   Delumeau, 'Commerce malouin', p 309.

6   J. Delumeau, 'La guerre de course française sous l'Ancien Régime', (Paper presented at the XV International Seminar on Maritime History held at the XIV International Congress of Historical Science, San Francisco 1975), pp 292–3.

7   Janine Lemay, 'La guerre de course à Saint-Malo pendant les guerres de Louis XV', *Positions des thèses soutenues par les élèves de l'École des Chartes*, (Paris 1948), p 88. It has not been possible to see the thesis from which these figures were taken.

8   Delumeau, 'Guerre de course française', p 290, gives totals of 46 privateers and 176 prizes.

9   Rennes Archives, 9B 435a–c, enregistrements des commissions de corsaires.

10 For the War of Austrian Succession, see *ibid* 9B 435d, and for the War of American Independence, Le Coz, 'La guerre de course à Saint-Malo sous Louis XVI (Diplôme d'Études Supérieures, Rennes 1957), Table A. The figures for the latter war are: below 15 tons 9, 16–50 tons 19, 51–100 tons 13, 101–200 tons 2, over 200 tons 5.

11 F. Robidou, *Les derniers corsaires malouins; la course sous la République et l'Empire, 1793–1814* (Rennes 1919), p 10.

12 Delumeau, 'Guerre de course française', p 290.
13 Lemay, 'Guerre de course', p 86.
14 H. Malo, *Les derniers corsaires: Dunkerque (1715–1815)*, (Paris 1935),
    p 45; Delumeau,' 'Guerre de course française', p 293; Archives
    Nationales AFIV 1199, report of de Cres to Napoleon, 6 September
    1811, quoted in Robidou, *Derniers corsaires malouins*, p 215.
15 *Ibid*, p 123.
16 For a detailed account of the cost of the ship, see Rennes Archives,
    Um 87, Napoléon.
17 Rennes Archives, Um 12, Tribunal de commerce de Saint-Malo, le
    Bougainville.
18 Rennes Archives 2 Um 7, 77.
19 Rennes Archives, C4 309, f 84, report of Pierre Beaugendre, master of
    the *Reine*.
20 J. S. Bromley, 'The importance of Dunkirk (1688–1713) reconsidered',
    (Paper presented at the XV International Seminar on Maritime History
    held at the XIV International Congress of Historical Science, San
    Francisco 1975), p 232. The following account of Dunkirk privateering
    is based on this excellent study.
21 Delumeau, 'Guerre de course française', p 287.
22 *Ibid*, p 283.
23 R. Richard, 'Le financement des armements maritimes au XVIIIe
    siècle. Une approche; le cas du Havre', *Bulletin de la Societé d'Histoire
    moderne*, xiv (1969), pp 11–12.
24 Cherbourg Archives, 2P/25/No 3, Inscription maritime 1745.
25 R. Thomas Lacroix, 'La guerre de course dans les ports des amirautés
    de Vannes et de Lorient (1744–83)', *Memoires de la Societé d'Histoire
    et d'Archéologie de Bretagne*, xxvi, (1946), p 167.
26 Delumeau, 'Guerre de course française', p 283.
27 Adm 1/1497, Botterell to Adm., Whitehaven, 26 June 1777.
28 A. Péju, *La course à Nantes aux XVIIe et XVIIIe siècles*, (Paris 1900)
    p 94; M. Launay, 'La guerre de course à Nantes pendant la Guerre de
    Succession d'Espagne' (D.E.S., Rennes 1962), p 172, quoted in J.
    Meyer, *L'armement nantais dans le XVIIIe siècle* (Paris 1969), p 83.
29 *Ibid*, pp 82, 114.
30 *Ibid*, p 81.
31 Adm. 1/3838, Fenwick to Adm., Elsinore, 7 August 1799.
32 Péju, *La course à Nantes*, pp 168–71. Prizes recorded at Nantes which
    were made by vessels from other ports have been excluded.
33 Meyer, *Armement nantais*, p 246.
34 A. M. de Boislisle, *Correspondences des Contrôleurs Généraux des
    Finances avec les Intendants des Provinces* (Paris 1883), ii, 245;
    Isambert, Decrusy, Taillandier, *Receuil général des anciennes lois
    françaises depuis l'an 420 jusqu'à la Révolution de 1789* (Paris 1833),
    xx, 136–7.
35 J. S. Bromley, 'Le commerce de la France de l'ouest et la guerre
    maritime (1702–12), *Annales du Midi*, 65 (1953), p 63.
36 R. Bélanger, *Les Basques dans l'estuaire du Saint-Laurent, 1535–1635*,
    (Montreal 1971), pp 33–58.
37 The extent of this decline during the wars with England is noted in A.

Lespagnol, 'Guerre et activites maritimes: l'example de Saint-Malo pendant la Guerre d'Amérique', (Paper read at the 14th Conference of the International Commission for Maritime History, July 1974), pp 11–18.

38 P. Rectoran, *Corsaires basques et bayonnais du XVe au XIXe siècle* (Bayonne 1946), p 281.

39 For a list, E. Ducéré, *Les corsaires sous l'Ancien Régime* (Bayonne 1895), p 269.

40 For the request to lift the embargo on privateering at Bayonne, Archives Nationales, F2/74–5, memorial on the necessity of continuing to fit out ships at Bayonne, undated with letter from de Grandbourg to the King, 31 May 1758.

41 Archives Nationales, B4/97, pp 136–45.

42 F. Jaupart, *L'activité commerciale de Bayonne au XVIIIe siècle* (Bayonne 1966), p 135.

43 Archives départementales des Basses Pyrénées, Amirauté de Bayonne, B Supplément, No 26, 8 December 1760.

44 *Ibid*, 8 May 1761.

45 *Ibid*, 8 September 1757.

46 *Ibid*, 8 April 1763.

47 Lacroix, 'Guerre de course', p 160.

48 Amirauté de Bayonne, B Supplément, No 26, 6 February, 6 March, 3 April 1747.

49 *Ibid*, 6 March 1747, 17 June 1746, 20 February 1758.

50 Archives Nationales, Marine B4/97, pp 136–45.

51 The *Labourt* received its first letter of marque on 23 October 1757 and its last prize was entered in the Amirauté records on 27 November 1761.

52 *Jupiter*, first letter of marque 21 May 1757, last prize 22 September 1759; *Grunvel* (?), letter of marque 21 October 1760; *Guerrier*, insurance policy 4 December 1760, last prize 15 January 1762; *Audacieux*, first letter of marque 28 January 1762, last prize 11 April 1763.

53 *Ibid*, 16 July 1759. He also ransomed the *Thila*(?) of New York for £6,000 and the *Mercury* of London for £900, both 16 July 1759.

54 Figures quoted in Jaupart, p 122.

55 G. Donin, *La Mediterranée de 1803 à 1805; pirates et corsaires aux Îles Ioniennes* (Paris 1917), pp 57–8, 98–104.

56 *Ibid*, pp 184–5.

57 *Ibid*, pp 191–2.

Chapter 2   *The Organization of Convoys and their Departure*

1 W. E. Minchinton, 'The merchants in England in the eighteenth century', *Explorations in entrepreneurial history*, December 1757, pp 62, 64, 66, 69.

2 W. Laird Clowes, *The Royal Navy* (2 vols, 1879, 1903), i, 198.

3 T. S. Willan, *The English coasting trade, 1600–1750* (Manchester, 1938), pp 28–9.

4 *Cal. S. P. Dom.*, *13 February 1689–April 1690* (reprint 1969), p 27, 16 March 1689, Earl of Nottingham to Adm.

5 J. A. Johnston, 'Parliament and the navy 1688–1714', (unpublished Ph.D. thesis, University of Sheffield, 1969), pp 227–9, 238, 243 ff.
6 Adm 3/2, minute of 20 Nov 1689.
7 Adm 2/378, Secretary to Chief Magistrate at Leith, 15 Aug 1689; Adm 2/379, Secretary to Mr Arthur Shallott, 13 Dec 1689.
8 J. Ehrman, *The navy in the war of William III 1689–1697* (Cambridge 1953), pp 301–2.
9 Adm 3/2, minute of 20 Nov 1689; correspondence is contained in Adm 2/169; 30/10 (Board to Committee).
10 L. Cullen, 'Ireland and Irishmen in eighteenth-century privateering' (paper presented at the XV International Seminar on Maritime History at the XIV International Congress of Historical Sciences, San Francisco 1975), p 470.
11 R. Davis, *The rise of the English shipping industry in the 17th and 18th centuries* (Newton Abbot 1972), p 316.
12 J. H. Owen, *War at sea under Queen Anne* (Cambridge 1938), pp 57–61.
13 Johnston, 'Parliament and the navy', pp 276–7.
14 Owen, *War at sea*, p 102.
15 6 Anne c 65; Johnston, 'Parliament and the navy', pp 281–4, 298–301.
16 A. D. Francis, *The wine trade* (1972), p 108.
17 Adm 1/4091, ff 71, 300, Secretary of State to Adm., 31 Oct 1706, 26 June 1707.
18 K. G. Davies, *The Royal African Company* (Atheneum ed, New York 1970), pp 186, 208, 210.
19 Defoe, quoted in R. C. Jarvis, 'Eighteenth century Dorset shipping', *Proceedings of the Dorset Natural History and Archeological Society*, XCII (1971), p 250.
20 R. W. Hidy, *The House of Baring in American trade and finance; English merchant bankers at work 1763–1861*, (Cambridge, Mass., 1949), p 5; W. G. Hoskins, *Industry, trade and people in Exeter 1688–1800* (2nd ed, Exeter 1968), pp 15–17, 63, 71–4.
21 Adm 1/5248, Order in Council dated 28 Feb 1688/9.
22 P. McGrath, *The merchant venturers of Bristol; a history of the Society of Merchant Venturers of the city of Bristol from its origin to the present day* (Bristol 1975), pp 81, 170.
23 S.R.O., R.H. 9/1/200, Account book of an Edinburgh merchant trading with France and Holland, 1711.
24 D. Swann, 'The pace and progress of port investment in England 1660–1830', *Yorkshire Bulletin of Economic and Social Research*, 12, pp 33–5.
25 L. F. Stock (ed), *Proceedings and debates of the British parliaments respecting North America, vol V 1739–54* (Washington D.C., 1941), p 122.
26 *Ibid*, p 125.
27 Adm 3/54, minute of 21 May 1746; Adm 1/1482, Hugh Bonfoy to Adm., *South Sea Castle*, in Plymouth Sound, 21 Nov 1746; Adm 3/52, minute of 25 Dec 1745.
28 Hoskins, *Industry of Exeter*, p 76.
29 Exeter R.O., 71/8, Journal of Samuel Milford, *passim*.
30 McGrath, *Bristol merchants*, p 171.

31 Adm 3/53, minute of 15 Feb 1745/6; J. Latimer, *The History of the Society of Merchant Venturers of the city of Bristol with some account of the anterior merchants' guilds* (Bristol 1903), p 201.
32 T. M. Devine, 'Glasgow merchants and the collapse of the tobacco trade 1775-1783', *Scottish Historical Review*, LII (1973), pp 53-6.
33 R. C. Jarvis, 'Eighteenth century Dorset shipping', *Proceedings of the Dorset Natural History and Archeological Society*, XCII (1971), p 252.
34 McGrath, *Bristol merchants*, pp 172-4.
35 Society of Merchant Venturers, Bristol, index of records; trade and public affairs, pp 78-9, Society to Adm, 12 May 1783 and 17 June 1784.
36 F. E. Hyde, *Liverpool and the Mersey; an economic history of a port 1700-1970* (Newton Abbot 1971), pp 31-4.
37 T. M. Devine, 'Glasgow merchants and the collapse of the tobacco trade 1775-1783', *Scottish Historical Review*, LII (1973), pp 50-74.
38 T. M. Devine, 'Glasgow merchants in colonial trade 1770-1815' (unpublished Ph.D. thesis, Strathclyde University 1971), pp 264-70.
39 Glasgow City Archives, Spiers Papers, Letterbook 1781-1789, no pagination, Alexander Spiers to Thomas Eden and Co., Glasgow, 8 Nov 1781.
40 Davis, *Rise of English shipping*, p 318.
41 Scottish Record Office, GD 150/2608, Morton Papers, Busta to Morton, 29 Dec. 1737, records that it was ten days before a boat could report the shipwreck of a vessel on the Island of Yell.
42 38 Geo III, c. 76.
43 H. S. K. Kent, 'The background to Anglo–Norwegian relations', *Norseman*, 11 (1953), p 154.
44 Society of Merchant Venturers, Bristol, index of records; trade and public affairs, pp 394-6, questions and trial relating to Captain Marshall's conduct in escorting a West India convoy, 6 and 17 November 1795, 6 January and 25 February 1796.
45 See below, p 96
46 A. N. Ryan (ed), *The Saumarez Papers; selections from the Baltic correspondence of Vice-Admiral Sir James Saumarez 1808-1812* (1968), pp 65-7.
47 Adm 1/3838, letters from British consuls, contains much information for the War of American Independence.
48 A. N. Ryan, 'The melancholy fate of the Baltic ships in 1811', *Mariner's Mirror*, 1, 1964, pp 123-34 and Commander W. E. May's comments, *ibid*, p 282.
49 Ryan, Saumarez Papers, pp xx-xxi.
50 Davis, *Rise of English shipping*, p 222.
51 G. J. Marcus, *A naval history of England; vol 2 the age of Nelson* (1971), p 370.
52 Adm 1/2046, Lynn to Adm., *Roebuck*, Hamoaze, 20 Dec 1757.
53 W. E. May, *A history of marine navigation* (1973), pp 32-3, 168-9.
54 Adm 1/306, Frankland to Adm., 18 Nov 1755.
55 A. Spencer (ed), *Memoirs of William Hickey, vol II (1775-1782)*, (1918) pp 12-13.

Chapter 3 *Marine Insurance*

1   The following account is taken from B. E. Supple, *The Royal Exchange Assurance* (1970), pp 9–30.

2   Quoted in C. Wright and C. E. Fayle, *A history of Lloyds* (1928), pp 68–70.

3   *An essay on insurances*, i, 430, quoted in A. H. John, 'The London insurance market of the eighteenth century', *Economica* (1958), p 127.

4   M. L. A. Boiteux, 'Contribution de l'assurance à l'histoire de l'économie en France', in *Les sources de l'histoire maritime en Europe*, M. Mollat (ed), (Paris 1962), p 454.

5   John, 'London insurance', p 136.

6   J. Cavaignac, *Jean Pellet, commerçant en gros 1694–1772* (Paris 1967), p 79; P. Viles, 'The shipping interest of Bordeaux 1774–1793', (unpublished Ph.D., Harvard University 1964), p 184. It is not clear whether all these were French rates.

7   For an account of the company's business in this war, see R. P. Crowhurst, 'Marine insurance and the trade of Rotterdam 1755–63', *Maritime History*, 2 (1972), pp 140–50; Alice Carter, 'How to revise treaties without negotiating: compromise, mutual fears and the Anglo–Dutch trade disputes of 1759', in *Studies in diplomatic history: essays in memory of D. B. Horn*, R. M. Hatton and M. S. Anderson (eds), (1970), pp 227–8.

8   John, 'Marine insurance', p 140.

9   *Ibid*, p 128.

10 Premiums at London and Liverpool in 1804–5, for example, can be compared in Janson and d'Aquilar's rate books, Add MSS 34, 669–70 and Liverpool Underwriters Association Rate Books A–C of d' Aquilar.

11 Wright and Fayle, *History of Lloyds*, pp 95–6.

12 His life is the subject of Lucy Sutherland, *A London merchant 1695–1774* (1933).

13 Wright and Fayle, *History of Lloyds*, p 190.

14 Sutherland, *London merchant*, p 69.

15 S. E. Morrison, *The maritime history of Massachusetts, 1783–1860* (Cambridge, Mass., new ed 1961), p 168. For an account of the development of American insurance in the eighteenth century, see C. Bradford, 'A premium on progress; an outline history of the American insurance market 1820–1970', *Newcomen Society of North America* (1970), pp 9–10.

16 38 Geo III c 76. The exceptions were East Indiamen, Hudson's Bay Company ships, vessels engaged in the Irish trade and fast, well-armed ships that were licensed to 'run', i.e. sail independently.

17 By 1764 surveys were carried out in fifteen ports; for an account of the methods of classification used for the Register of 1797–8, see G. Higgins, *Annals of Lloyds Register* (1934), pp 18, 20, 25.

18 *Williamson's Liverpool Advertiser*, 28 May 1756 and Janson's premiums quoted in Wright and Fayle, *History of Lloyds*, p 190.

19 Add MSS 34, 669, ff 31v, 32, Rate Book of Janson.

20 *Ibid*, ff 36v, 37.

21 Viles, 'Bordeaux shipping', p 184.

22 L. F. Stock (ed), *Proceedings and debates of the British Parliament respecting North America* (5 vols, Washington 1924–41), v, 523.

23 The following are taken from the records of the Maatschappij van Assurantie, Discontering en Beleening der Stad Rotterdam, Assurantie Boeke, in the Gemeente Archief, Rotterdam.

24 *Herbert v Pigou*, J. A. Park, *A system of the law of marine insurances* (1787), pp 387–90; there was a duty for the commodore to provide convoy and not ask for reward, J. Weskett, *A complete digest of the theory, laws and practice of insurance* (1781), p 138.

25 Park, *Marine insurance*, pp 398–9.

26 *Ibid*, p 399.

27 There were a number of variations, but Mansfield ordered in *Lilly v Ewer*, in February 1779, that fine distinctions ought to be suppressed; *English Reports*, vol 99, p 52.

28 *Ibid*, vol 171, p 21. See also *Gordon v Morley*, *ibid*, vol 93, p 1171 and *Campbell v Bardieu*, 2 Strang 1265.

29 *English Reports*, vol 126, pp 746–7.

30 *Ibid*, vol 171, pp 18–9.

31 *Hibbert v Pigou*, May 1783, *ibid*, vol 99, pp 624–7.

32 *Manning v Gist*, April 1782, *ibid*, vol 99, pp 545–6.

33 *Cohen v Hinckley*, 1 Taunton 249.

34 *Laing v Glover*, June 1813, *English Reports*, vol 128, pp 604–6.

35 Weskett, *Digest of insurances*, p 140; see also the case of the *Ranger* merchant ship in Park, *Marine insurance*, pp 38–40.

36 *Ibid*, pp 430–2. No date is given.

37 Weskett, *Digest of insurances*, p 171; Park, *Marine insurance*, p 341.

38 Weskett, *Digest of insurances*, pp 8–9, Park, *Marine insurance*, p 133; also *Hog v Gouldney* in W. Beawes, *Lex mercatoria rediviva: or the merchant's directory* (4th ed 1783), p 310.

39 Park, *Marine insurance*, pp 252–7, Weskett, *Digest of insurances*, pp 281–8.

40 13 Geo 2 c 4, f 18 and 29 Geo 2 c 34 f 24 quoted in Park, *Marine insurance*, p 157.

41 *Ibid*, pp 167–70.

42 *Ibid*, pp 178–86.

43 *Ibid*, pp 187–9.

44 Weskett, *Digest of insurances*, pp 19–20; Magens on the other hand advised underwriters always to pay the cost of cables, N. Magens, *Essay on insurances* (2 vols, 1755), i, 52–3.

45 *Barclay v Etherington*, Beawes, *Lex mercatoria*, p 309.

46 See below, p 255. For account of the attack, see R. P. Crowhurst, 'D'Estaing's cruise in the Indian Ocean; a landmark in privateering voyages', *Studia*, 35 (1972), pp 60–2.

47 Park, *Marine insurance*, pp 205–17; Weskett, *Digest of insurances*, pp 119–23.

48 Quoted in Park, *Marine insurance*, p 217.

Chapter 4 *The Northern States and Canada*
1 Elizabeth B. Schumpeter, *English overseas trade statistics 1697–1808* (Oxford 1960), tables V and VI, pp 17–18.

2   D. R. McManis, *Colonial New England; a historical geography* (New York 1975), p 49.

3   *Ibid*, pp 103–5.

4   H. A. Innes, *The cod fisheries; the history of an international economy* (Toronto 1940), p 161 and C. and Roberta Bridenbaugh, *No peace beyond the line. The English in the Caribbean 1624–1690* (New York 1972), p 343.

5   G. S. Graham, 'The naval defence of British North America 1739–63', *Transactions of the Royal Historical Society*, 4th ser, XXX (1948), p 103, footnote.

6   Sir Charles Whitworth, *State of the trade of Great Britain in its imports and exports progressively from the year 1697* (1776), p 63.

7   McManis, *Colonial New England*, p 109.

8   Adm 1/1776, Stafford Fairborne to Adm., *Tilbury*, St John's, Newfoundland, 13 Sept 1700.

9   Adm 1/5248, Orders in Council, Kensington, 27 Jan 1696/7.

10 Adm 2/378, Adm. to Torrington, 12 Sept 1689.

11 L. F. Stock (ed), *Proceedings and debates of the British Parliament respecting North America, vol III, 1702–1727*, (Washington 1930), p 39.

12 *Ibid*, p 107.

13 *Ibid*, p 112.

14 G. F. Dow and J. H. Edmonds, *The pirates of the New England coast 1630–1750* (New York 1968), p 68.

15 *The maritime history of Massachusetts 1783–1860* (Cambridge, Mass., 1961), pp 6–7.

16 T. E. Norton, *The fur trade in colonial New York 1686–1776* (Madison, Wisconsin 1974), pp 6–7.

17 B. and L. Bailyn, *Massachusetts shipping 1697–1714; a statistical study* (Cambridge, Mass., 1959), p 21.

18 L. H. Leder and V. P. Carosso, 'Robert Livingston (1654–1728): businessman of colonial New York', *Business History Review*, XXX (1956), pp 33, 37.

19 C. Bridenbaugh, *Cities in the wilderness. The first centuries of urban life in America 1625–1742* (New York, new ed. 1960), p 176.

20 Bailyn, *Massachusetts shipping*, p 56.

21 *Calendar of Treasury Papers, 1556–7 – 1696* (1868), p 517, Report of the Commissioners of the Navy to the Lords of the Treasury, 5 June 1696. Great quantities of pitch, tar and turpentine were shipped to England; A. Dewar (ed), *The voyages and travels of Captain Nathaniel Uring* (new ed 1928), p 79.

22 Bailyn, *Massachusetts shipping*, p 53.

23 Bridenbaugh, *Cities in the wilderness*, p 175.

24 G. B. Nash, 'Slaves and slave owners in colonial Philadelphia', *William and Mary Quarterly*, 3rd ser., XXX (1973), pp 223–56.

25 *Calendar of State Papers, 1708–1714* (1879), p 36, vol CVII, Col. Robert Quary to the Lord High Treasurer, 20 April 1708.

26 J. H. Plumb, *Sir Robert Walpole. The making of a statesman* (1956), p 121; *Sir Robert Walpole, the King's minister* (1960), pp 246–7.

27 The creation of this interdependent economy on a European scale

between the sixteenth and the eighteenth centuries is the subject of R. Davis, *The rise of the Atlantic economies* (1973), *passim*.

28 R. Davis, *The rise of the English shipping industry in the seventeenth and eighteenth centuries* (Newton Abbot 1972), p 68.
29 Davis, *Rise of the Atlantic economies*, p 272.
30 H. A. Innes, *The cod fisheries; the history of an international economy* (Toronto 1940), p 161.
31 *Ibid*, p 136. These had displaced Havre, Dieppe and the Norman ports early in the eighteenth century.
32 McManis, *Colonial New England*, p 106.
33 J. Gwyn, *The enterprising admiral; the personal fortune of Admiral Sir Peter Warren* (Montreal 1974), pp 12–13. The naval documents relating to the siege are given in J. Gwyn, *The Royal Navy and North America: the Warren Papers, 1736–1752* (Navy Records Society, 1973), pp 83–115.
34 G. S. Graham, *Empire of the North Atlantic; the maritime struggle for North America* (Toronto 1950), pp 123–5.
35 *Ibid*, p 127.
36 *Ibid*, pp 127–8.
37 Dewar, *Voyages of Captain Uring*, p 85.
38 G. S. Graham, 'The naval defence of British North America 1739–1763', *Transactions of the Royal Historical Society*, 4th ser., XXX (1948), p 97.
39 *Ibid*, p 98.
40 Adm 1/2653, Peter Warren to Adm., 8 June 1741/2.
41 Adm 1/2640, Thomas Smith to Adm., *Princess Mary*, Lisbon River, 7 Jan. 1743/4.
42 Adm 1/2640, Richard Spry to Adm., *Comet*, Boston, 7 Nov. 1744.
43 Davis, *Rise of the Atlantic economies*, pp 273–5.
44 P. L. White, *The Beekmans of New York in politics and commerce 1647–1877* (New York 1956), p 362; E. Edelman, 'Thomas Hancock. Colonial merchant', *Journal of Economic and Business History*, I (1928–9), p 94.
45 The following account is based on a series of letters in Treasury and Admiralty papers: T 1/385, Baker to Clevland, 20 Jan. 1759; T 1/389, Clevland to Martin, 20 Jan. 1759; T 1/389, Baker to Martin, 14 Mar. 1759; T 1/389, Colebrooke and Nesbitt to Treasury, 25 Apr. 1759 and 10 May 1759; T 1/415, Colebrooke and Nesbitt to Martin, 2 July 1762; T 1/418, Colebrooke to Dyson, 12 Nov 1762; T 29/33, minute of 7 Feb 1759, Adm 1/4286, Martin to Clevland, 8 Feb 1759, Adm 3/66, minute of 23 Apr 1759.
46 S. F. Chyet, *Lopez of Newport; colonial American merchant prince*, (Detroit 1970), pp 84–5.
47 *Ibid*, p 76; Virginia D. Harrington, *The New York merchant on the eve of the Revolution* (New York 1935), p 173.
48 Graham, *Empire of the North Atlantic*, p 208.
49 *Ibid*, pp 323–4.
50 *Ibid*, p 220.
51 *Ibid*, p 325.
52 White, *Beekmans of New York*, p 449.

Chapter 5 *The Southern States*

1   Stella H. Sutherland, *Population distribution in colonial America* (New York 1936), p 186.
2   Sir Charles Whitworth, *State of the trade of Great Britain in its imports and exports progressively from the year 1697* (1776), p 69.
3   R. Davis, *The rise of the English shipping industry in the 17th and 18th centuries* (Newton Abbot 1972), p 273.
4   Sutherland, *Population distribution*, p 183.
5   *Ibid*, p 184.
6   In view of the continuing debate on slavery it is impossible to say whether the plantation economy was dependent on slave imports to maintain tobacco production at the end of the seventeenth century.
7   A. P. Middleton, 'The Chesapeake convoy system 1662–1763', *William and Mary Quarterly*, III, 3rd ser (1946), p 18. Unless otherwise stated, information on the Chesapeake convoys between 1689 and 1713 is taken from this source.
8   Davis, *Rise of shipping industry*, p 184.
9   *Ibid*, p 59.
10 Freight rates are a good guide to shipping activity. The normal peace time rate was £5 to £5 10s per ton, but in the wars after 1689 rates of £12 or £13 charged for long periods; *ibid*, p 289.
11 J. M. Price, *France and the Chesapeake. A history of the tobacco monopoly, 1674–1791, and of its relationships to the British and American tobacco trades* (2 vols, Ann Arbor, Michigan, 1973), i, 179.
12 P. G. E. Clemens, 'The rise of Liverpool, 1665–1750', *Economic History Review*, 2nd ser, XXIX (1976), p 215.
13 H. F. Rankin, *The golden age of piracy* (Williamsburg, Va., 1969), p 52.
14 Elizabeth Donnan, 'Eighteenth-century English merchants; Micajah Perry', *Journal of Economic and Business History*, IV (1931–2), p 90, reports one occasion, in 1708, when London merchants overcame their scruples in this regard because they were afraid that the colonists might try to manufacture their own linen and woollen cloth.
15 Adm 1/1692, Francis Dove to Adm., *Warwick*, 17 Sept. 1702; L. F. Stock (ed), *Proceedings and debates of the British parliaments respecting North America, vol III, 1702–1727* (Washington 1930), p 3. The same dominance of the London trade is shown in a convoy list for 1700: of 57 ships, 26 were bound for London, 5 for Bristol, 5 for Liverpool and the balance to British outports; C O 5/1311, No 10 (iii), pp 400–1, list of fleet from Virginia on 9 June 1700 under *Essex Prize*, quoted in Middleton, 'Chesapeake convoy', pp 204–7.
16 Donnan, 'Micajah Perry', p 90.
17 Davis, *Rise of shipping industry*, p 285.
18 For ship sizes:

LONDON SHIPS: TONS SERVED PER MAN

	For Virginia and Maryland
1686	9.8
1726	10.8
1736	11.0

Source: Davis, *Rise of shipping industry*, p 59.

AVERAGE SIZE OF VESSELS TRADING IN THE CHESAPEAKE

Year	Average size of vessels	Observations
1693–1700	113.3	538
1726	89.5	220
1732–5	58.5	528

Source: J. F. Shepherd and G. M. Walton, *Shipping, maritime trade and the economic development of colonial North America* (Cambridge 1972), p 195.

19 The role of credit in the rise of Glasgow is emphasized in J. M. Price, 'The rise of Glasgow in the Chesapeake tobacco trade, 1707–1775', *William and Mary Quarterly*, 3rd ser, XI (1954), pp 194–7.

20 Middleton, 'Chesapeake convoys', p 192.

21 Details of losses in 1745 are from *ibid*.

22 *Ibid*, p 193.

23 *Ibid*.

24 *Ibid*, p 194.

25 Stock, *Proceedings*, v, 131, 185.

26 Price, *France and the Chesapeake*, i, 388.

27 Shepherd and Walton, *Shipping*, p 195.

28 PRO 30/8, vol 95, part II, f 158, James Buchan, Thomas Hanbury, William Anderson, John Buchanan, Edward Athawes to William Pitt, London, 6 January 1757. They claimed the trade was worth £700,000 a year to Britain, as well as another £100,000 on items other than tobacco.

29 Adm 1/1443, Adams to Clevland, Diana, at Spithead, 1 April 1762.

30 F. C. Huntley, 'The seaborne trade of Virginia in mid-eighteenth century: Port Hampton', *Virginia Magazine of History and Biography*, LIX (1951), pp 301–2; the figures are for 1752. Dinwiddie's estimate is taken from R. A. Brock (ed), *The official records of Robert Dinwiddie*, (2 vols, Richmond, Va., 1883–4), i, 385.

31 P. H. Giddens, 'Trade and industry in colonial Maryland, 1753–1769', *Journal of Economic and Business History*, IV (1931–2), p 254.

32 The account of this convoy's return from the Chesapeake is taken from Adm 1/1443, Adams to Clevland, *Diana*, 1 and 4 April 1762.

33 For an account of the cruise by four French naval vessels, *La Malicieuse*, *Le Courageux*, *L'Hermione*, and *Le Sage* off the American coast when returning to France from service in the West Indies, see Archives Nationales, Marine, B4/103, ff 283–5, de Longueville to Berryer, Vigo, *La Malicieuse*, 22 August 1761, f 297, Kerguelin Trémarec to the King, *Le Sage*, 17 August 1761, ff 304–5, copy of a letter to Berryer, Vigo, *L'Hermione*, 22 August 1761.

34 Archives Nationales, Marine B4/78, f 48, Frégats pour croiser aux côtes de la Virginie et des autres colonies anglaises de l'Amérique Septentrionale, 26 April 1758.

35 Archives Nationales, Marine, B4/103, ff 216–8, Le Vassor de la Touche no doubt expected that he would be ordered to sail with his frigate and be able to earn prize money.

36 Whitworth, *Trade of Great Britain*, p 53.

37 *Ibid*, p 69.

38 Stock, *Proceedings*, v, 127.

39   The construction date of the *Phoenix* is unknown. The fifth vessel to carry this name was a fifth rate, burnt in 1692; the next recorded was the eighth, a sixth rate built in 1743; T. D. Manning and C. F. Walker, *British warship names*, (1959), p 342. Details of rates, construction and disposal of naval vessels are taken from this source.

40   Details of the clash between Captain Fanshawe and the Carolina merchants is contained in Stock, *Proceedings*, v, 127–8.

41   C. Bridenbaugh, *Cities in revolt. Urban life in America, 1746–1776* (New York 1955), p 46; F. B. C. Bradlee, *Colonial trade and commerce, 1733–1774* (Salem, Mass., 1927), p 12.

42   Anne Bezanson, R. D. Gray and M. Hussey, *Prices in colonial Pennsylvania* (Philadelphia 1935), pp 89–92.

43   Quoted in Bridenbaugh, *Cities in revolt*, p 46.

44   Sutherland, *Population distribution*, p 262.

45   Whitworth, *Trade of Great Britain*, pp 53–4.

46   Sutherland, *Population distribution*, pp 249–50.

47   Add MSS 32, 866, p 289, Lyttleton to Newcastle, Charles Town, 19 July 1756.

48   No convoys sailed from Charleston in 1756. Captain Hale with the frigate *Winchelsea* was there for a time in mid-summer, but his duty was to guard the Acadians; Adm 1/1891, Hale to Clevland, *Winchelsea*, 3 August 1756.

49   There is no official record of convoys sailing from Charleston in 1759 or 1760, although Robert Man escorted a convoy from England to the port in 1759, and in March 1760 was reporting to the Admiralty as escort for the Bristol trade; Adm 1/2112, Man to Adm., *Milford*, in Kingroad, 26 Mar 1760. It appears from the port records of Charleston that the convoy sailed from there in mid-May 1759; C.O. 5/510, pp 74–6, shows that seven ships were cleared out from Charleston between 3 and 11 May, of which two were bound for London, one for Poole, one for Cowes – all of which required convoy to the English Channel – two from Bristol and one from Glasgow. The same comments apply to the convoy for 1760, for which there is no record.

50   C.O. 5/510, ff 55–94, *passim*.

51   It is clear from the attempts of the Halifax merchant, Joshua Mauger, in March 1757 to buy as much molasses, pork, butter and peas in the American colonies and England that foodstuffs were in great demand; Archives Nationales, Marine B4/95, f. 86, Joshua Mauger to Mrs Sarah Nickelson, Halifax, 28 March 1757.

52   Adm 1/2110, Man to Adm., *Penguin*, Spithead, 12 Mar. 1758; Adm 1/2111, Man to Adm., *Penguin*, Dover Road, 23 Apr. 1759.

53   There is no record of trade between the outports and Georgia until 1760; Customs 3/56–60, *passim*, and this is supported by the records of payments of 'seamen's sixpences' by Bristol merchants, which do not show any vessel sailing to Savannah; Society of Merchant Venturers, Bristol, annual list of ships.

54   Adm 1/2112, Marlow to Clevland, *Dolphin*, Charles Town, 15 May 1761; a vivid eye witness account of the hurricane is given in the *South Carolina Weekly Gazette* for 6 May 1761, a copy of which is enclosed in C.O. 5/20, f 133, Bull to Pitt, Charles Town, 16 May 1761.

55 Adm 1/2113, Marlow to Adm., *Dolphin*, Charles Town, 15 May 1761, enclosing letters from William Bull dated 30 Mar. and 15 Apr.
56 Adm 1/2111, Man to Adm., *Penguin*, Dover Road, 23 Apr. 1759. The minimum number of ships for a Carolina and Georgia convoy was six; Adm 1/1442, Antrobus to Adm., *Surprize*, Downs, 11 May 1759.
57 Adm 1/1606, Cuming to Adm., *Blandford*, South Carolina, 22 Aug. 1758, and enclosure Hale to Cuming, Coopers River, 7 Aug. 1758; Cuming to Adm., *Blandford*, in St Mary's Sound, at Scilly, 29 Oct. 1758.
58 Adm 1/1893, Hale to Adm., Port Louis, 20 Nov. 1758; Saunders gives a similar account, except that he gives the date of the storm as the 27th instead of the 16th; Adm 1/90, Saunders to Adm., off Brest, 28 Oct. 1758; J. K. Laughton, 'On convoys', *The Naval Journal* (1894), p 238.
59 D. Syrett, *Shipping and the American war 1775–83; a study of British transport organization*, (1970), p 78 for example states 'British carrying trade with the American mainland ceased'.
60 G. S. Graham, *Empire of the North Atlantic; the maritime struggle for North America* (Toronto 1950), pp 222–3.

Chapter 6 *West Indies*
1 R. S. Dunn, *Sugar and slaves, the rise of the planter class in the English West Indies 1624–1713* (1973), p 312.
2 C. and R. Bridenbaugh, *No peace beyond the line. The English in the Caribbean 1624–1690* (New York 1972), p 276.
3 Whitworth, *Trade of Great Britain*, p 49.
4 *Ibid*, p 69.
5 Adm 2/379, Admiralty to Blathwayt, 27 Dec. 1689.
6 M. Pawson and D. Buisseret, *Port Royal Jamaica* (1975), p 43.
7 J. Ehrman, *The navy in the war of William III, 1689–1697*, (Cambridge 1953), p 609.
8 Pawson and Buisseret, *Port Royal*, p 43.
9 Dunn, *Sugar and slaves*, p 220.
10 Pawson and Buisseret, *Port Royal*, pp 45, 65.
11 Dunn, *Sugar and slaves*, p 203.
12 Adm 1/3814, Popple to Burchett, Whitehall, 15 Dec 1703.
13 R. Davis, 'English foreign trade 1700–1774', in *The growth of English overseas trade in the 17th and 18th centuries*, W. E. Minchinton (ed), (1969), table p 118.
14 Davis, *English shipping industry*, quoted in Dunn, *Sugar and slaves*, p 207.
15 Adm 1/3814, Popple to Burchett, Whitehall, 17 Nov. 1703.
16 Sir Alan Burns, *A history of the West Indies*, p. 414.
17 *Cal. S. P. Dom., 1703–1704* (1924), p 75, Southwell to Nottingham, 4 Aug. 1703.
18 Adm 1/3814, Popple to Burchett, Whitehall, 17 Nov. 1704.
19 *Cal. S. P. Dom., 1702–1703, vol 1*, (1916) p 720, warranted by Rear-Admiral Whetstone to Captain Huntingdon, Port Royal, 17 May 1703.
20 For the proposal, Stock, *Proceedings*, iii, 28.
21 *Ibid*, p 178. It is not clear whether the sums of money are in sterling or colonial currency.

22 Adm 1/4091, ff 114, 220, Board of Trade and Plantations to Admiralty, 11 Dec. 1706/7.
23 Adm 2/428, p 97, Admiralty to Popple, 23 Feb. 1708/9.
24 Stock, *Proceedings*, iii, 157–8.
25 Adm 1/1823, Gordon to Admiralty, 29 Sept. 1707.
26 R. Pares, *War and trade in the West Indies, 1739–1763* (Oxford 1936), p 116.
27 B. Mc L. Ranft (ed), *The Vernon Papers* (1958), p 52, Merchants of Jamaica, Kingston to Vernon, 21 Jan. 1739–40.
28 Pares, *War and trade*, p 80.
29 *Ibid*, p 309.
30 For delays in this and subsequent years, see Adm 1/235, Cotes to Adm, *Malborough*, Port Royal, 24 May and 7 Aug. 1757, 10 Feb. and 19 June, 1 Nov. 1759.
31 Adm 1/87, Martin to Adm, *Captain*, in Plymouth Sound, 17 Mar. 1744–5.
32 For Holmes' report, see Adm 1/236, Holmes to Adm, 23 July 1761.
33 E. Long, *The history of Jamaica* (3 vols, 1744), i, 311.
34 Captain Nathaniel Uring recounts one occasion when, from personal experience, the master of a merchant ship insisted that the island he saw was the South Keys. He was wrong; it was the Grand Cayman Island, which he had visited many times before; A. Dewar (ed), *The voyages and travels of Captain Nathaniel Uring* (new ed 1928), p 164.
35 Adm 1/1893, Hobbs to Adm, *Eagle*, Spithead, 14 Dec. 1758.
36 Adm 1/1895, Innes to Adm, *Enterprise*, Plymouth, Downs, 26 June, 6 July 1761.
37 Adm 1/931, Durell to Adm, Portsmouth, 26 Jan. 1760; Adm 1/235, Holmes to Adm, 30 Aug. 1757, Adm 1/654, Smith to Adm, *Royal Sovereign*, Downs, 12 Nov. 1757.
38 Pares, *War and trade*, p 306, considers, quoting HCA 3/284, that the Admiralty sued the master for the securities given when the letter of marque was issued. The warrant for the arrest of the master, dated 6 Oct. 1759 in HCA 14/77 refers to 'A breach of our instructions and a contempt for our colours and authorities'.
39 Pares, *War and trade*, pp 182–3.
40 Sir John K. Laughton (ed), *Letters and papers of Charles, Lord Barham, Admiral of the Red Squadron 1758–1813, vol 1*, (1906), p 31.
41 The convoy which sailed under the *Litchfield* in June 1758 numbered 162; Adm 1/1489, Barton to Adm, *Litchfield*, off Cape Clear, 16 July 1758.
42 Pares, *War and trade*, pp 231–2.
43 Customs 3/58, f 188.
44 Adm 1/241, Parker to Adm, *Bristol*, Port Royal, Jamaica, 19 Apr. 1778.
45 G. J. Marcus, *A naval history of England; vol. 1 the formative centuries* (1961), p 442.
46 The main acts were, 27 Geo III cap. 27, 32 Geo III cap. 43 and 45, and 45 Geo III cap. 57.
47 B. Edwards, *The history, civil and commercial, of the British colonies in the West Indies* (4th ed, 1807), pp 411, 425.
48 L. J. Ragatz, *Statistics for the study of British Caribbean history* (1927),

table III, quoted in L. F. Horsfall, 'The West India trade' in C. N. Parkinson (ed), *The trade winds* (1948), p 167.

Chapter 7 *East Indies*

1 Whitworth, *Trade of Great Britain*, pp 9, 10.
2 C. N. Parkinson, *Trade in the eastern seas 1793–1813* (Cambridge 1937), pp 167–9.
3 See below pp 242–3.
4 The incident is recorded in I.O.R., Marine Records, Miscellanies, 21, minutes of 4, 11, 18 August, 1, 27 September 1756.
5 See below p 241.
6 Parkinson, *Trade in eastern seas*, p 231.
7 C. Lloyd (ed), *The health of seamen. Selections from the works of Dr James Lind, Sir Gilbert Blane and Dr Thomas Trotter* (1965), p 178.
8 I.O.R., Miscellanies, 13, p 7, James to Captain Edwin Carter, *Chesterfield*, Francis Fowler, *Walpole*, John Williams, *Hector*, 4 Feb. 1756.
9 Adm 1/2245, O'Brian to Adm., *Colchester*, Funchall Road, 19 Apr. 1757.
10 W. E. May, *A history of marine navigation* (1973), pp 32–3.
11 The following account is based largely on Parkinson, *Trade in eastern seas*, pp 99–108.
12 *Ibid*, p 297.
13 War ended before d'Estaing could attempt this.
14 Quoted in Parkinson, *Trade in eastern seas*, pp 100–1.
15 For an account of the loss of the *Dodington* see the *London Chronicle*, 3, 5 and 28 January 1758. The ship was probably lost on the Doddington Rock, which lies in lat. 33° 50' S, long. 26° 17' E.
16 J. H. Parry, *Trade and dominion* (1974), p 117.
17 I.O.R., Records of Fort St George, Despatches to England 1701–2 to 1710–11 (Madras 1925), pp 5, 10, Abstracts 5 November 1703, 28 January 1704.
18 G. J. Marcus, *A naval history of England, vol 2; the age of Nelson* (1971), pp 377–8; Sir Evan Cotton, *East Indiamen; the East India Company's maritime service* (1949), pp 170–2.
19 R. P. Crowhurst, 'The voyage of the *Pitt* – a turning point in East India navigation', *Mariner's Mirror*, 55, (1969), pp 43–56.
20 Parkinson, *Trade in eastern seas*, pp 51–6.
21 V. T. Harlow, *The founding of the second British empire, 1763–1793* (2 vols 1952), i, 101.
22 S. C. Hill, *Notes on piracy in eastern waters* (Bombay 1923), pp 169–70.
23 C. Gill, *Merchants and mariners of the eighteenth century* (1961), pp 24–5.
24 Parry, *Trade and dominion*, pp 116–17.
25 *Ibid*, p 95.
26 Schumpeter, *English overseas trade*, pp 52, 55.
27 Parkinson, *Trade in eastern seas*, p 96.
28 For additional details of the cruise, see R. P. Crowhurst, 'D'Estaing's cruise in the Indian Ocean; a landmark in privateering voyages', *Studia*, 35 (1972), pp 53–65.

29   I.O.R., Records of Fort St George, Despatches from England 1711–14, p 78, General Letter 14 October 1712.
30   Marcus, *Age of Nelson*, pp 111–13, 376–84.
31   H. A. Colgate, 'Trincomalee and the East Indies squadron 1746–1844', (unpublished M.A. thesis, London University, 1959), pp 44–5.
32   Adm 1/2245, O'Brian to Adm., *Colchester*, Funchall Road, 19 Apr. 1757 enclosed a petition from eight sailors of the *Delaware*, St Helena Road, 27 July 1757.
33   Parkinson, *Trade in eastern seas*, p 258.

Bibliography

Only those sources actually mentioned in the notes have been included.

Manuscript Sources

England

British Museum
Rate Book of Janson, Add. MSS. 34, 669–70.
Newcastle Papers, Add. MSS. 32, 866.

India Office Records
Marine Records, Miscellanies, 13, 21, 504A.
Records of Fort St George, Despatches from England, 1711–14.

Public Record Office
Admirals' Despatches, Channel Fleet, Adm. 1/87, 90.
Admirals' Despatches, Jamaica, Adm. 1/235, 236, 241.
Admirals' Despatches, Leeward Islands, Adm. 1/306.
Admirals' Despatches, Downs, Adm. 1/654.
Admirals' Despatches, Portsmouth, Adm. 1/931.
Captains' Letters, Adm. 1/1442–3, 1482, 1489, 1497, 1606, 1692, 1776, 1823, 1891, 1893, 1895, 2046, 2110–3, 2245, 2640, 2653.
Letters from Colonial Governors, Adm. 1/3814.
Letters from British Consuls, Adm. 1/3838.
Letters from the Board of Trade and Plantations, Adm. 1/4091.
Letters from the Treasury, Adm. 1/4286.
Order in Council, Adm. 1/5248.
Lords' Letters to Secretary of State, Adm. 2/378–9.
Secretary's Letters, Adm. 2/428.
Board's Minutes, Adm. 3/2, 4, 52–3, 66.

Letters from Colonial Governors to the Colonial Office, C.O. 5/510, 520, 1311.
Chatham Papers, PRO 30/8, vol. 95.
Records of the Board of Customs, Customs 3/56–60, 75–80.
Letters to the Board of Treasury, T.1/385, 389, 415, 418.
Minutes of the Board of Treasury, T.29/33.

Exeter City Library
Milford Journal, 71/8.

Liverpool Underwriters Association
Rate Books A–C of d'Aquilar.

Society of Merchant Venturers, Bristol
Annual list of ships.
Index of records; trade and public affairs.

Scotland

Scottish Record Office
Morton Papers GD 150/2608.

Glasgow City Archives
Photostat copies of Spiers Papers, Letterbook 1781–9.

France

Archives Nationales, Paris
Prize dossiers, B4/78, 95.
Prize lists, F2/74–5.
Naval vessels lent for privateering, B4/97, 103.

Archives départementales des Basses Pyrénées, Pau
Amirauté de Bayonne, registration of privateers, B Supplément.

Archives départementales d'Ille-et-Vilaine, Rennes
Amirauté de Saint-Malo, registration of privateers, 9B/435.
Tribunal de Commerce, 2 Um/7, 12, 77, 87.
Fonds Vignols, 1F/1930.

Archives de la Marine, Cherbourg
Amirauté de Cherbourg, Inscription Maritime, Saint Valéry sur Somme, 2P/251.

Holland

Gemeente Archief, Rotterdam
Maatschappij van Assurantie, Discontering en Beleening der Stad Rotterdam, Assurantie Boeke.

Printed Sources

Primary

Calender of State Papers, Domestic 13 February 1689 to April 1690 (reprint 1969).

Calender of State Papers, Domestic, 1702–1703, vol. 1 (1916).

Calender of State Papers, Domestic, 1703–1704 (1924).

Calender of State Papers, 1708–1714 (1879).

Calender of Treasury Papers, 1556–7 – 1696 (1868).

Bezanson, Anne, Gray, R. D. and Hussey, M., *Prices in colonial Pennsylvania* (Philadelphia 1935).

Boislisle, A. M. de, *Correspondences des Contrôleurs Généraux des Finances avec les Intendants des Provinces* (Paris 1883).

Brock, R. A. (ed), *The official records of Robert Dinwiddie*, (2 vols, Richmond, Va., 1883–4).

Cole, A. H., *Wholesale commodity prices in the United States 1700–1861* (Cambridge, Mass. 1938).

Dewar, A. (ed), *The voyages and travels of Captain Nathaniel Uring* (new ed. 1928).

English Reports

Isambert, Decrusy and Taillandier, *Receuil général des anciennes lois françaises depuis l'an 420 jusqu'à la Révolution de 1789* (Paris 1833).

Laughton, Sir J. K. (ed), *Letters and papers of Charles, Lord Barham, Admiral of the Red Squadron 1758–1813, vol 1*, (1906).

Lloyd, C. (ed), *The health of seamen. Selections from the works of Dr James Lind, Sir Gilbert Blane and Dr Thomas Trotter* (1965).

London Chronicle

Mitchell, B. R. and Deane, Phyllis, *Abstract of British historical statistics* (Cambridge 1971).

Ranft, B. Mc L. (ed), *The Vernon Papers* (1958).

Records of Fort St George, Despatches to England 1701–2 to 1701–11 (Madras 1925).

Ryan, A. N. (ed), *The Saumarez Papers; selections from the Baltic correspondence of Vice-Admiral Sir James Saumarez 1808–1812* (1968).

Schumpeter, E. B., *English overseas trade statistics, 1697–1808* (Oxford 1960).

Spencer, A. (ed), *Memoirs of William Hickey, vol II (1775–1782)* (1918).

Stock, L. F. (ed), *Proceedings and debates of the British parliaments respecting North America* (5 vols, Washington 1924–41).

Whitworth, Sir Charles, *State of the trade of Great Britain in its imports and exports progressively from the year 1697* (1776).
Williamson's Liverpool Advertiser and Mercantile Register.

Secondary

Allen, G. W., *Massachusetts privateers of the Revolution* (Massachusetts Historical Society 1927).
Bailyn, B. and L., *Massachusetts shipping 1697–1714; a statistical study* (Cambridge, Mass. 1959).
Beawes, W., *Lex mercatoria rediviva: or the merchant's directory* (4th ed. 1783).
Bélanger, R., *Les Basques dans l'estuaire du Saint-Laurent 1535–1635* (Montreal 1971).
Bird, J., *The major seaports in the United Kingdom* (1969).
Boiteux, M. L. A., 'Contribution de l'assurance a l'histoire de l'economie en France', in *Les sources de l'histoire maritime en Europe*, M. Mollat (ed) (Paris 1962).
Bradford, C., 'A premium on progress; an outline history of the American insurance market 1820–1970', *Newcomen Society of North America* (1970).
Bradlee, F. B. C., *Colonial trade and commerce 1733–1774* (Salem, Mass. 1927).
Bridenbaugh, C., *Cities in the wilderness. The first centuries of urban life in America 1625–1742* (New York, new ed. 1960).
Bridenbaugh, C., *Cities in revolt. Urban life in America, 1746–1776* (New York 1955).
Bridenbaugh, C. and Roberta, *No peace beyond the line. The English in the Caribbean 1624–1690* (New York 1972).
Bromley, J. S., 'Le commerce de la France de l'ouest et la guerre maritime (1702–1712)', *Annales du Midi*, 65 (1953).
Bromley, J. S., 'The importance of Dunkirk (1688–1713) reconsidered' (Paper presented at the XV International Seminar on Maritime History held at the XIV International Congress of Historical Science, San Francisco 1975).
Burns, Sir Alan, *A history of the West Indies.*
Carter, Alice C., 'How to revise treaties without negotiating: compromise, mutual fears and the Anglo-Dutch trade disputes of 1759' in *Studies in diplomatic history: essays in memory of D. B. Horn*, R. M. Hatton and M. S. Anderson (eds) (1970).
Cavaignac, J., *Jean Pellet; commerçant en gros 1694–1772* (Paris 1967).

Chyet, S. F., *Lopez of Newport; colonial American merchant prince* (Detroit 1970).

Clemens, P. G. E., 'The rise of Liverpool, 1665–1750', *Economic History Review*, 2nd ser, XXIX (1976).

Clowes, W. Laird, *The Royal Navy* (2 vols, 1879, 1903).

Colgate, H. A., 'Trincomalee and the East Indies squadron 1746–1844' (unpublished M.A. thesis, London University 1959).

Cotton, Sir Evan, *East Indiamen; the East India Company's maritime service* (1949).

Crowhurst, R. P., 'Bayonne privateering 1744–1763' (paper presented at the XV International Seminar on Maritime History held at the XIV International Congress of Historical Sciences, San Francisco 1975).

Crowhurst, R. P., 'D'Estaing's cruise in the Indian Ocean; a landmark in privateering voyages', *Studia*, 35 (1972).

Crowhurst, R. P., 'Marine insurance and the trade of Rotterdam 1755–1763', *Maritime History*, 2 (1972).

Crowhurst, R. P., 'The voyage of the *Pitt* – a turning point in East India navigation', *Mariner's Mirror*, 55 (1969).

Cullen, L., 'Ireland and Irishmen in eighteenth-century privateering' (paper presented at the XV International Seminar on Maritime History at the XIV International Congress of Historical Sciences, San Francisco 1975).

Davis, R., 'English foreign trade 1660–1700', 'English foreign trade 1700–1774' in *The growth of English overseas trade in the 17th and 18th centuries*, W. E. Minchinton (ed), (1969).

Davis, R., *The rise of the Atlantic economies* (1973).

Davis, R., *The rise of the English shipping industry in the seventeenth and eighteenth centuries* (Newton Abbot 1972).

Davies, K. G., *The Royal African Company* (Atheneum ed., New York 1970).

Delumeau, J., 'Le commerce malouin sous l'Ancien Régime d'après les registres de l'Amirauté' in *Les sources de l'histoire maritime en Europe du Moyen Age au XVIIIe siècle*, M. Mollat (ed) (Paris 1962).

Delumeau, J., 'La guerre de course française sous l'Ancien Régime' (paper presented at the XV International Seminar on Maritime History held at the XIV International Congress of Historical Sciences, San Francisco 1975).

Devine, T. M., 'Glasgow merchants and the collapse of the tobacco trade 1775–1783', *Scottish Historical Review*, LII (1973).

Devine, T. M., 'Glasgow merchants in colonial trade 1770–1815' (unpublished Ph.D. thesis, Strathclyde University 1971).

Donnan, Elizabeth, 'Eighteenth-century English merchants; Micajah Perry', *Journal of Economic and Business History*, IV (1931–2).

Dow, G. F. and Edmonds, J. H., *The pirates of the New England coast 1630–1750* (New York 1968).

Donin, G., *La Mediterranée de 1803 à 1805; pirates et corsaires aux Îles Ioniennes* (Paris 1917).

Ducéré, E., *Les corsaires sous l'Ancien Régime* (Bayonne 1895).

Dunn, R. S., *Sugar and slaves, the rise of the planter class in the English West Indies 1624–1713* (1973).

Edelman, E., 'Thomas Hancock. Colonial merchant', *Journal of Economic and Business History*, I (1928–9).

Edwards, B., *The history, civil and commercial, of the British colonies in the West Indies* (4th ed. 1807).

Ehrman, J., *The navy in the war of William III, 1689–1697* (Cambridge 1953).

Francis, A. D., *The wine trade* (1972).

Giddens, P. H., 'Trade and industry in colonial Maryland, 1753–1769', *Journal of Economic and Business History*, IV (1931–2).

Gill, C., *Merchants and mariners of the eighteenth century* (1961).

Graham, G. S., *Empire of the North Atlantic; the maritime struggle for North America* (Toronto 1950).

Graham, G. S., 'The naval defence of British North America 1739–1763', *Transactions of the Royal Historical Society*, 4th ser., XXX (1948).

Gwyn, J., *The enterprising admiral; the personal fortune of Admiral Sir Peter Warren* (Montreal 1974).

Gwyn, J., *The Royal Navy and North America; the Warren Papers, 1736–1752* (1973).

Gupta, B. K., *Sirajuddaullah and the East India Company, 1756–1757. The background to the foundation of British power in India* (Leiden 1966).

Harlow, V. T., *The founding of the second British empire 1763–1793* (2 vols 1952).

Harrington, Virginia D., *The New York merchant on the eve of the Revolution* (New York 1935).

Hidy, R. W., *The House of Baring in American trade and finance; English merchant bankers at work 1763–1861* (Cambridge, Mass. 1949).

Higgins, G., *Annals of Lloyds Register* (1934).

Hill, S. C., *Notes on piracy in eastern waters* (Bombay 1923).

Hoskins, W. G., *Industry, trade and people in Exeter 1688–1800* (2nd ed. Exeter 1968).

Horsfall, Lucy F., 'The West Indian trade', in *The trade winds; a study of British overseas trade during the French wars 1793–1815*, C. N. Parkinson (ed) (1948).

Hyde, F. E., *Liverpool and the Mersey; an economic history of a port 1700–1970* (Newton Abbot 1971).

Huntley, F. C., 'The seaborne trade of Virginia in the eighteenth century: Port Hampton', *Virginia Magazine of History and Biography*, LIX (1951).

Innes, H. A., *The cod fisheries; the history of an international economy* (Toronto 1940).

Jarvis, R. C., 'Eighteenth century Dorset shipping', *Proceedings of the Dorset Natural History and Archeological Society*, XCII (1971).

Jaupart, F., *L'activité commerciale de Bayonne au XVIIIe siècle* (Bayonne 1966).

John, A. H., 'The London insurance market of the eighteenth century', *Economica* (1958).

Johnson, J. A., 'Parliament and the navy 1688–1714' (unpublished Ph.D. thesis, Sheffield University 1969).

Kent, H. S. K., 'The background to Anglo-Norwegian relations', *Norseman*, 11 (1953).

Latimer, J., *The history of the Society of Merchant Venturers of the city of Bristol with some account of the anterior merchants' guilds* (Bristol 1903).

Lacroix, R. T., 'La guerre de course dans les ports des amirautés de Vannes et de Lorient (1744–1783)' *Mémoires de la Societé d'Histoire et d'Archéologie de Bretagne*, XXVI (1946).

Laughton, J. K., 'On convoys', *The Naval Journal* (1894).

Le Coz, J., 'La guerre de course à Saint-Malo sous Louis XVI', (Diplôme d'Études Supérieures, Rennes 1957).

Lemay, J., 'La guerre de course à Saint-Malo pendant les guerres de Louis XV', *Positions des thèses soutenues par les élèves de l'École des Chartes* (Paris 1948).

Leder, L. H. and Carosso, V. P., 'Robert Livingston (1654–1728): businessman of colonial New York', *Business History Review*, XXX (1956).

Long, E., *The history of Jamaica* (3 vols, 1744).

Lespagnol, A., 'Guerre et activités maritimes: l'example de Saint-Malo pendant la Guerre d'Amérique' (paper read at the XIV Conference of the International Commission for Maritime History, Greenwich, July 1974).

McGrath, P., *The merchant venturers of Bristol; a history of the*

Society of Merchant Venturers of the city of Bristol from its origin to the present day (Bristol 1975).

McManis, D. R., *Colonial New England; a historical geography* (New York 1975).

Magens, N., *Essay on insurances* (2 vols, 1755).

Malo, H. *Les derniers corsaires; Dunkerque (1715–1815)* (Paris 1935).

Marcus, G. J., *A naval history of England; vol 2, the age of Nelson* (1971).

May, W. E., *A history of marine navigation* (1973).

Minchinton, W. E., 'The merchants in England in the eighteenth century', *Explorations in entrepreneurial history* (1957).

Morel, A., 'Les armateurs malouins et le commerce interlope', in *Les sources de l'histoire maritime en Europe du Moyen Age au XVIIIe siècle*, M. Mollat (ed) (Paris 1962).

Morrison, S. E., *The maritime history of Massachusetts, 1783–1860* (Cambridge, Mass., new ed. 1961).

Meyer, J., *L'armement nantais dans le XVIIIe siècle* (Paris 1969).

Middleton, A. P., 'The Chesapeake convoy system 1662–1763', *William and Mary Quarterly*, III, 3rd ser. (1946).

Nash, G. B., 'Slaves and slave owners in colonial Philadelphia', *William and Mary Quarterly*, 3rd ser., XXX (1973).

Norton, T. E., *The fur trade in colonial New York 1686–1776* (Madison, Wisconsin 1974).

Owen, J. H., *War at sea under Queen Anne* (Cambridge 1938).

Pares, R., *War and trade in the West Indies, 1739–1763*, (Oxford 1936)

Park, J. A., *A system of the law of marine insurances* (1787).

Parkinson, C. N., *Trade in the eastern seas 1793–1813* (Cambridge 1937).

Parry, J. H., *Trade and dominion* (1974).

Pawson, M. and Buisseret, D., *Port Royal, Jamaica* (1975).

Péju, A., *La course à Nantes aux XVIIe et XVIIIe siècles* (Paris 1900).

Plumb, J. H., *Sir Robert Walpole. The making of a statesman* (1956).

Plumb, J. H., *Sir Robert Walpole, the King's minister* (1960).

Price, J. M., *France and the Chesapeake. A history of the tobacco monopoly 1674–1791, and of its relationship to the British and American tobacco trades* (2 vols, Ann Arbor, Michigan 1973).

Price, J. M., 'The rise of Glasgow in the Chesapeake tobacco trade, 1707–1775', *William and Mary Quarterly*, 3rd ser., XI (1954).

Rankin, H. F., *The golden age of piracy* (Williamsburg, Va. 1969).

Rectoran, P., *Corsaires basques et bayonnais du XVe au XIXe siècle* (Bayonne 1946).

Richard, R., 'Le financement des armements maritimes au XVIIIe siècle. Une approche; le cas du Havre', *Bulletin de la Societé d'Histoire Moderne*, XIV (1969).

Robidou, F., *Les derniers corsaires malouins; la course sous la République et l'Empire, 1793–1814* (Rennes 1919).

Ryan, A. N., 'The melancholy fate of the Baltic ships in 1811', *Mariner's Mirror*, 1 (1964).

Shepherd, J. F. and Walton, G. M., *Shipping, maritime trade and the economic development of colonial North America* (Cambridge 1972).

Supple, B. E., *The Royal Exchange Assurance* (1970).

Sutherland, Stella H., *Population distribution in colonial America* (New York 1936).

Swann, D., 'The pace and progress of port investment in England 1660–1830', *Yorkshire Bulletin of Economic and Social Research*, 12.

Sutherland, Lucy, *A London merchant 1696–1774* (1933).

Syrett, D., *Shipping and the American war 1775–83; a study of British transport organisation* (1970).

Viles, P., 'The shipping interest of Bordeaux 1774–1793', (unpublished Ph.D., Harvard University, 1964).

Walker, C. F. and Manning, T. D., *British warship names* (1959).

Weskett, J., *A complete digest of the theory, laws and practice of insurance* (1781).

White, P. L., *The Beekmans of New York in politics and commerce 1647–1877* (New York 1956).

Willan, T. S., *The English coasting trade, 1600-1750* (Manchester 1938).

Wright, C. and Fayle, C. E., *A history of Lloyds* (1928).

Index

Acadians, 22
Adams, Captain, 156
Aghulas Bank, 225
Aghulas Current, 225
Albany, 115, 118, 122
Albemarle Sound, 155
Alexandretta, 41
Algiers, 41
Allen, G. W., 135
Amicable Society for a Perpetual
  Assurance Office, 83
Amoy, 228, 235
Amsterdam, 84, 95, 115, 120
Ancona, 40
Annapolis, 152, 155
Antigua, 78, 101, 178, 181, 183–4, 193–4
d'Anville, 125
Archangel, 52, 72, 75
Arendal, 74
Ashley, R., 158
Asiatisk Kompagni, 44
Azores, 40

Baetman, Captain, 26
Bahamas, 159
Bailyn, B., 116
Baker, William, 129–30, 184
Baltimore (Ireland), 49, 50
Bantry, 50
Barbados, 48, 51, 57, 77–9, 170–2, 175,
  177–85, 192–4, 199
Bardsey, Island, 28
Barnstable, 146, 153
Bart, Jean, 15, 25–6
Basseterre Road, 181, 194
Batavia, 95
Bayonne, 31–5, 37–40, 42, 123
Beck, Sir Justus, 84

Beckford, William, 95, 184
Beekman, Gerard, 129
Belfast, 94
Belfast Lough, 68
Bellomont, Lord, 115
Benbow, Vice-Admiral, 176
Bencoolen, 220, 233, 237
Bergen, 74
Berkeley, George, 47, 66
Bermuda, 94, 139
Beverly, 92
Bideford, 146, 150, 152–3
Bilbao, 110
Billingsgate, 49
Billingsley, Case, 84
Bird, J., 69
Blanckmann, Jean, 26
Bluefields Bay, 97, 181, 189
Board of Trade and Plantations, 49
Bombay, 219, 220, 227–8, 241
Bonet, Pierre, 37
Book of Rates, 121
Bordeaux, 28, 30–1, 34, 42, 88–9, 95,
  123
Boston, 38–9, 51, 92, 107–8, 110, 114,
  116–19, 125
Boys, Commodore, 26
Braund, Thomas, 91–2
Bréhat-Paimpol, 25
Brereton, William, 83
Brest, 27–8, 54, 152
Bristol, 37, 45, 48, 57, 61–3, 66–7, 77,
  90, 112, 118, 143, 146, 150, 153–4,
  187, 195, 203
British Association Insurance Club, 96
Brittany, 25
Bruges, 57
Bubble Act 1720, 87
Buchanan, John, 154

Cabinet Council, 50
Cadiz, 95
Calais, 42
Calcutta, 219, 220, 227, 242
Calico, 215
Canary Islands, 48, 223
Candeler, Richard, 82
Canton, 95, 219–20, 228, 232
Cape Alta Vela, 79
Cape Antonio, 189
Cape Beata, 79
Cape Caxine, 41
Cape Fear, 157
Cape of Good Hope, 224, 225–6, 244–5
Cape Hatteras, 157
Cape Lookout, 157
Cape Matapan, 41
Cape Sviatoi Nos, 76
Cape Verde Island, 223
Carlisle Bay, 194
Carolina, 51, 138, 144, 157, 160–2, 164, 166
Carthagena, 185
Celebes, 220, 231
Ceuta, 40
Charleston, 99, 117, 144–5, 158, 160–4, 167, 191
Chesapeake, 51, 139–43, 146, 148, 151, 154, 157
Chetwyn's Insurance, 86
China, 137, 219
Christiansand, 74
Ciboure, 32, 38
Cider, 17
Clyde, 94
Coffee, 119, 186, 242
Co-Hong, 234, 236
Colbert, 33
Colden, Cadwallader, 118
Cole, A. H., 162
Committee for the Affairs of Ireland, 49
Committee for Trade and Plantations, 49
Committee of Trade of the Port of Lancaster, 66
Committee of West India merchants, 63
Compagnie d'Assurance générale, 88
Compagnie française des Indes orientales, 17, 44, 211
Compagnie pour la Mer du Sud, 17
Connecticut, 121
Connecticut River, 105
Conseil des Prises, 25
Convoy Act 1798, 71

Convoys and Cruisers Act (1708), 54
Conyngham, 28
Cook v Townson, 99
Corinth, 41
Cork, 68, 77
Cotton, American, 112, 119; West Indian, 172, 178
Court of Assurances, 82
Coz, J. N. le, 20
Crete, 41
Crooked Island, 187
Cruger, Henry, 132
Cuninghame, Findlay & Co., 151
Cuninghame, William, & Co., 151
Cyclades, 41

Dale, James, 222
Dalrymple, Alexander, 230
Dance, Nathaniel, 229
Danzig, 74
Darnard, Etienne, 37
Dartmouth, 56, 112
Davers, 185
Davis, R., 45, 213, 216
Deal, 146
Deerskins, 157, 160–1
Delaware River, 115, 121, 129
Delumeau, J., 18, 22, 28
Demarara, 94
Dickinson, Jonathan, 118
Dingle, 50
Dinwiddie, Governor, 155
Dogger Bank, 52, 73
Dominica, 79
Dufourcq, Samson, 39
Du-Guay Trouin, 54–5, 58
Dunkirk, 15, 25–6, 28, 31, 42, 50, 54
Dunster, William, 84
Duplat, Joseph, 39
Dutertre, Jean, 243
Dymock, 83

East India Company, 43, 44, 59, 208–48
East River, 115
Edinburgh, 28, 58
l'Eguille, Frogier de, 246
Ellenborough, Lord, 96
Elsinore, 52, 74
Elton, Abraham, 58
English Harbour, 102, 194, 203
l'Epine, Noel Danycan de, 17
d'Estaing, Comte, 102, 198–9, 224, 232, 237–40, 246
Evance, Sir Stephen, 117
Exeter, 57, 61, 66, 90, 112, 116

Falmouth, 77, 94, 146, 150

False Bay, 225
Fanshawe, 159
Faroe Islands, 30
Faulkner, Captain, 191
Fernando Noronha, 224
Fielding, Thomas, 91
Finch, Captain, 144
Fishbourn, William, 118
Flekkefjord, 96
Florida, 166, 167
Florida Strait, 180, 181, 188–90, 203
Forbin, Chevalier de, 15, 25
Forestier, Captain, 37
Forrest, Captain, 192
Fort Malborough, 102–3, 238–40
Fort St George, 220, 227
Frankland, Admiral, 78
Frontenac, Governor, 115
Funchal, 77

Gambia, 56
Genoa, 40, 80
George, John, 114
Georgia, 105, 161–4, 166
Gibraltar, 41, 80
Gillstone Ledges, 54
Ginger, 172
Glasgow, 44, 58, 63, 68–9, 143, 150, 152–4, 167, 169, 195
Glen, Governor, 160
Gothenburg, 74
Grand Banks, see Newfoundland Fishery
Gravesend, 220–1
Great Belt, 74
Great Migration, 108
Greenock, 153, 154
Grimsby, 58
Guadeloupe, 174, 177, 182, 192–4, 202
Gunfleet, 49
Gupta, B. K., 242

Halifax, 98, 135, 136, 167–8
Hamburg, 52, 62, 76
Hamburg Company, 57
Hamelin, Jacques, 244–5
Hamoaze Dockyard, 77
Hampton Roads, 155–6
Hancock, Thomas, 129
Hanö Bay, 74
Harrison, John, 77, 223
Hawke, Admiral, 23
Havana, 152, 189
Heligoland, 52, 76
Helyar, John, 175
Hendaye, 32

Hickey, William, 78
Hispaniola, 79
Hobbs, Captain, 190
Holmes, Rear-Admiral Charles, 188
Honduras, 182
Howland Wet Dock, 219
Hudson Bay, 72, 76
Hudson's Bay Company, 43, 59, 76, 110, 114, 134
Hull, 73, 116
Humber, 52
Huntingdon, Captain, 177
Hyde, F. E., 67

d'Iberville, 114
Île de France, see Mauritius
India, 44
Indian Ocean, 17
Indigo, 158, 160, 172, 178, 215
Iroquois, 115
Isle of Man, 143

Jamaica, 51, 57, 62, 78–9, 94, 99, 126, 170–205
Janina, 41
Jaupart, F., 35
Jones, John Paul, 28, 67
Jourdan, Jean, 17

Kempenfelt, Captain, 222
Kerguelen, Trémarec, 246
Kerr, Commodore, 179, 180
Killigrew, Sir William, 83
Kingston, 180, 181
Kinsale, 57, 222
Knipe, Sir Randolph, 84

Lacroix, R. T., 27
Lafargue, Martin, 37
Lagos Bay, 83
La Hogue, 18, 46
Lancaster, 143
La Pérouse, 135
La Rochelle, 123
Lascelles, Henry, 184
Law, John, 88
Lebat, Dominique, 39
Leghorn, 40, 62, 80
Le Havre, 27
Leith, 49, 75, 247
Lemay, Janine, 21
Lemême, François, 243
Levant Company, 41, 43, 45, 84
Le Vassor de la Touche, 157
Leveille, Louis, 26
Lignum vitae, 119, 186

Lime juice, 221, 224
Linen, 17
Linois, Admiral, 229
Lisbon, 25, 38, 80, 110, 112, 223
Liverpool, 44, 58, 61–3, 66–7, 77, 92, 94, 116, 137, 143, 146, 150, 153, 154, 168–9, 187, 195, 203
Liverpool Underwriters Association, 92
Lloyd, Thomas, Junior, 118
Lloyds Coffee House, 61, 87, 90
Lloyds List, 61, 87–8, 93
Lockhart, Captain, 63
Lofoten Island, 75
Logwood, 119, 178, 182, 186, 196
London, 42, 44, 46, 56, 69, 72, 81, 88, 94, 96, 98, 99, 101–2, 140, 150, 153, 168, 188, 202
London Assurance Company, 89–90
Long Island Sound, 105, 115
Long Sand, 51
Lopez, Aaron, 131–2
Lorient, 27–8
Louisbourg, 110, 118, 122–5, 157, 162
Lynn, 60, 101
Lynn, Captain, 77

Maatschappij van Assurantie, Discontering en Beleening der Stad Rotterdam, 89
Madagascar, 150, 224, 226–7
Madeira, 40, 77–8, 101, 221–3
Madras, 219, 222, 227–8, 235, 240, 243
Magalhaens v Bushar, 97
Magens, Nicholas, 88
Mahogany, 119, 186
Maine, 121
Mallerousse, 243
Malta, 41
Man, Captain, 163
Manila, 218, 228, 234
Manning, Edward, 184–5
Mansfield, 81, 93, 96, 101–3
Marblehead, 38, 92, 107, 109, 123
Marine Coffee House, 86
Marine Insurance Act, 1906, 96
Marine Insurance Corporation, 83
Martinique, 78, 174, 176–7, 181, 192, 194, 201–2, 204
Maryland, 68, 102, 105, 138–69, 172
Maskeleyne, N., 223
Massachusetts, 108, 121, 123, 135, 137
Massachusetts Bay, 105, 107–8, 114–15
Mast ships, 114, 132
Masters, Thomas, 118
Mauritius 237–9, 241, 243–6

Mayer, T., 77, 223
Medway, 42, 72
Mercer's Hall Company, 84, 90
Merchant ships, American, *Delight*, 39, *Duke*, 39, *Frise*, 39, *Seaflower*, 39; Dutch, *Elizabeth*, 27; East Indiamen, *Canterbury*, 228, *Cassandra*, 226, *Dodington*, 226, *Duchess*, 242, *Duke of Richmond*, 221, *Falmouth*, 222, *Fox*, 217, *Grantham*, 221, *Greenwich*, 226, *Nottingham*, 217, *Pitt*, 230–2, *Prince Edward*, 217, *Scaleby Castle*, 224, *Suffolk*, 221; English, *Arundel*, 97, *Bedford Galley*, 146, *Boneta*, 175, *Ellis*, 192, *George and Henry*, 99, *Gloster*, 164, *John and Joan*, 96, *Lively*, 30, *Mills Frigate*, 93, 99, *Nightingale*, 50, *Pomona*, 96, *Prosperous Esther*, 102, *Roundburst Galley*, 180, *Sally*, 37, *Selby*, 101, *Somerset Frigate*, 180, *Success*, 39, *Venus*, 163, *Walthamstow Galley*, 180
Methuen Treaty, 34
Meyer, J., 29
Milford, Samuel, 61
Milford Haven, 57, 100, 113
Minbielle, Jean, 37, 39
Mineral and Battery Works, 85
Mines Royal, 85
Mitchell, B. R., 59, 65, 165, 201
Moliet, Michel, 38
Montserrat, 79, 181, 183–4, 194
Morlaix, 25, 28
Morrison, S. E., 114
Mozambique Channel, 226
Mull of Kintyre, 28, 68
Murray, Rear-Admiral George, 168
Muscovy Company, 75

Naguille, Pierre, 39
Nantasket, 114
Nantes, 28–30, 88
Nantucket, 92, 121
Nantucket Shoals, 127
Narragansett Bay, 107
Nattal, 103
Nautical Almanac, 77
Naval ships, English, *Acheron*, 41, *Alarm*, 62, *Aldborough*, 62, *Améthyste*, 157, *Antelope*, 62, *Arethusa*, 68, *Arrow*, 41, *Assistance*, 172, *Association*, 54, *Basilisk*, 37, *Blandford*, 164, *Bonetta*, 168, *Brume*, 157, *Colchester*, 222, *Comet*, 127, *Coventry*, 54, *Defence*, 75, *Deptford*,

Naval Ships—*cont.*
78, *Diana*, 156, *Dolphin*, 163, *Dover Prize*, 144, *Drake*, 172, *Dumbarton*, 144, *Dunkirk*, 177, *Experiment*, 179, *Flamborough*, 158, *Fly*, 60, *Garland*, 58, *Greenwich*, 177, *Guernsey*, 174, *Henry Prize*, 144, *Hero*, 75, *Humber*, 191, *Kingston*, 177, *Licorne*, 157, *Looe*, 62, *Mordaunt*, 174, *Penguin*, 163, *Phoenix*, 159, *Prevoyante*, 168, *Prince Edward*, 62, *Roebuck*, 77, *Rose*, 114, 159, *St George*, 75, *Sapphire*, 62, *Sauvage*, 157, *Seaford*, 68, *Success*, 163, *Swan*, 174, *Swift*, 60, *Tartar*, 62, 159, *Thetis*, 168, *Thisbe*, 168, *Winchelsea*, 163, *Winchester*, 78; French, *Bellone*, 244, *Bizarre*, 164, *Caroline*, 244, *Hermione*, 152, *Hortense*, 41, *Incorruptible*, 41, *Manche*, 244, *Marengo*, 243, *Minnion*, 164, *Sultana*, 152, *Thétis*, 157, *Vénus*, 244
Nelson, Captain Horatio, 41–2
Nevis, 79, 99, 112, 177–8, 181, 183–4, 194
New Bedford, 92
Newburyport, 92
Newcastle, 49, 51, 54, 60
Newfoundland, 54, 56
Newfoundland fishery, 16–18, 38, 42, 51, 64, 80, 109, 110, 112–13, 118–19, 133–4
New Hamsphire, 121
New Jersey, 104
New Lloyds Coffee House, 91
Newport (Rhode Island), 115, 117–18, 131
New York, 51, 107, 110, 112, 115, 117–18, 121–2, 125, 127, 129, 131–3, 144, 167
Nieuport, 25
Nore, 52, 72–3, 75–6, 221
Norfolk (North Carolina), 155
North Cape, 52, 75
North River, 108
North West Company, 134
Norway, 52
Norwich, 61, 66
Nova Scotia, 22, 133, 136
Nugent, 63

Office of Assurances, 83
Opium, 228, 235, 242
Oporto, 38, 60, 69, 80
Orkneys, 76
Ostend, 25, 56–7

Pantelleria Island, 41
Parkinson, C. N., 70
Pawson, M., 174
Péju, A., 31
Penn, William, 115
Pennsylvania, 104, 131, 133, 137, 144
Pepper, 103, 215, 237, 247
Pepperell, William, 123
Pepys, Samuel, 49
Perry, Micajah, 147
Philadelphia, 39, 107, 115, 117–18, 125, 127–8, 137, 160
Pillau, 74
Pimento, 186
Piscataqua, 107, 114, 123
Piscataqua River, 108
Pitch, 155
Plymouth, 57, 60, 77, 113, 146
Plymouth (Massachusetts), 107
Poole, 48, 56, 112
Pope's Head Alley, 91
Port Hampton, 155
Port Louis, 27–8, 79
Portobello, 184
Port Royal (Bay of Fundy), 118
Port Royal (Jamaica), 172, 174–5, 180–1, 203
Portsmouth, 66, 72, 76, 96–7
Price, J. M., 153
Prince of Wales Island, 233
Privateer ships, American, *Bonhomme Richard*, 28, *Chasseur*, 28, *Crawford*, 28, *Lexington*, 28, *Reprisal*, 28; English, *Falcon*, 37, *George*, 99; French, *Aigle*, 37, *Aigle Volant*, 27, *Audacieux*, 37, *Aurora*, 101, *Bellone*, 39, *Bougainville*, 24, *Cantabre*, 39, *Cartier*, 243, *Clarisse*, 243, *Comte de Noailles*, 38, *Comtesse Brionne*, 30, *Condé*, 238, *Confiance*, 243, *Emilie*, 243, *Expédition*, 238, *Flambeaux*, 37, *Fortune*, 244, *Grunvel*, 39, *Hermine*, 27, 38, *Jupiter*, 39, *Labourt*, 39, *Marsouin*, 24, *Minerve*, 24, *Napoléon*, 24, *Reine*, 25, *Revenant*, 244, *St Joseph*, 37, *St Philippe de Merliment*, 27, *St Vincent*, 27, *Samson*, 39, *Speculateur*, 24, *Ville Hélie*, 27
Providence, 107, 121
Purvis, Captain, 144

Quary, Colonel Robert, 115, 118, 147
Quebec, 72, 118, 134–5
Quimper, 28

Ram's Insurance, 86

Randolph, Edward, 139
Ransom, 18
Rappahannock River, 143, 156
Rennes, 17
Rice, American, 105, 158–63, 167; Indian, 242
Riga, 74
Rigais, François, 95
Rio de Janeiro, 224
Robidou, F. 21, 23
Rotterdam, 89, 95
Royal Adventurers into Africa, 45
Royal African Company, 43, 45, 56
Royal Exchange, 48–9, 61, 84, 87, 94, 120, 247
Royal Exchange Assurance, 87
Rum, 112
Russell, Colonel John, 83
Russia, 44, 55
Russia Company, 45, 51

St Augustine, 152, 158, 162
St Christopher, see St Kitts
St Croix, 194–5
St Eustatius, 68, 95, 165–6, 194, 199, 200
St George's Channel, 66
St Helena, 52, 223, 225, 241, 245
St Jean-de-Luz, 32, 34, 35, 39
St John's, 112, 126
St Kitts, 79, 97, 100, 165, 174, 178, 181, 183–4, 194, 199–200
St Lucia, 198–9, 202
St Malo, 15–25, 28–9, 31, 34, 42, 88, 114, 123, 152
St Pierre et Miquelon, 136
Saint-Pol, 54–5, 58
St Thomas, 94
Salem, 92, 107–8, 110, 116–17
Saltpetre, 206, 215, 242, 248
San Sebastian, 152
Santa Cruz, 95
Sarsfield, Patrick, 49
Saumarez, Captain, 63
Sausse, Captain, 26
Savannah, 158, 161, 163, 167
Scanderoon, 54
Scarborough, 116
Schumpeter, E. B., 104, 136, 148, 150, 177, 182, 196, 213, 214
Scilly Islands, 66
Scituate, 116
Sheerness, 114
Shepherd, J. F., 154
Ship Bank, 151
Shippen, Edward, 118

Shirley, Governor William, 123–4
Sicily, 41
Sierra Leone, 56
Silk, 161, 215, 242
Silver, 228
Skagerrak, 73
Smith, Captain Thomas, 126
Smyrna, 47, 54, 80, 83, 95
Society of Merchant Venturers, Bristol, 57–8, 62–3, 66, 68, 90
Spermaceti candles, 121
Spiers, Alexander, 69
Spry, Captain Richard, 127
Stalpaërt, Jean, 30
Stevenson v Snow, 98
Stockholm, 74
Stockton-on-Tees, 50
Straits of Gibraltar, 38, 40, 54
Straits of Messina, 41
Sumatra, 102–3, 217, 219, 227, 238, 240
Surat, 227, 235
Surcouf, Robert, 23, 240, 243–4
Surinam, 95, 115
Surnam, Captain, 78

Tar, 155
Tarife, 40
Taylor v Woodness, 96
Tea, 206–48
Texel, 76
Thames, River, 56, 72, 219, 221, 247
Thurot, François, 26, 63
Tin, 228
Tobacco, 68, 105, 112, 138–69, 171
Tobago, 94, 199, 201
Topsham, 66
Torbay, 77
Tortoiseshell, 186
Tortola, 97, 194–5
Tory Island, 63, 66, 195
Toulon, 40, 54
Toussaint l'Ouverture, 79
Townsend, Captain, 159
Trieste, 40
Trincomali, 241
Tumeric, 215
Tunis, 41
Turkey, 44
Tyne, 52

United Company of Merchants Trading to the East Indies, 44
Uring, Captain Nathaniel, 124

Valentia, 49
Vannes, 27–8, 38

Vazeley and others v St Barbe, 101
Venice, 81
Vereenigde Oost Indische Compagnie, 44, 211, 232
Vermont, 121
Vernon, Admiral Edward, 60, 184–5
Viana, 38, 80
Viborg, 101
Vignols, L., 18–19, 22
Vigo, 27
Vingå Sound, 74
Virginia, 56–8, 68, 101–2, 138–69, 172
Vitré, 17

Walker, Sir Hovenden, 118
Warren, Commodore Peter, 123, 126
Warwick v Scott, 96
Watson, Rear-Admiral Charles, 222
Webb v Thomson, 97
West India Association, 66
Weymouth, 56, 64, 146
Whale fishery, 18
Whale oil, 121

Wheeler, Commodore, 174
Whetstone, Vice-Admiral, 177
Whitaker, Sir Edward, 52
Whitby, 116
Whitehaven, 153, 155
Whitworth, Sir Charles, 121, 131, 145, 150, 157, 162, 178, 183, 213–14
Wickes, 28
Wilkes, John, 90
Williams, Sir John, 84
Windward Passage, 181, 187–8
Winthrop, Governor Francis, 109
Wood, Thomas, 179
Wright, Captain Lawrence, 174
Wylie, Hugh, 68

Yarmouth, 116
York River, 143, 156

Zante, 41, 80
Zeeland, 30
Zemba Island, 41